THE PROUSTIAN COMMUNITY

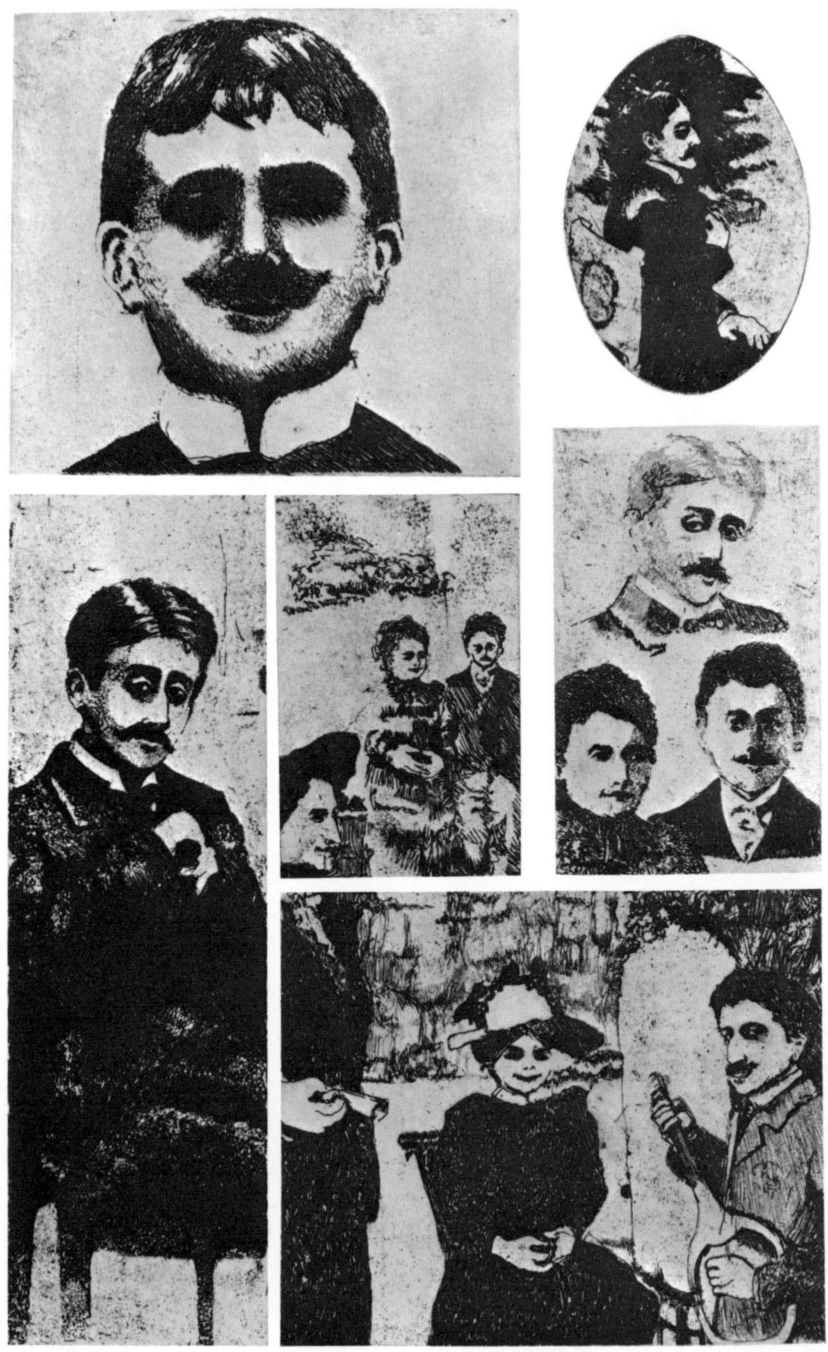

"Remembrance of Things Proust." Courtesy of Eleanor Rappe.

THE PROUSTIAN COMMUNITY

Seth L. Wolitz

New York University Press
New York 1971

Library of Congress Catalog Card Number: 73-171349
ISBN: 8147-9153-0
Manufactured in the United States of America

To
JAMES CHANEY
ANDREW GOODMAN
MICHAEL SCHWERNER
and those who participated in the Movement

"I woke up this morning with my mind
set on Freedom."

ACKNOWLEDGMENTS

I wish to thank Eleanor Rappe, the San Franciscan artist, for permission to reproduce her etching *Remembrance of Things Proust,* and also the Vorpal Galleries where shc exhibits. I am grateful for the gracious permission given me by Rapho Guillumette Pictures to reproduce the photographs of J. H. Lartigue, and by the Librairie Académique Perrin to reproduce a photograph from Philippe Jullian's book, *Prince of Aesthetes: Count Robert de Montesquiou 1855-1921.* My thanks go also to the Duc de Gramont for use of the photograph of the Comtesse Greffülhe.

I greatly appreciate the permission given by the following for use of passages from the works cited:

From REMEMBRANCE OF THINGS PAST, by Marcel Proust, translated by C. K. Scott-Moncrieff, and Frederick Blossom. Copyright 1924, 1925, 1927, 1928, 1929, 1930, 1932 and renewed 1952, 1953, 1955, 1956, 1957, 1958, 1960 by Random House, Inc. Reprinted by permission of Random House, Inc., Mr. George Scott-Moncrieff, and Chatto and Windus, Ltd., London.

From THE LITTLE COMMUNITY, by Robert Redfield. Copyright 1955 by The University of Chicago Press. Reprinted by permission of the publisher.

A literary work always has the same character: a coherent universe within which the events unfold, the psychology of the characters is presented, and the author's unconscious stylistic patterns are integrated within his coherent verbal structure.

Lucien Goldmann, "Méthodologies, Problèmes, Histoires," Revue Internationale des Sciences Sociales, *vol. XIX (1967), no. 4.*

PREFACE

Critics have often invited us to look upon an artistic creation as a living world, and in fact many nineteenth-century artists—Balzac, Thackeray, Zola, and Tolstoy to name a few—consciously attempted to create a world which would constitute an immense fresco of an age. Proust belongs to this tradition of epic novelists. But whereas others maintained an omniscient but removed third-person narration, Proust, under the name of Marcel, placed himself in the center of his work by using a non-omniscient first-person narrative form. The world of the narrator, therefore, became a microcosm of French life circa 1900, for the author consciously created a small but varied community about the persona.

The fascinating world which Marcel describes led me to question the esthetic function, in the novel, of the community in which the narrator lives. Why did Proust devote so many pages to analyzing the society of his age? How does his portrayal of society affect the structure of the novel? What is the author's "point of view" (I, p. 649; PI, p. 864), in fact, of society? These questions and many others, it seemed to me, might best be answered by applying not only the tools of literary criticism but methodology from other fields. In Robert Redfield's *Little Community,* a theoretical study of anthropological methodology, I found what I believed would be fruitful new approaches. Following Redfield, I shall examine the community created by Proust from several angles: as a whole, in historical perspective; as a cluster of groups arranged in social hierarchy; and as a framework of social institutions, in which individuals move up and down the social ladder with the passage of time. But this is a literary, not an anthropological (or sociological), study. My purpose is to reveal the various esthetic functions of society in the magnificent structure of *A la Recherche du Temps Perdu.*

Every aspect of the community interests Proust, but he concentrates especially on "high society" and the social movement around it, since being accepted by it is the goal of all the members of his narrator's world. High society does more than bring out the basic drives of the individual and his caste; it is in itself, by its form, its changes, its reactions to external events, and its ethos, a reflection of Man at one point on a time-space continuum.

The several chapters of this study will approach the Proustian community from different angles, proceeding from the general to the particular. In Chapter I, "The Historical Perspective," we shall review the political, economic, and especially the social conditions of the age and Proust's own role in society. This chapter is intended to serve as a point of reference for later discussions of the Proustian vision of society. In Chapter II, "Concept and Composition," we shall define the nature of the social theme and examine the ways in which it will be developed. In Chapter III, "The World View," we shall show that the novel is a reflection of Proust's belief in the unity of the personal world as against the fragmentation of the external world. In Chapter IV, "The Social Institutions," two major institutions of the community, the salon and the resort, will be studied as elements in the structure of the novel. We shall emphasize the construction and evolution of these institutions as well as the roles of the characters who move within them. In Chapter V, "The Biographical Perspective," we shall emphasize the role of the individual in society and examine the effects of an important external event, the Dreyfus Affair, upon the individuals in the novel. In this final chapter, we shall study an important social caste, the Jews, and particularly the individuals who represent this caste, Swann and Bloch.

By examining closely the nature, structure, and function of the community about the narrator, I wish to promote a greater appreciation of Proust's artistry in shaping historical fact to serve his esthetic vision. By applying Robert Redfield's anthropological approaches to an esthetic creation, I wish to contribute a new source of methodology for literary criticism and scholarship.

All the extracts from *Remembrance of Things Past* are borrowed from the two-volume Random House edition of Scott Moncrieff's masterful translation published by Chatto and Windus, Ltd., of London. American orthography, however, has been substituted for the English one. Immediately following the page reference to the English translation, we have cited the reference to the Pléiade edition edited by Pierre Clarac and André Ferré to serve both the informed reader and the scholar. All the other translations in the text have been rendered by the author.

Hopefully this study will offer a new perspective of the narrator's experience of empirical reality and of Marcel Proust's esthetic vision of human existence.

CONTENTS

LIST OF ILLUSTRATIONS

following page 178:

The Dreyfus Affair. Caption I: "Above all, let's not talk of the Dreyfus Affair!" Caption II: "They talked about it . . ."

At Dieppe in 1880. Left to right: Count Robert de Montesquiou, Marquis du Lau (friend of Comtesse Greffülhe), the Prince de Sagan, Prince Edmond de Polignac, Charles Haas (Proust's Swann), and an unknown person. Photograph courtesy of the Librairie Académique Perrin.

AUTHOR'S NOTE

The origin of this book was an incident which occurred in Federalsburg, Maryland, during the early days of the Civil Rights Movement. I, with others, had gone South to help fulfill our vision of the American Dream; we were greeted by a group of high school youth who ran up to us screaming "Freedom Riders," and threw hot coffee in our faces.

As we drove away from Federalsburg, I was reminded of Proust's soliciting names for a petition protesting Dreyfus' condemnation. The appeal for social justice appeared identical. The world of Marcel Proust's novel loomed suddenly before me and time seemed to evaporate. . . .

I suggested the subject of this book to Henri Peyre, my mentor at Yale, who welcomed it and assisted me. His astute comments and continued encouragement over what he once called "the long pregnancy" of this book have served me well. I appreciate deeply his unstinting attention.

I wish to acknowledge the enormous help Nancy Sendler provided in proofreading the first draft. It is with intense sorrow that I learned of her tragic death. She was a splendid woman whose few years were too often marred by misfortune.

I wish to thank all my friends, colleagues, students and departmental secretaries who offered suggestions and encouragement for this work both at Yale and at the University of California, Berkeley. I am especially grateful to Philip Bertocci, Melvin

Edelstein, Robert Griffin, Hurst Hannum, Richard Kuisel, Martin Kanes, Raymond Poirier, Beverly Ornstein, David Radin, Harry Senn, Peter Stern, and Gene Tanke—all of whom made invaluable suggestions for the manuscript.

The New York University Press has been especially kind to me. The enthusiasm for the project from Chris Kentera and Anthony Meisel is greatly appreciated, and the sure workmanship of the staff provided much assistance.

I owe so much to my parents for their constant concern, love, and generosity. From them I learned that "As you sow in tears, so will you reap in joy." They taught me the meaning of social justice and introduced to me the world of art.

My wife has been a devoted companion whose love, patience and endless support have brought this book to fruition. She is the source of my happiness. "Dignity and honor are her garb: She smiles looking at the future."

THE PROUSTIAN COMMUNITY

1900! The exhibition! Cosmopolitanism triumphant! From every corner of the world, a formidable avalanche came sweeping down on Paris! From this time forward, one sees everything there . . . everything except a society.

—*Marquis de Castellane*
Men and Things of my Time *(1912)*

We no longer have a single salon that is a salon and nothing more; for society though grown to monstrous proportions lacks a head.

—*Arthur Meyer (editor of* Le Gaulois*)*
40 Years of Parisian Society *(1912)*

Proust (Marcel), boulevard Haussmann 101 (VIIIe), Telephone 292 - 05, Palo.

—Tout-Paris *(1912)*
[*The French Social Register*]

Chapter I

THE HISTORICAL PERSPECTIVE

We are present at a Requiem Mass in honor of a departed pope in the great cathedral of Notre-Dame de Paris:

> A little farther, toward the nave, the Comte de Paris, whose wife was traveling, has taken his place on the Gospel side opposite the Prince and Princesse Napoléon on the Epistle

> side. Next, still in the choir, in white cape, came the Knights of the Holy Sepulchre, led by Prince Xavier de Bourbon-Parme who accompanied the grand prior Mgr. Bressolles. Also, on the Epistle side, the Knights of Malta, led by the Prince de Polignac, black capes covering their red tunics.[1]

With such personalities in attendance we might guess the time to be 1800 or perhaps even 1900; but this was the mass for John XXIII, held on June 11, 1963. Our eyes are drawn to the princes of the Church and especially to the bearers of the great names of France which still live: the Comte de Paris, a descendant of the House of Orleans and pretender to the throne of France; Prince Napoléon, heir to the Bonaparte Empire; Prince Xavier de Bourbon-Parme, a true Bourbon, descendant of the ruling house of Parma and heir to the Carlist throne of Spain; and the Prince de Polignac, a member of one of the oldest noble families of France and President of the Knights of Malta. As cardinals in violet gowns of mourning serve the solemn mass, a ceremony so ancient and so omnipresent, before these persons whose splendid costumes alone give them airs of demigods, whose titles contain the history of France, whose very ancestors, throughout the ages, fulfilled these same functions in this cathedral which they ordered built, is it timelessness we sense at such an occasion?

The historian and sociologist might cry, "This is an anachonism in 1971. The aristocracy is a fossil which should have disappeared in the French Revolution." And they might blame the conservative forces such as the Catholic Church for preserving antiquated social distinctions. But these remarks were already shouted seventy years ago. The poet, on the other hand, might be enchanted and would gather these precious remains from another age and use them in his creative efforts. If so, it is not hard to imagine that almost one hundred years ago, when the aristocracy was still a meaningful caste, a hypersensitive young Marcel Proust perhaps did see some bejeweled Duchesse de Guermantes surrounded by her ancestors glowing in the stained glass window of a country church one Easter Sunday; that he became infatuated with aristocracy, climbed the social rungs, and discovered the humanity and inhumanity of these costumed people who bore imposing titles; and that when his dream was crushed by reality, he revolted against them and himself, found his vocation as an artist, and saved the various moments of his social life as material for his novel, recreating the dreams of his youth with the reality of his maturity.

In the morning of June 11, 1963, at Notre Dame, the Prince de Bourbon-Parme, dazzling in his white cape, in the distant choir among his knights, looked like a heroic marble statue to the bourgeois seated in the apse not far from the West Porch. In the afternoon in the upper chapel of Sainte Chapelle, built by Saint Louis in 1241 to house the holy crown of thorns which only a direct descendant can touch, this Prince de Bourbon-Parme, standing at the altar surrounded by the magnificence of the stained glass, was approached by the faithful so that he might touch the crown of thorns and bless them; face to face he appeared, in spite of the magic of his name and uniform, a tired old man, with bags under his eyes and protruding thick veins on his bald head. Thus the initial charm and mystery of a distant titled figure could be shattered by a single encounter with the man himself. Marcel Proust learned this lesson well seventy years ago when he realized the difference that exists between dream and reality, between one point of time and the next, between one angle of vision and another. He developed a new technique of character presentation, a new view of reality, and an efficient means to demonstrate his concept of time through the changing personalities of those who people the worlds of *A La Recherche du Temps Perdu.*

One discovers the function of the aristocracy and the fascination which it still holds for the ordinary Frenchman in spite of his joke, "he is a count of no account," if one considers that in this same year, in the early spring of 1963, the star of the gala opening of *Lawrence of Arabia* at a Champs-Elysées cinema was the Duchesse de la Rochefoucauld (no doubt serving in the classic function of aristocracy as panache for the land); that a high percentage of French diplomats are still drawn from the aristocracy, albeit the petty nobility; that the finest clubs such as the Jockey or the Union are still presided over by the most respected names, the Duc de Broglie, Duc de Doudeauville, Duc de Luynes, and Comte de Miramont Fitz-James, for example; [2] that the petty attentions and services of daily life still give aristocrats precedence, especially if they enjoy pecuniary comfort. One can see it when he reads the lavish articles the mass newspapers and weeklies continually present about the Comte de Paris and other French noble families and European royalty. Clearly the aristocracy endures as a class and seems to have adapted itself to the exigencies of modern living while preserving as many prerogatives and customs as it can.

The bourgeoisie, though it had economic and political control, lacked prestige and coveted social acceptance from the class it had deprived of power. The aristocrat, aware of the bourgeois' need for acceptance, would not yield easily his one asset, social privilege; rather, he exploited the myth of his own class and used the weapon of exclusion to reinforce his social dominance. It would appear, then, that the French bourgeoisie, unable to convince itself of its superior social worth and thereby combine its political power with social dominance, as the aristocracy had done centuries earlier, preserved the old social order with aristocrats as the social leaders. Thus by divorcing political power from social dominance, the bourgeoisie allowed the enemy class to survive, to serve as an unnecessary goad to worthless social ambitions and to offer a possible political threat. Though titles had been abrogated following the Revolution in 1790, Napoleon introduced them again in 1804,[3] and they survive in kingdoms, empires, and republics to the present day.

Let us consider briefly the political importance of the aristocracy in 1871, the year of Marcel Proust's birth. After her humiliating defeat in the Franco-Prussian War, France was in a political turmoil not unlike the pitiful one to come in 1940. A National Assembly was called at Bordeaux to restore political stability to the land. Of the 630 members elected to the Assembly, no less than 400 were royalists and mainly of noble birth.[4] Though they were divided between Orleanists and Legitimists, the possibility of the Comte de Chambord (the legitimate heir) becoming Henry V, King of France, was very real. Only one obstacle kept him from his crown: the Assembly would not accept his demand that the French fly the white flag with the Bourbon fleur-de-lis. For two years his followers begged him to yield to the tricolor, and though his namesake, Henry IV, had said "Paris is worth a mass," Henry V held firm.

In 1873 a conservative government was installed, and Orleanist nobles, who revered parliamentary institutions, played the major role.[5] The Legitimists, from lack of knowledge or interest and from great hostility to this form of government, were ineffectual. The Duc de Broglie became Prime Minister and other Orleanist nobles such as the Ducs Decazes and Audiffret-Pasquier filled important posts in the government. Although a monarchy could not be restored, at least the royalists could control the Republic.[6] In this same year the Comte de Chambord, childless, named the Comte de Paris (Orleans branch) as his successor.

In 1875 a constitution for the Republic was completed, and any hope for a Legitimist or Orleanist restoration was destroyed. And with the fall of the Duc de Broglie in the year 1877, the end of conservative rule and of government dominated by nobles was consummated.[7] Though the Chamber of Deputies and the Senate would continue to seat nobles, most left, never to return.

Naturally there were rumors that the monarchy would return. For example, in 1885 the Comte de Paris, who had become the pretender after the death of Chambord in 1883, and was living like a sovereign, so frightened the Republicans that they exiled the royal family. A few years later when the Boulanger movement, so heavily supported by the Duchesse d'Uzès, collapsed, the monarchists were hurt considerably; another stunning blow came in 1892, when the Church under Leo XIII disassociated itself from the royalist cause. Following the Dreyfus Affair, the royalists lost their last strong support, the army, and they became completely discredited. From then on, only the proto-fascist *Action Française* led by Charles Maurras and Léon Daudet (a friend of Proust's) nurtured the dream of restoration. Clearly the political decline of the aristocracy at a time when everything favored its political renaissance showed how it had forgotten its ancient role; the aristocrats had but one place to turn to in order to preserve themselves as a class—the salon.

The salon is part of high society, Society with a capital "S," or in French, "Le Monde." High society brings people generally of the same background (title, family, wealth) together in a series of leisured events such as parties, balls, hunts, and races. The lower levels are peopled with upper bourgeois, such as doctors, lawyers, rich businessmen, and acceptable artists and scholars, the middle sections by the fabulously wealthy bourgeois and petty nobility, and the upper echelons, generally known in Proust's time as the Faubourg Saint-Germain,* by old noble families and some particularly appreciated bourgeois.

To enter high society one must be *seen* by others, be a constant participant, and look for an invitation to a more socially prominent salon. Missing a series of major social events could eventually lead to failure, for the people with whom one associates may have a weak memory for faces; nonetheless they also fear they are being snubbed if a person does not associate with them. The most vulnerable people are the reigning queens and the members of their salons; time inevitably works against these exclusive salons because they must bring in new faces in order to offer variety and to avoid boredom—which is a cardinal sin. Society is in flux because its distinctions, such as which queen reigns and what is good form, constantly change. Believing in these ephemeral distinctions, however, creates the illusion of reality. He who accepts this way of life is a snob, and he who chases after the select group and forgets his own origins is a social climber. Proust's hero, Marcel, and other characters will be victims of the delusion; only Marcel and the artists will be cured. Let us look then more closely at this society.

On June 23, 1903, the following item was recorded in the

---

* The Faubourg Saint-Germain is the area of Paris in which the nobility settled after the Restoration and in which they continued to live during the nineteenth century. By the end of the Second Empire, however, many nobles were living on the Right Bank. The Faubourg Saint Germain then became synonymous with aristocratic society, and throughout the Third Republic, the Faubourg Saint-Germain was used in its figurative sense.

"Mondanités," the social column of the popular society newspaper, *Le Gaulois:*

> A small gathering but of supreme elegance the night before last at the home of Comtesse Greffülhe, nee La Rochefoucauld, who did the honors, aided by her daughter-in-law, Comtesse Greffülhe, nee Caraman-Chimay, and her granddaughter Mlle Elaine Greffülhe. Present: Prince Murat, Duc de Gramont, Duc d'Harcourt, Prince Borghese, Comte de Dampierre, Comtesse de Guerne, Duchesse de Trévise, Comte A. de la Rochefoucauld, Comte Albert de Mun, Comtesse d'Hinnisdal, Duc de Bassano, Comte de Castellane, Comte H. de Ségur, Princesse G. de Caraman-Chimay, Comtesse Murat, Comte de Gabriac. . . .

The people at this little party, according to all memoirs of the age, are certainly the cream of French aristocratic Society. The newspaper, in its very choice of words, underlines the importance of the people present; "a small gathering" means not only "small" and "limited" but highly "selected" (another key word). And when "of supreme elegance" is added, this means we are in the presence of the finest element, the *"ne plus ultra"* of the Faubourg Saint-Germain.

Let us analyze the Faubourg from just this one social event. Notice that the gathering is given by the Comtesse Greffülhe nee La Rochefoucauld. She and her daughter-in-law particularly were considered queens of society by memorialists of the time.[8] We have here, I believe, an "ideal type" in Weberian terminology. Their salon was truly "smart" and "elegant" because it integrated —a new fashion in 1900—the "pick" of Legitimist, Orleanist, and Empire nobilities (as well as visiting high European nobility).[9] Obviously Prince Murat, Duc de Bassano, and the Duc de Trévise are First Empire titles; Prince de Caraman-Chimay, Duc de Gramont, Duc de Luynes, and Comte A. de la Rochefoucauld are *ancien régime* titles, the families of which have medieval sources. But a great salon in the Faubourg Saint-Germain is more than a gathering of the great names of Europe; it is also one continuous family gathering of "my cousins" as Oriane de Guermantes would say—a sign of acceptance. Comtesse Greffülhe nee La Rochefoucauld is a cousin of Comte Aymery de la Rochefoucauld; Comtesse Greffülhe nee Caraman-Chimay is the sister of the Prince de Caraman-Chimay, who himself married the Princesse Hélène de Brancovan (a Romanian House), who herself is the sister of the poetess Anna de Noailles nee Brancovan-Bibesco (a friend of Proust's). The Comte H. de Noailles (not present) married the sister of the Duc de Gramont (present), whose son, the Duc de Guiche (Proust's friend) married Mlle Elaine Greffülhe a year later.[10] And so on. Everyone is related by blood, marriage, and genealogy. Broglie, Uzès, Gramont, Brissac, Guermantes, Luynes, La Trémoïlle form one vast clan, a little community. Unconcerned with economics, inactive though devoted to a lost political cause, they had leisure, enough leisure to develop the most intense social life seen since the court of Louis XIV. Etiquette, precedence, and status followed the traditions of the royal court. They lacked only a king, who was in exile at Twickenham.

Let us observe now some of the constant social activity in the months of May and June of the same year, 1903. On May 19, a cousin of the Comtesse Greffülhe nee Chimay, Comte Robert de Montesquiou, Proust's friend and patron in society, partial model of the Baron de Charlus, dandy and social king of his age, held a reception from four to seven at his Pavillon des Muses. Among those present were the Comtesse Greffülhe nee Chimay, Comte A. de la Rochefoucauld, Comtesse de Castellane, and Comtesse de Dampierre. On May 19, Mme Standish nee des Cars, a cousin of the Comte de Montesquiou, gave a charity party for the same people. On June 4 the Comte and Comtesse de Gabriac reciprocated with a *soirée musicale*. The same faces were present. And on June 1 and on June 8 the Comtesse E. de Pourtalès had two magnificent receptions; present were Ducs de Luynes, de Noailles, de la Trémoïlle, Prince Murat, Prince A. de Broglie, Comtesse Greffülhe, Comtes Jean, Boni, Stanislas de Castellane, Comtesse d'Haussonville, Comtes G. and A. de la Rochefoucauld, and others.[11] We are with the innermost core of the Faubourg Saint-

Germain: it is one large family constantly meeting—the world of the Guermantes.

This is the world Mme Verdurin calls "the bores" but desires intensely. This is the dream world of Marcel; this is the "chic" world of Odette, the world of "success" for Morel and Rachel, and the land of "final acceptance" for Bloch. The Faubourg remained closed to them during the seventies; but with the fall of aristocratic political power, a slow thaw set in in the eighties and was hastened by the political events of the nineties.[12] Intimate and isolated, the Faubourg needed new faces, something exotic like Jews and reformed demi-mondaines, artists for cultural inebriations, and selected rich bourgeois who could be watched burning in envy and who made rich marriages. But did those who were finally allowed to enter become *part* of the Faubourg, or were they simply in it? Let us turn to Marcel Proust and observe this society from a different perspective.

Proust came from the high bourgeoisie strata of society, which had a basic prerequisite for possible social advancement: money. His father, an Inspector-General of Public Health, had placed his wife's money so well that Marcel never had to work for an income. His social group, therefore, was as leisured as the aristocrats were. Though the individual was generally directed toward the bourgeois disciplines of law or medicine, many preferred the slippery but colorful career of social climbing. The extremely wealthy bourgeois imitated the aristocratic life: he owned a chateau, he rode to hounds, he gave cotillions in Paris, he cheered his horses at Chantilly, he sailed a yacht at Deauville; he had, in short, every accoutrement but position.

To live outside the Faubourg, though imitating it, must have been frustrating, not unlike kissing a woman through a veil. But eventually the bourgeois used his economic means to penetrate first the impoverished noble society and eventually, by social osmosis, the inner Faubourg. The Lebaudy family, the great sugar merchants, did this, as did the Wendels and the Schneiders, the Carnegies of France; and the French symbol of supreme wealth, the Rothschilds, who even received an Austrian title, though Jewish, and whose daughters in 1900 were married to such distinguished noblemen as the Prince de Wagram and the Duc de Gramont. Marriage remained the assured way to obtain and secure entrance.

Besides rich Jewish maidens who became ennobled through marriage, there were American girls such as Anna Gould, who married Comte Boni de Castellane, and Mattie Mitchell, who married the Duc de la Rochefoucauld; they offered rich dowries and were absorbed quickly. (The Princesse de Monaco nee Kelly continues the tradition in our time.) The name of the families was continued, but the origins of the bearer are radically different.

Proust's treatment of high society would be in fact a study more of the bearer and how he or she rose to the Faubourg than of the history or mystique of the title. The great truth which Proust would reveal about society is that it constantly changes within each strata, as an audience does every night in a theater (II, p. 544; PIII, p. 236).

Young Proust, on the fringes of high society, held several advantages besides the necessary wealth: intelligence, urbanity, artistic inclinations, and the exoticism of being half Jewish. He began the climb early. Through his lycée friend Jacques Bizet he entered his first literary bourgeois salon, that of his friend's mother, Mme Straus—a rather good beginning.[13] This salon mixed artists with artistically inclined nobles. In 1890 he met Gaston de Caillavet, who took him to his mother, Mme Arman de Caillavet, who charmed the leading writer Anatole France to her gilded cage and thus created the leading bourgeois salon of the Belle Epoque.[14] Through this salon Proust received invitations to other literary bourgeois salons and met enlightened nobles. He was able to meet the Empire nobles in the salon of the Princesse Mathilde, whose salon was not difficult to enter.[15] In 1893 Proust met the Comte de Montesquiou at Madeleine Lemaire's salon. According to Jacques-Emile Blanche, Proust's friend and portraitist, Proust had not really circulated among the "gratin" of the Faubourg until Montesquiou made it possible.[16]

Proust then began to frequent the salons of the Murat, Wagram, Polignac, and Gramont.[17] It was in 1894 at the Princesse de Wagram's that he saw the queen of the Faubourg, Comtesse

Greffülhe nee Chimay.[18] Excited, Proust wrote the following to Montesquiou: "But all the mystery of her beauty is in the radiance; in the enigma above all of her eyes. I have never seen so beautiful a woman. I don't feel I can introduce myself to her and I will not ask that even of you because apart from the indiscretion which could result, it seems to me that I would suffer a rather painful anxiety to speak to her." [19] (Another talent we see Proust exploited was flattery.) Shortly after, Proust was introduced to her, but he never really became a member of her set. On May 21, 1898, Proust was mentioned in *Le Gaulois* as being at a "very elegant dinner, Monday night at the home of the Marquise de Brou." Present were the Duchesse d'Uzès, dowager, Comte and Comtesse Laugier-Villars, Marquise de St. Paul, M. M. Le Myre de Vilers, M. Dumber, M. E. Pailleron of the Académie Francaise, M. Grosclaude, Marcel Proust, Prince Aymon de Lucinge. It may appear that it was a select party, but in truth it was rather mixed: literary people and "intellectual" nobles—the usual fare for Proust. By 1904 he seems to have become quite friendly with the Princesse Bibesco, a novelist, and Anna de Noailles, a poetess: "I dined last night at the Noailles, where I dine rather often." In the same year he thought of joining a club and approached Antoine Bibesco, but he quickly withdrew when Antoine did not display much concern.[21] By 1905 Proust commanded enough respect to invite to his party Comte Aymery de la Rochefoucauld, les Guiches (son of the Duc de Gramont and his new wife Elaine Greffülhe), Comtesse d'Haussonville, Duchesse de Gramont, Princesse de Chimay, and Madeleine Lemaire, who all came.[22] Obviously, this is the same "gratin" which attended the great receptions of 1903.

It is of interest to note that salons constitute the first part of Proust's early literary effort, his *Chroniques*—articles originally published in *Le Figaro*—which were flowery evocations of the "elite" salons which Proust attended in the last years of the century: the salon of Princesse E. de Polignac, Comtesse d'Haussonville, Comtesse de Guerne, and so on. Proust, therefore, was already at work taking notes for his masterpiece. His active social life continued until a little after 1900 when inspiration at last rescued him.

Was Proust a social success? It appears so; apparently he knew some of the highest members of the Faubourg. But was he a full member of the Faubourg? We may doubt it. He was not part of high society like the successful climber Charles Haas, who was the only Jew to become a member of the Jockey Club and who did know superficially the Comte de Paris and the Prince of Wales (whom Proust did not know). Actually Proust was friendly mainly with the "intellectually" inclined members of the Faubourg and not with the horsey set.[23] His acquaintance with such really great society names as Brissac, Fitz-James, d'Harcourt, and La Trémoïlle, which are continually mentioned in *A la Recherche,* seem to have eluded Proust in life; that is, he probably met them but he never knew them intimately. And Lucien Daudet, his friend, was no doubt correct when he said of Proust: "He failed to be received in the genuine and constant intimacy of some Madame de Guermantes or other, in order to see the inner workings of some French families apart from the formal hours." [24] This is supported by the Comte de Luppé, who said: "[Proust] knew the public life of society, but he did not penetrate its intimacy. The club life, the chateau—important in society—Proust never penetrated." [25] This may explain in part why the aristocracy in the novel appears mainly in salon scenes.

Proust seems to have served as an ornament to the salon (like a Bloch) and did not become an integral member. The strange Charles Briand in his book *Le Secret de Marcel Proust,* the *Kama-Sutra* of French criticism, states that Proust's role in Society was at best that of a "reporter of social events" for *Le Figaro.*[26] This may be overstating the case, but there is strong evidence from those who saw him in society that "Proust appeared to be a non-conformist," [27] because of his old-fashioned mannerisms, excessive flattery, his constant interests in genealogy and protocol; [28] in short, because of his exotic personality, which was no doubt the original reason he was admitted into high society. It is clear, then, that Proust was a small figure in the Faubourg; he enriched it by his presence but he was not a full member. He fulfilled by his conversation and wit the same role as other artists in society: that of the entertainer. He was, one could say, a *jongleur* to the court and perhaps *Hofjude*. It is the error of later generations to see Proust as an important member of his chosen society. No doubt the narrator Marcel, moving nimbly from one social success to the other in the masterwork, might give this impression; but until Marcel Proust received the Goncourt Prize in 1919, the author was always known as "our little Marcel," a witty, sensitive hypochondriac.

Since snobbery and social climbing are supposedly the great motivating factors of the Faubourg and its members, let us discover Proust's position: Was he a snob, was he a social climber? To answer this question means considering many contradictory opinions. No subject—not even the novel—has so fired the imaginations and quills of critics. They are evenly divided. George Painter, the biographer, the English critics Stephen Hudson and Ralph Wright, the maudlin Cattaui, and the great Curtius absolutely reject the thought that Proust was a snob.[29] Revel goes farther and says that Proust never even conceived of Le Monde.[30] Maurois, Nathan, and Pierre-Quint are perhaps less assured and declare that if he did social climb or practice snobbery, it was to probe into the relations of human beings and the social machine.[31] In contrast Proust's friends Georges de Lauris and the Princesse Bibesco as well as Henri Bonnet, Miss Haldane, and Louis Auchincloss accept Proust's social ambitions as real and are not very concerned.[32] Those that really accused him were mainly those who saw him in high society: Baron Seillière, Jean Cocteau, Duchesse E. de la Rochefoucauld, Duchesse de Clermont-Tonnerre, Maria-Anne Cochet, Clive Bell, André Germain, and the inimitable Charles Briand.[33] For them Proust's sin is that he pursued the bearers of great titles and imitated their ways.[34]

It seems to me ridiculous to defend Proust against the charge that he had youthful social ambitions (as witness his "friends"), but it seems equally foolish to make him appear a snob all his life. One would be hard pressed to protect Proust on the basis of the *Chroniques* alone, for such phrases as the following are clearly flattery: "The charming company of M. and Mme d'Haussonville is like those waters which are more exquisite taken from their very source, but which one can use very well in

Paris" (*Chroniques,* p. 52); and, speaking of the voice of the Comtesse de Guerne, "It is probably the only example of a voice without physical support, of a voice not only pure but so spiritualized that it seems more a sort of natural harmony" (*Chroniques,* p. 3). In his youth he obviously played the social game and enjoyed it. But it did not take him long to see that part of his early motivations were snobbish. This did not stop him from enjoying the salon, but it placed his social life in a new perspective: it was not really very important. Society eventually became the material he exploited for his fictions. Proust's first work, *Les Plaisirs et les Jours,* already displays social satire, and *Jean Santeuil* clearly exposes Proust's view of high society: "Moreover, society life is preoccupied with three things . . . snobbism, that is to say admiration of that which in others is independent of their personality; scandal, namely the extreme attention given most of the time (under the pretext of criticism) to appearances; social conventions and etiquette, the erection of formalism in things real and even more real than all the rest" (JS II, p. 129). And in *A la Recherche* the social experience of the hero, who is Proust's mouthpiece, is meant to reveal the "emptiness of salon life" (PII, p. 416). Mauriac quotes a letter from Proust in which we read, "I Guermantized the other evening and my most amiable hosts appeared to me rather stupid." [35] "I had been among society folk enough to know that they, not the electrical workers, are the real illiterates" (II, p. 1008; PIII, p. 888). Examples are numerous concerning Proust's mature feeling about high society; the *chef-d'oeuvre* reveals his total rejection of it.[36] However, one striking example of Proust's social relationship which offers his final attitude toward society, satire, appears in the following letter written in 1918 about his friend, the Duc d'Albuféra.

> What do you think of this judgement of Albu (Duc d'Albuféra, one of Proust's few noble friends of the "horse set")?

Telephone conversation:

—But my dear Louis, did you read my book?
—Read your book, have you written a book?
—Yes Louis, I even sent it to you.
—Ah, my little Marcel, if you sent it to me, I have certainly read it, only I wasn't certain of having received it. (Sic) [37]

It would seem to follow that social relationships had little to do with friendship, common interests, or understanding. Proust discovered this fairly early. "I realize how little a 'strong friendship' amounts to in the fashionable world" (II, p. 98; PIII, p. 852). And one could say that in his novel each character is alone; all friendships are superficial. This highly pessimistic attitude, no doubt, expresses his life's experience. Let us therefore look at his friendships to discover who they were and how they were conducted. It has been reliably reported that Proust's lycée friends were mainly Jewish or half Jewish.[38] They were Robert Dreyfus, Daniel Halévy, Jacques Bizet, Fernand Gregh, Reynaldo Hahn, and Léon Brunschvicg. They all had in common a lively literary interest, which was expressed in a little revue they published. Proust would maintain weak relationships with these school friends for the rest of his life, but these were never smooth. He was known as an excessive flatterer throughout his life. He exploited flattery well, though, for it helped him enter the salon of Mme Straus and Mme de Caillavet, through a devoted cultivation of their sons. And flattery proved especially effective with the Comte Robert de Montesquiou, who opened the gates of high society for him. Between 1900 and 1906 Proust's friends were mainly nobles: the Marquis Bertrand de Fénelon, Prince Antoine Bibesco, Duc de Guiche, Marquis d'Albuféra, and Prince Léon Radziwill.[39] By Proust's friendship patterns we can see that he did climb socially, and apparently quite willingly.

Flattery for Proust was a means to an end and possibly his sole way of communicating with the outside world. Here is an example of flattery directed to his literary friend Mme de Noailles. "I beg of you stop being so kind, because I can no longer bear its burden of happiness of recognition, of emotion, of stupefaction which is so strong I would die of it."[40] Perhaps Proust did feel this way at the time, but he would later reveal his sentiments in a letter to Louis de Robert: "while looking through some papers, some letters from her [Mme de Noailles] written for the most part after each of my articles in *Le Figaro,* or a long telegram from her under the pretext of complimenting me, rewrote the article for the better."[41] Gide, who knew them both, said these revealing words: "but Proust knowing Mme de Noailles sufficiently, knew her to be vain and quite incapable of criticism, and hoped that the most outlandish praise appeared to her the most worthy, the most sincere; he used her as he used everybody."[42] Proust exploited friends; that is rather clear, but that he "used everybody" seems a cruel accusation. Proust admittedly did not put much stock in friendship, but I think the answer lies not in his unpleasant encounters but within himself.

Being a homosexual, Proust felt set apart from the normal world. He desired, however, like any normal person, some deep meaningful friendship. But Proust knew that if he revealed his true inclinations, the friendship would end and he would be ostracized. Proust, therefore, was frustrated in his friendships. They could be only superficial for him and underline his isolation. Gide, of course, emphasized Proust's homosexuality in his *Journals.* "Far from denying or hiding his uranism, he displays it, and I could almost say, boasts of it."[43] But Proust went out of his way in public—as with his friend Walter Berry—to deny any possible incriminating association. In his letters to Berry, when he talks of love or expresses deep feelings for the American, he constantly repeats, "Nothing of Charlus."[44] In a biting letter to Paul Souday, Proust attacks the critic for using the adjective *féminine* in regard to himself: "From feminine to effeminate, there is only one step. Those who have served me as witnesses in duels will tell you if I have the softness of effeminates."[45] Proust was highly sensitive to his homosexual problem and ashamed of this aberration. A disciple of Proust's, Emmanuel Berl, recalled: "He taught the solitude of man and the fatality of passions."[46] The significance of friendship and homosexuality will of course be important in the work as a disruptive element in high society. Proust demonstrated what odd friendships develop around this theme.

Art for such a man as Proust was the sole means by which he could communicate to the world.[47]

It is well known that Proust's mother was Jewish, nee Weil, of Alsatian origin. This fact had an important effect on Proust and has been made much of by critics.[48] But although his mother was from a rich Jewish middle-class home, Proust was raised and died a Catholic. More important, religion obviously played no role in his life, and must have meant little to his parents. (If intermarriage between Jew and Gentile is still frowned upon by both groups, can one imagine how much more daring was it in earlier times?) We may safely doubt that Proust received any occult initiation into the mysteries of Gallicism or circumcision. It would be better to view him as the best product of a Third Republic education.

In the novel, the Jewish question arises only in terms of high society and the Dreyfus Affair. It is true that Proust climbed into the Faubourg through the Jewish and half-Jewish salons of Mme Straus, widow Bizet nee Halévy, and Mme de Caillavet nee Lippmann. He was aware of the antisemitism of Montesquiou and other arrogant nobles, but he achieved a certain acceptance by bowing, in part, to their prejudices. Yet when the Dreyfus Affair struck the Faubourg, Proust defended Dreyfus and identified when necessary with the Jews.[49] "*La Libre Parole* [an antisemitic paper, a forerunner of the *Action Française*] had said that a certain number of young Jews including M. Marcel Proust, etc., vilified Barrès [an anti-Dreyfusard]. In order to correct this, it would have been necessary to say that I was not a Jew and I didn't want to. Thus I let it be said that I had demonstrated against Barrès, which was not true." [50]

Proust, in fact, though not active in the Dreyfusard movement, was a Dreyfusard and was very proud of this fact throughout his life. He watched in dismay and fascination as the Affair split society into factions. He was shocked to see Jews ostracized from salons and recorded these events in both *Jean Santeuil* and *A la Recherche*. In his later years he complained to J. E. Blanche, in great indignation, that such anti-Dreyfusard aristocrats as the Princesse de Monaco, mother of the Duc de Richelieu and of the Comtesse G. de la Rochefoucauld, joined by the Princesse Wagram and the Duchesse de Gramont, left the Straus salon because its mistress was a Dreyfusard—though these "ladies" were born with such names as Heine and Rothschild.[51] Such actions are bad enough when carried out by old aristocrats, but when *parvenus* commit such acts because it is "the thing" to do—and reject their own origins—it is not only self-destructive but also the clearest evidence of the social disease of snobbery. Obviously the *arriviste* must slavishly imitate the old noble to excess so that he can remain in the good graces of the alien society he has elected to make his own. By honoring his own principles Proust jeopardized his social ambitions, revealing himself to be an intellectual first and a *mondain* second.

Proust, in fact, was not unaware of the foibles he encountered among Jewish Frenchmen, and he seemed to joke continually about them.[52] In fact, the character of Bloch springs out of Proust's comic spirit. He believed, nevertheless, that total assimilation of all Jews in France was possible, which certainly placed him within the mainstream of liberal thinking in his age. Proust had evidence in the person of Charles Haas, the one Jew to enter the Jockey Club as well as being one of the most successful *mondains* of the age. Proust apparently wished to imitate his success. One could then say that Charles Haas was Proust's yardstick to social success in life as Swann is to the narrator Marcel in the work. The role and function of the Jews in the novel will be further discussed in Chapter V.

The novel which Proust constructed spans the Belle Epoque (from 1870 to 1925) and reflects not only the personal vision of the author but the historical events of the age through the lucid broodings of Marcel the narrator.

And I understood that all these materials for literary work were nothing else than my past life. . . .
—Marcel Proust (II, pp. 1015-16; PIII, p. 899)

It is the artist who portrays what is more real than reality itself.
—Leo Lowenthal, Literature and the Image of Man

Indeed, we may perhaps remark that the greater part of the vague images and sensations that come to us even after childhood is over, and in the rest of our life, are nothing but a memory of that time —a recollection, a repetition, an echo, or a reflection of that ancient image.
—Giacomo Leopardi, Zibaldone

Chapter II

CONCEPT AND COMPOSITION

For Proust, beauty is revealed when great truths are unearthed and explained. "And since art is a faithful recomposing of life, around the verities which one has finally found within oneself there will always float an atmosphere of poetry (II, p. 1015; PIII, p. 898). It is not surprising that critics trained to think of art in terms of explicitly defined genres should face a problem upon discovering that *The Remembrance of Things Past* fits no standard pattern that exists for French novels. Proust was forming his own mold. Casting aside traditional plot and continued action, somewhat as did Sterne in *Tristram Shandy* or possibly Diderot in *Jacques le Fataliste,* Proust conceived of his work as an interpretation, a critical analysis, of his narrator's life. "The duty and the task of a writer are those of a translator" (II, p. 1009; PIII, p. 890). The novel is not an invention of a tale but an explication of the tale which is one's own past life. Art, then, captures, distills, and recasts for Proust the lived experience.

The problem which arises in viewing this new form of novel is to discover what central theme, what essential idea, knits the work together. Everyone admits that Proust treats of time, art, space, society, reality, love, the search for a vocation, and so forth. But there seems to be no agreement as to what constitutes the backbone of the work. Most think time is the central theme. Their argument may be crudely summed up in this way: Proust goes back and discovers the different "selves" captured by time; he exhumes them by the voluntary memory, orders them, and immortalizes them in a work of art (something "timeless"); thus man conquers time.

The theme of the occupational search is also popular. The critic Edmond Kinds presents this point of view succinctly: *"La Recherche du Temps Perdu* is the novel of a vocation: the only plot thread which does not break between the first and the last volume." [1] He bases his strongest argument on a little sentence from *Past Recaptured:* "And so my entire life up to that day could—and, from another point of view, could not—be summed up under the title, *A Vocation*" (II, p. 1016; PIII, p. 899). There is also his reference to "that invisible vocation of which these volumes are the history" (I, p. 1002; PII, p. 397).

Kinds and his group may convince us that there is a vocational theme, but they cannot deny the importance of the time theme. Proust himself warned against using general titles to prove a point: "often with readers the title is more or less a symbol, an image that must be taken in a sense more general, more poetic than the reader of the book will give it" (*Contre Sainte-Beuve,* p. 206). Time and vocations are significant, but by offering different titles Proust suggests that neither alone is adequate. The vocational theme, furthermore, may have a corollary, the art theme. The novel constantly treats of artists, artistic problems, and the author's attempt to make the work itself immortal art; but it can be argued that there is no sustained treatment of art, that it appears and disappears.

Consideration of these three themes—time, vocation, and art—were the most popular for critics of Proust until the nineteen fifties. Since then, with the growing interest in bringing psychology, philosophy, and sociology to bear on literary criticism, highly sophisticated works by Jauss, Brée, Zéphir, Picon, and Bersani have appeared. Zéphir renewed critical interest in the narrator and his life as the backbone of the work: "Thus the first object of Proust in his novel was to discover his 'real self,' his profound personality, and at the same time to evolve from his observation, from his experience of life and of men, a conception of the human person." [2] Ian Watt, the fine comparativist, effectively supports this agreeable theme and offers Hume as Proust's philosophic ancestor.[3] It is self-evident that the omnipresence of the narrator and his relations is a constant in the work, yet the originality of the Zéphir and Watt studies becomes clear only when we realize that the narrator's personality is defined in time. Thus even the narrator's life is not the only backbone: the time theme is still required. Moss, Picon, and Bersani also take up this new viewpoint, but they attempt to redefine the central idea of the work. Moss sees the grand theme as the narrator's attempt to cope with the meaning of reality, again in a time context.[4] Picon's originality is in offering as the central theme the deception which external reality imposes upon the narrator—thereby joining the abstract themes of the earlier critics with the personal themes of the more recent ones. Picon's concept of the work, however, seems to me basically a more highly refined expression of yet another theme: Proust's search for reality.[5] Bersani, in other words, agrees with Picon when he states that the novel "shows how the disappointments the narrator suffers as a result of his extraordinarily rich imagination lead him to give up novelizing in life to reminisce about the way he used to novelize, in art." [6]

Reality versus unreality has been a most fruitfully developed theme since 1950, and critics as varied as Martin-Deslias, Picon,

Maurois, and Turnell have called it the central idea of the work. (Picon's most original contribution is to demonstrate that Proust approaches reality as an experiment rather than accepting reality as the basis of an experience.)[7] But the reality theme, however valid, does not invalidate the claims of the art, time, or vocational themes. In short, I believe that no single theme can be called central.

The Remembrance of Things Past is so vast a work that Proust, who was trying to put his whole essence into it, needed more than one central idea upon which to rest his themes, illustrations, and general laws. At this point an analogy may be useful. In Proust's work, each episode of the simple, direct narrative can be thought of as a pearl on a strand. If each episode is a pearl, many of them will become too heavy for one strand to hold. What could one do? Through the perforation in each pearl send two or more finely twined silk threads. This, I believe, is exactly analogous to what Proust did: he entwined the themes of time, space, art, reality, vocation, and so forth. But the one theme which is evident on every page of the novel is the social theme: it is embodied in every episode. Marcel depicts society, in its sociological and worldly senses, from Aunt Léonie's house to the farewell to the "worldly" life at the matinee of the Princesse de Guermantes. All the events, all the actions in the novel take place in the external world. We are constantly watching Marcel and his relationships with other groups and individuals with whom he attempts to communicate, be it for reasons of love or snobbery.[8] One cannot really open any page and say here is time itself, or art itself, but Marcel's relations with the external world are on every page. The paradox is that the written work as a whole is the product of the internal world, but in the recounting it is just at that moment when Marcel enters the inner world that the novel ends! Thus the text presents the narrator's interpretation of his experiences in the external world.

The origins of Proust's effort to describe and interpret society have deep roots in French literary history. Balzac made the first attempt. He was not, of course, the first to deal with different strata of society, but he was the first to attempt to describe all the aspects of an age in literature. Balzac taught Proust the cyclical use of character and the love of meaningful detail as well as the grouping of works under one inclusive title.

The French literary tradition was chiefly concerned with portraying the rich bourgeoise and aristocrat, who were fascinated with descriptions of themselves, especially in idealistic poses. From the epics and Breton tales of medieval France to the portraits *chez* Rambouillet, high society was likened to the ideal or gallant image of the age. It is with the rise of the novel that idealism dissolved into reality—though only at a slow pace. The Scudéry tradition still painted knights errant wandering about the mythic map of Tendre. The real turning point, in my opinion, is Furetière's *Roman Bourgeois,* in which upper middle-class society is presented in a life-like manner. In fact, when the critic Harry Levin defines the novel as having the quality of a human document and a work of art, he is referring to this realist tradition of the novel.[9] However, the use of material drawn from the life around one was first exploited by dramatists. From the medieval farce to Molière, through Dancourt to the *comédie larmoyante,* theater treated everyday realities more incisively. It was in the middle of the eighteenth century, that Marivaux and later Restif de la Bretonne evolved the realist novel. But realism in the novel tended to treat lower-class elements, whereas the comic theater portrayed the upper classes.

The writers of memoirs also recorded society. Saint-Simon, in his massive memoir, thrashed an entire generation when he recorded the life of high society in the French court at the beginning of the eighteenth century. This highly personal genre, the memoir, permitted not only a retelling but a critique of one's life or one's image of an age. Proust read Saint-Simon avidly and did not fail to learn from him genealogies, stylistic devices, dramatic anecdotal situations, and Saint-Simon's view of class struggles from his own entrenched position. Herbert De Ley's valuable *Proust and Saint-Simon* demonstrates the important influence of memorialists upon Proust. In *Mémoires d'Outre-Tombe* of Chateaubriand we encounter poetic reminiscences which offer a justification of the author's existence as well as an image of the great man against the backdrop of his age. Chateaubriand, acting as a born writer by dramatizing his existence, offers a highly personal vision of society as reflected through his own careers. The technique of the interpretation of the macrocosm through the microcosm, the individual, greatly appealed to Proust, who eventually used the first-person narrative in this fashion.

The emergence of Balzac, the social novelist, in the early nineteenth century is not *sui generis.* At the same time Auguste Comte was writing his *Cours de Philosophie Positive,* which was the beginning of the social sciences. By the end of the century the social sciences were in full bloom: it was the age of Marcel Mauss, A. Van Gennep, L. Lévy-Bruhl, Henri Hubert, and Emile Durkheim. With the scientific study of society, it was hardly possible that interest in the changes within society would go unobserved by writers. The beginning of the Third Republic offered a durable example: Zola.

General laws of society were being proposed, determinism was brought to the arts by Taine, and Zola was the outcome. Taking Balzac's panorama of society and grafting it onto a pseudo-scientific deterministic theory of behavior, Zola watched the descent of a few generations of the Rougon-Macquart family in the Second Empire. One can argue today about the proof of his theories, but few critics would question Zola's powers as a storyteller and observer of an age. Proust disliked Zola for his poor style, *roman à thèse* elements, simple presentation of character, and the purely external world in which the characters move. But Proust has much in common with Zola. Both wished to establish laws, Proust deductively, Zola inductively. Both selected families and developed them throughout their novels. Both take us into scenes of depravity and leave us with an image of the corruption of mankind. And both are indebted to Balzac and the positivist and determinist movements.

By 1900, in fact, the theater and the novel were portraying the modern age. In the theater Henri Becque's *Les Corbeaux* set off a series of bourgeois melodramas, which Curel, Porto-Riche, and Brieux assiduously developed. In the novels preciosity was mixed with bitter social observations by Bourget, Hervieu, and France. It is little wonder that Proust, who knew all these men, absorbed their interests as he wandered in high society with them.

Proust, then, is a focal point for the different ways and means to treat society. Proust's original contribution to the use of the social theme is to portray society as it can be seen through the eyes of a child, a young man, and a graying man. This method offers different perspectives of society by an observer who admits he is not omniscient, and society is revealed as a reflection of one man's changing vision. The persona is in the center of the world he creates, and we accept it as the world of the age he is presenting. It is this element which gives the book not only the sense of authenticity but also the flavor of a memoir or an autobiography. We see what he sees, we correct our views when he corrects his, we can watch the fantasy of a child's image of life dissolve slowly into the reality of worldly existence. In short, the author, by use of the first person, is directly involved in the work, whereas traditionally such a panoramic vision in literature uses the third person singular, a technique which creates a falsely detached vision.

Proust concentrates on portraying characters in high society to observe human behavior closely in a social situation. By watching the social movement he not only acts as a chronicler of his age but reveals the mechanism that causes change in society, whether due to personal whim or external events. In short, Proust, not unlike Thackeray in *Vanity Fair,* offers a panorama of his age, but, as I have said, he also analyzes closely a particular portion—high society.

However, the novel is no *roman à clef*. Proust was interested in forming characters who are individuals in their own right as well as representatives of some class in society. By showing everything in movement—by choosing a specific day or evening across the years and intensely analyzing the narrator's reactions and his impressions of the external world, and by observing what other members of society are doing—Proust not only reveals but easily compares the society from one period to another; laws of social behavior are deduced and the sense of time—that great theme—is underlined as the narrator seeks his vocation in this external world of complex interpersonal relations. Therein lies the originality of Proust's treatment of society and its members. Whereas Paul Hervieu, a decent writer, observes with bitter irony a person at a ball, Proust not only observes his presence, notes his quirk, but analyzes how he has changed, how he has not changed, what are the hidden social motives in his mannerisms and speech, how he represents a class, his function vis à vis the hosts, and his relations with the narrator. Thus the society is treated in terms of person, class, institution, and as a whole: the external world. I shall attempt to examine that society in the same way.

Until the last hundred pages of the work, the narrator defined reality itself as the external world. In the first part of his life Marcel sought happiness and meaning in the outside world through social climbing and a love affair. In these aspects Marcel was following Swann, who acted as his Vergil. Whereas Swann withered on the vine by accomplishing nothing meaningful for himself or others, Marcel avoided death in life—which is Swann's existence—because he was determined to conquer life by understanding the self. This determination is exposed to the world in the form of art (the one real act of being in his life), which is, in Proust's terms, the only means to communicate with another. "Only by art can we get outside ourselves" (II, p. 1013; PIII, p. 895).

M. Picon effectively shows that the *moi* in Proust which is dissatisfied with living upon itself can only find fulfillment outside of itself by contact with the external world. Yet in this contact the author is deceived because of his false expectations.[10] But the author never abandons his desire to make contact with reality, the external world of society. His means of attack are unique. Proust is not content to live upon himself as a hermit; on the contrary, the world outside himself, the other being, would fulfill his own life if only he could communicate satisfactorily with others. There is a misconception among critics who think Proust believed man to be so alone that he cannot communicate. If Proust believed this, he would never have written the novel. It is precisely because Proust wished to make external contact that he did write the novel. Other forms of communication, such as conversation, friendship, or love are little more than clichés, ramblings, and salon banter. Proust and the narrator realize that they have gained little, that their own participation in society has yielded only superficiality. Proust needed to discover his own real self, not the external *moi*, in order to re-evaluate his existence and find some basis for happiness. The sole means of communication, then, became art. "Life as it really is, life disclosed at last and made clear, consequently the only life that is really lived, is literature" (II, p. 1013; PIII, p. 895).

In the novel, then, Proust uses his portrayal of society as a structural element to serve as the *reflection* or impression of the external world that exists in a single man's mind, a mind through which the author reviews and explains to the outside world the different stages of his existence; he does not offer direct descriptions of what he sees (in the manner of contemporary writers). Like Velasquez in *Las Meninas,* he uses a mirror to capture himself and the world around him in their proper relationship and proportion. In this vast panorama Proust, not unlike the sociologist, was looking for general laws: "Whereas I had sought great laws, they called me one who grubs for petty details" (II, p. 1118; PIII, p. 1040). "Was it not more worthwhile that I should study the gestures they made, the words they uttered, their lives, their natures, and endeavor to plot the curve and induce the general law?" (II, p. 1080; PIII, p. 986). Compare this statement to one by Mr. Evans-Pritchard, the noted anthropologist: "The aim of social anthropology is to reduce all social life to laws of general statements about the nature of society which allow prediction." [11] We could say that Proust attempts to unite the creative intuitive act with the scientific deductive method. He offers a *coup de théâtre* at the end of the work in which he explains that this external world which we have seen so brilliantly exposed is the false world, hence the paradox: he must now retreat into himself to write the work we have just read. He must explore inner reality and discover himself. At that point—the last one hundred pages—the novel turns on its axis, and takes on a circular form. We can begin the work again and this time catch the proofs of his deductive laws of human behavior and understand how he sidestepped his true vocation. Through art, then, he has discovered himself and the road to meaningful communication. (This concept is not unlike Platonic thought, for Plato has man seek the Good, discover it, and then go back to lead others to it. The external society in that case may well be explained as being the shadows on the wall of the cave. Proust was the lucky slave who broke his chains, sought the sunlight, and recounted his arduous pilgrimage in the novel after the experience had been digested and understood.)

We are therefore interested in looking at society from a literary-anthropological point of view when we examine its social classes, world view, institutions, and biography. The value of this approach is that it permits us to study a work of art and perhaps make a contribution to social history at the same time. Proust takes this course and accordingly serves as the chronicler and portraitist of his age: the book becomes a microcosm of the Belle Epoque. Proust actually was aware of his multiple role as artist. "My dear friend, you tell me that there is a certain social sense as well as some repercussions in this book; I accept this double compliment; you will see that it is true when you are acquainted with the other two volumes." [12]

The salon is an important social institution in the novel. In the salon Proust can observe people, their idiosyncrasies and their reactions to other people, events of the age (the Dreyfus Affair and World War I), and the effects time had on society from 1870 to approximately 1925. "And the interest of these salon transformations was that they were also an effect of lost time and a phenomenon of memory" (PIII, p. 993). By choosing to study society, chiefly through the salon, Proust chose the major social institution. (*Le Figaro,* and *Le Gaulois,* the leading society papers of the day, devoted most of their second pages to salon events).

Society, especially high society, is not static in Proust. The word "transformation" is the key to an understanding of the social theme: everyone is in flux. Proust accordingly seeks out the laws which govern social movement and necessarily follows the minute changes in the character and clientele of a salon. What is more astounding than the rise of Odette? Her constant mobility is barely perceptible and yet, while the sand runs out of an hour glass, Odette is transformed from a demi-mondaine into a wife and finally metamorphosed into a countess. Chronological time appears only now and again with the off-hand observation that Odette has a new affectation.

The transformation of society is not a new theme, but it has not occupied the attention of critics and literary historians significantly until the last ten years. Benjamin Crémieux and Léon Pierre-Quint were the first to underline the importance of Proust's function as a chronicler.[13] Later Baker, Coelho, Mansfield, Brée, Moss, and especially Revel and Bersani have presented interesting chapters on the same theme.[14]

While I tend to agree with the above-mentioned critics—insofar as they comment on the importance of society—I find certain of their views contestable. When Turnell and Krutch talk of Proust's treatment of society as "Apollonian" and say that it is "a relief to turn to a writer who doesn't take sides," I believe they are in error.[15] Be it a question of politics (the Dreyfus Affair), class distinctions, or homosexuality, though Proust makes "many thousand distinctions," he clearly informs us of his feelings. Like Pirandello, Proust may see different sides of the truth, but he does not shirk from expressing an opinion. In fact, Proust has Marcel bitterly attack Swann's inability to take a stand: "But now I found myself slightly shocked by this attitude which Swann invariably adopted when face to face with generalities. He appeared unwilling to risk even having an opinion, and to be at his ease only when he could furnish, with meticulous accuracy, some precise but unimportant detail. But in so doing he did not take into account that even here he was giving an opinion, holding a brief (as they say) for something, that the accuracy of his details had an importance of its own" (I, p. 75; PI, p. 98).

A favorite attack upon Proust's treatment of society is its "limited" panorama. When March attacks Proust's "realistic panorama of society" as "far inferior in scope to Balzac's *Comédie Humaine*," I think we are faced with a critic's fumble with analogy.[16] Proust set out to record society through the reflection of one man's life, whereas Balzac had the pretension to want to capture an entire society. Thus their goals were different. To say "inferior" or "superior" treatment is therefore unnecessary. However, a direct attack on Proust's "limitations" can be found in these comments by Van Meter Ames: "His life was so restricted externally that vast tracts of the modern scene he never saw at all—which is partly the reason why his novel takes his reader away from the dull reality as much as Arabian tales. Business does not exist in his pages except for its ancient form surviving in a picturesque fringe of small shopkeepers and street-hawkers. He ignored the industrial revolution." [17]

The "modern" world is not absent from the work, for who are the Verdurins, the Blochs, and the Swanns, if not the great entrepreneurs, financiers, and capitalists. They were products of the business world who did not worry about financial security—which is a very telling point about the age. Moreover, though money is hardly mentioned in the novel it is the lubricant of high society. And not all the nobles were unemployed. Norpois is a diplomat and Saint-Loup's father is President of the Suez Canal (I, p. 566; PI, p. 748).

Now Proust no doubt liked the picturesque quality of street-hawkers and small shopkeepers, but we must remember that Parisian society of 1900, with which he is dealing, had little industry in the city itself; even today the industrial complexes are outside the city. Paris is still a city of shopkeepers and a commercial center. Proust is not wrong in recording a city not yet braced to "modern industrial living." In daily life, the industrial revolution had little meaning, yet modern inventions such as the telephone, car, airplane, and electricity have their place in the novel.

That world of high society in 1900 may seem fantastic, but Proust's bitter words and sharp portrayals strip the masks from that escapist society. In fact, the whole attempt of the novel is to destroy any *Arabian Nights* vision of the contemporary world. The novelist reveals the atmosphere and the soul of the age. Witness the remarks of the anthropologist Robert Redfield:

> The characterizations of the artist and of the sensitive reporter are of course not precise at all; but very much of the whole is communicated to us. We might call them all portraits. They communicate the nature of the whole by attending to the uniqueness of each part, by choosing from among the parts of them for emphasis and by modifying them and rearranging them in ways that satisfy "the feeling" of the portrayer. Writers of novels . . . do a sort of verbal portraiture of the little community.[18]

> What Lafcadio Hearn wrote about the national character of the Japanese commands my assent, as does what Balzac wrote about the provincial bourgeois, and both Hearn and Balzac gave us plenty of evidence. Indeed the command exercized of my assent to the truth of those characterizations may be more powerful upon me than the command exercized by many a scientific study of group personality.[19]

Proust himself was aware of his role as a chronicler. In *Jean Santeuil* he makes the following remarks: "The chapter that we are going to write would not be less out of place in a psychological study on the different varieties of ambitious persons (*arrivistes*), in a historical study on society at the end of the nineteenth century, than in the most modern story of *Jean Santeuil*" (JS, I, p. 249).

To appreciate fully the social question it is vital to understand the Proustian character. Everyone who could climb into society and come in contact with the narrator is represented. The Proustian character represents the different events or transformations in society brought on by time, external events, and personal development. He is the microcosm of a social class in society. This is especially important because plot is unimportant—if existent—and it is the development of relationships between the individuals which is important in terms of construction and meaning for the social theme. Proust underlines the importance of the individual person in his work: "People foolishly imagine that the vast dimensions of social phenomena afford them an excellent opportunity to penetrate farther into the human soul; they ought on the contrary, to realize that it is by plumbing the depths of a single personality that they might have a chance of understanding those phenomena" (I, p. 953; PII, p. 33). And so Proust chiseled such individuals for the many different representatives in his novel: Odette the demi-mondaine, Verdurin the high bourgeois, Bloch the Jew, Morel the artist of peasant origins, Guermantes the aristocrat, and Françoise the maid.

Though Proust created representative types, his novel is not a *roman à clef*. Certainly he used characteristics of people he knew or had heard of, but that is typical of many a writer. However, when people recognize, for example, in Mme Verdurin, both Mme Aubernon and Mme Caillavet, they are not mistaken. When Mme Verdurin talks of "our dinners of conversation" (II, p. 550; PIII, p. 550), or of her "Anatole France" (II, p. 544; PIII, p. 236), contemporary readers correctly recognized Mme Aubernon or Mme Caillavet because Proust deftly caught the two personalities and fused them with others to make Mme Verdurin, a representative type. M. Léon Brunschvicg, Proust's schoolmate, saw himself portrayed as Bloch; the Marquise de Chevigné saw herself as Oriane while others saw Comtesse Greffülhe. That so many people can recognize so many different persons of their own time in the portraits shows that Proust was very accurate in recording what he saw: "there is not a single fictitious name of a character under which he could not write the names of sixty persons he has actually seen, one of whom posed for the grimace, another for the monocle, etc." (II, p. 1016; PIII, p. 900). The character grows like a mosaic fashioned from many pieces and expertly set. (We will discuss the composition of the character and his place in the structure of the novel in a later chapter.)

In studying the Proustian character we will watch what he desires from society, how he helps transform society, and how the society affects him. We will watch his mobility in both directions. The method called in anthropology "the biographical study" will permit a "depth" study of society. The characters whom Proust chose, I hope to prove, were not arbitrarily selected; they came from specific groups in society which were climbing into high society, and they were in direct contact with the customs and institutions of the age. The characters, by their actions, will permit Proust, in fact, to display his laws of human behavior. The very last words of the novel underline the importance of the character: "I would therein describe men . . . as occupying in Time a place far more considerable than the so restricted one allotted them in space, a place, on the contrary, extending boundlessly . . . in Time" (II, p. 1124; PIII, p. 1048).

The social theme provides the basis for the work and the people who populate the composition. They will congregate in the salon, the major social setting of the novel. As the work proceeds we really move from one salon to another. I agree with Revel, Poulet, Chaumeix, and Jauss that the novel is made of a series of fragments of time and space.[20] But the salon is the polarization point. People are either coming or going to one, and most of the scenes are within one. Mr. Moss has underlined eight major social events in his book,[21] but there are others which, if less formal, are still social gatherings at someone's home. Each salon affords a new look into the kaleidoscope of external life. The people seen in one salon change or disappear in the next one. And Proust notes: "for this writer . . . would need to prepare his book with minute care, constantly regrouping his forces as if for an attack" (II, p. 1112; PIII, p. 1032). The battle takes place in the salon. Each salon, then, like an old daguerrotype, links past years to present ones.

Chronology is basic to the social theme and the portrayal of the age. Recently much work has been done by Linn, Houston, Jaquillard, and especially Hachez and Jauss, to prove that Proust was conscious of a continued chronology.[22] (In the first chapter I have already given a synopsis of the political, social, and economic history of the time, so we need not concern ourselves with that here.) Linn, Houston, and Jauss have pointed out certain dates as hints to the *Zeitraumen* of each novel. Hachez has made the most detailed study and attempts to give the exact years for each novel. This may be overzealous but it shows that by and large Proust did conceive of each novel as being set within some time-space between the years 1870 and 1925.

Proust employs chronology in an original manner to give us a point of reference. Instead of stating a year he mentions some event. Sometimes it is a literary event, a new book or a theatrical success, sometimes a political event, a social scandal, or some disaster. This subtle means of pointing to chronology permits a certain floating world of time but it hardly varies more than five years. That Proust chose this method to record dates is consonant with his attitude toward time: we remember events, not dates.

I have worked out my own time sequences, which do not vary greatly from those of the above-mentioned authors except that I have added some of my own discoveries of particular time references.[23] There are, of course, strange errors in dates. The Russo-Japanese War of 1904 is placed in *In a Budding Grove* (I, p. 254; PIII, p. 331); Agadir 1911 is mentioned in *The Guermantes Way* (I, p. 1013; PII, p. 412); and L'Affaire Landru of 1920 is in *The Captive* (II, p. 523; PIII, p. 205); but these discrepancies are not a real problem. Proust in fact wanted some anachronisms, "our life being so careless of chronology, interpolating so many anachronisms in the sequence of our days" (I, p. 488; PI, p. 642). Mlle Brée, with much insight, states: "on the whole, and in spite of some dates interfering, the novel in its entirety advances slowly and chronologically." [24]

Since the different events occur in short periods of time, it should not be shocking to discover that almost all the first part of *Guermantes Way,* from the meeting of Saint-Loup and Rachel to the end of the Villeparisis salon scene, takes place in one day and each of the salon scenes in but a few hours. Proust concentrates on one small given moment and place and discovers the true meaning of the gathering as well as the reason for a person's presence at it. He chose with great care and efficiency people, places, and times he needed to illustrate his major themes and integrate them into his concept of a work of art.

One may list in an interminable description the objects that figured in the place described, but truth will begin only when the writer takes two different objects, establishing their relationship—analogous in the world of art to the sole relationship in the world of science, the law of cause and effect—and encloses them in the necessary rings of a beautiful style, or even when, like life itself, comparing similar qualities in two sensations, he makes their essential nature stand out clearly by joining them in a metaphor, in order to remove them from the contingencies of time. (II, p. 1008-9; PIII, p. 889)

The World View of a people is its characteristic outlook. It is the inside view, the ways in which a person of the group typically sees himself in relation to his world. It includes his mapping of that world, that is to say, the categories he uses in his perception of the familiar and of the strange. It includes the emphasis he places on what he sees, the choices he makes from among the alternatives he knows.
—David G. Mandelbaum,
Village India

I had removed one of my gloves,
When some remembrance of an act
Darted across my mind that made
Me leave the other one intact.
—Ishikawa Takuboku
(1885-1912)

Chapter III

THE WORLD VIEW

Robert Redfield has said: "Every world view is made of the stuff of philosophy, the nature of all things and their interrelations." [1] In short, the world view is "an inside view of the whole meaningful world of the native." [2] Proust's novel is the effort of one man to translate in terms of art a personal world view—and its structural components. The novel recreates through the narrator the quest of the author, who has sought to find meaning and order from his life experiences. When the narrator discovers that hidden behind the flotsam and jetsam of mundane existence there exists a meaningful unity within the narrator, who serves as the axis of his universe, he is filled with ecstatic happiness. But more significantly, the structure of the novel reproduces the world view of the narrator and of the author. The novelist has the craftsmanship, however, to delay the final revelation of the total world view until the last scene of the novel. Throughout the work, though, the author has used the structure of social settings which hint at the unity of the novel and the world view: involuntary memories, art works, dreams and journeys which, when drawn together at the right moment, will overwhelm Marcel with the realization of the unity of his existence. All that once seemed arbitrary, at loose ends, will appear meaningful, and the world view of the narrator will become apparent.

In the last major scene of the novel, a tired and frustrated old man arrives at the matinee of the Princesse de Guermantes. It is Marcel. As he emerges from the car, musing as usual, existence seems to him more than ever an endless fragmentation of possibilities that can never be crystallized, a series of unrelated, directionless moments waiting for final extinction. In this muted though lugubrious state, he trips upon two uneven cobblestones. (In musical terms, the recapitulation of the work begins at this moment.) Cobblestones! Marcel is suddenly happy, joyous, vibrant. The cobblestones serve as a catalyst, which for some mysterious reason release an intense emotional experience. Shortly thereafter, in the library of the Prince, the same extraordinary sense of felicity passes through Marcel; it is triggered by the teaspoon tapping against the plate, the napkin brushing his lips, and the discovery of an edition of *François le Champi.* By a little rational effort he realizes that the cobblestones had revived a memory of Venice; the teaspoon, a forest clearing; the napkin, Balbec; and *François le Champi,* Combray. Once again the power of the involuntary memory to revive the past and fuse it with the present into timelessness overwhelms Marcel with happiness. He decides he must uncover the meaning of these distinctly happy experiences.

Leaving the library, Marcel enters the salon and finds that most of the people he knew have grown old, and persons were present whom he never dreamed would frequent the house of Guermantes. The very house of Guermantes had gained a bourgeois Princess! Social life truly appeared kaleidoscopic, and once again life itself seemed utterly fragmented. In a melancholy state, Marcel encounters Mme de Saint-Loup, nee Gilberte Swann, who introduces him to her daughter, Mlle de Saint-Loup. Suddenly felicity pervades Marcel's being. Mlle de Saint-Loup "seemed to me like my own youth" (II, p. 1112; PIII, p. 1032). She draws him back to his youth because she is symbolically the meeting point of his life's experiences, all of which grow out of Combray. She unites the two families which most impressed Marcel in youth, the Swanns and the Guermantes. Gazing at her youthful face, Marcel realizes how time has passed over him from Combray to the present.

Mlle de Saint-Loup functions in the novel as the human Méséglise, the town which links by road Swann's home and the Guermantes' château, the keystone which joins Swann's Way and Guermantes' Way and thereby completes the Proustian world. She represents the fusion of the aristocracy and the upper bourgeoisie—the social movement which is a constant in the work. Mlle de Saint-Loup completes the cycle of Marcel's worldly existence by incarnating the two paths of his worldly interests: social climbing (Guermantes' Way) and love (Swann's Way). She knits together into a totality the seemingly fragmented worlds of Marcel's life, both intellectual and emotional, as is best represented by the symbol of the two ways (human possibilities) which merge at last. And by drawing Marcel back to his youth in Combray, to his hopes and joys, to the unsolved mystery of the two ways, she emphasizes that the Méséglise of his youth was clearly beyond his youthful scope because Méséglise itself is much more than a town or junction: it is the symbol of unification and order in life. Yet Marcel had the chance to discover the real meaning of Méséglise many years earlier at the beginning of *Past Recaptured,* when Gilberte surprised him by revealing that Guermantes could be reached from Tansonville via Méséglise. (Though this discovery was already foreshadowed during the narrator's evening walk with his parents.) At the time, Marcel did not search for the deeper meaning of this geographic discovery. Had he only done so then! "This work of the artist [is] to seek to discern something different underneath material, experience, words" (II, p. 1013; PIII, p. 896). But he was still not ready. Finally, at the matinee, at this late hour, meeting Mlle de Saint-Loup enables him to perceive his total temporal and spatial existence.

When Marcel discovered that Méséglise unites the two ways in Combray into a geographic unity at the beginning of *Past Recaptured,* he had partially resolved the mystery of Méséglise. But Mlle de Saint-Loup leads Marcel to the psychological meaning of the fusion: Guermantes' Way and Swann's Way, which he had heretofore considered *external* to himself, as separate worlds, were revealed as integral parts which had fused together to make up the unity of his existence. Marcel, then, in Combray could not be allowed to reach Méséglise, for it symbolized the attainment of his internal unity, the end of the quest. Only at the matinee does Marcel comprehend that Mlle de Saint-Loup, Swann's granddaughter and Oriane de Guermantes' nephew's daughter, crystallizes by her presence the major ways which he had passed through in life. As Méséglise unites the two ways in

Combray, so Mlle de Saint-Loup fuses Marcel's experiences from childhood to the matinee into a meaningful whole. Greater than the cobblestone, teaspoon, napkin, or *François le Champi,* which revive periods of the past, Mlle de Saint-Loup acts as the catalyst which integrates all the parts of his life into a whole.

Marcel's perception of the whole scope and order of his existence is what causes his happiness. The lack of unity and direction, conversely, had frustrated and demoralized him. But now, Marcel experiences direction and order in his life. Let us see then how Mlle de Saint-Loup helped develop Marcel's world view, in which everyone can be related to the narrator and to the other characters.

Before the matinee scene, Marcel floated in a world of chaos, but when he discovers the order of his internal world, he conceives of it as a series of interlocking, self-contained worlds (such as Combray, Balbec, Paris, La Raspelière, the matinee) which cluster about his life line and are bounded peripherally by Swann's Way and Guermantes' Way (which start at Aunt Léonie's house and end in the person of Mlle de Saint-Loup). The Ways and contained worlds are welded together by the people who cross back and forth Marcel's lifeline. They are therefore related not only to the narrator but eventually to everyone else. That this integrated world view mirrors the structure of the novel is revealed by the extraordinary encounter with Mlle de Saint-Loup:

> Like most persons, moreover, did she not resemble the starlike crossroads in a forest where paths leading from the most different points converge, also for our life? Many were the paths of my life which met Mlle de Saint-Loup and radiated outward from her. First of all, there came to an end in her the two principal "ways" where I had taken so many walks and dreamed so many dreams: through her father, Robert de Saint-Loup, the Guermantes way; through Gilberte, her mother, the Méséglise way, which was Swann's way. One of them, through the young girl's mother and the Champs-Elysées, led me to Swann, to my evenings at Combray, to the Méséglise way; the other,

through her father, to my afternoons at Balbec, where I saw him again beside the sunlit sea. And straightway, cross-roads between these two main roads defined themselves. For this very real Balbec where I had met Saint-Loup—it was largely on account of what Swann had told me about the churches, especially about the Persian church, that I had so much wanted to go there; and on the other hand, through Robert de Saint-Loup, nephew of the Duchesse de Guermantes, I came out on the Guermantes way again at Combray. But Mlle de Saint-Loup led to many other points of my life besides—to "the lady in pink," for example, who was her grandmother and whom I had seen at my great-uncle's. A fresh crossroad here, because the great-uncle's valet, who opened the door to me that day and who later, through the gift of a photograph, made it possible for me to identify "the lady in pink," was the father of the young man who had been loved, not only by M. de Charlus but also by the same father of Mlle de Saint-Loup, who had thereby made her mother unhappy. And was it not Mlle de Saint-Loup's grandfather, Swann, who had been the first to mention to me Vinteuil's music, just as Gilberte had been the first to speak to me of Albertine? Now, it was while talking with Albertine about Vinteuil's music that I had discovered who was her closest girl friend and had begun that life with her which had led to her death and had brought me so much sorrow. Moreover, it was also Mlle de Saint-Loup's father who had gone to try to get Albertine to come back to me. And there even passed before my eyes again my entire society life, both in Paris, in the Swann and Guermantes salons, and quite at the other extreme, at Balbec, at the Verdurins'—which thus brought up alongside the Combray "ways" of the Champs-Elysées and the beautiful terrace of La Raspelière. Moreover, whom have we known whose friendship with us we can recount without being necessarily obliged to place him in all the most widely different settings of our existence? A life of Saint-Loup painted by me would extend through all the various scenes of my own life and involve my entire

> existence, even those portions of it to which he was a stranger, such as my grandmother and Albertine. Furthermore, however far apart they were, the Verdurins were connected with Odette through the latter's past, with Robert de Saint-Loup through Charlie, and in their house, what a role Vinteuil's music had played! Finally, Swann had been in love with the sister of Legrandin, who had known M. de Charlus, whose ward young Cambremer had married. . . . And my introduction to Mlle de Saint-Loup was going to take place in the home of Mme Verdurin, . . . that same Mme Verdurin who, before I loved Albertine, had brought about and then broken off the love between the grandfather and grandmother of Mlle de Saint-Loup. All about us were paintings by Elstir, who had introduced me to Albertine. And, the better to fuse together all the past periods of my life, Mme Verdurin, like Gilberte, had married a Guermantes. (II, p. 1110-1111; PIII, p. 1029-1031)

The paragraph was written at an early period so that if Proust should die before the work was completed, the original concept would live on. Proust had written to his "friend" Louis de Robert quite early, "You have seen that there were two ways around Combray, the Méséglise-la-Vineuse Way and Swann's Way. And these two ways take on a significance for my internal life." [3] Thus from the beginning the work was solidly ordered. The world of the narrator is contained within the paragraph. Yet Proust has sketched in only the most essential lines. We could add many more names and little worlds—for example, Doncières and Venice. Each is tied to each by mystic threads, so that "life is ceaselessly weaving other threads between human beings and events, that life crosses these threads with one another and doubles them to make the fabric heavier, so that, between the tiniest point in our past life and all other points, a rich network of memories leaves us only the choice of which road to take" (II, p. 1111; PIII, p. 1030).

Therefore, a Swann in the internal world view is as much

related to people on the Guermantes side as he is to people on the Swann side. One could easily imagine a line drawn from Swann to the Duchesse, to Charlus, to the Prince de Guermantes, and to Saint-Loup. Each person becomes a "star-like crossroads" in the Proustian community. Only those roads, however, which cross Marcel's life or relations are relevant to the novel, but it is clear that the mystery of another person's existence can never be dissipated entirely, for who knows how many other crossroads emanate and skirt Marcel's life and the community in the novel? According to Proust, we can only know so much about another being—what we hear and see. Therefore Proust insists that we concentrate on uncovering and elucidating our own world order rather than seeking vainly to comprehend the totality of someone else.

Proust had a tendency toward drawing parallels and interrelationships to underscore the fact that a community of persons does exist. It is no accident that Odette, for example, is Jupien's first cousin (II, p. 855; PIII, p. 674); that the father of Mme Sazerat of Combray was the lover of Mme de Villeparisis, whom Mme Sazerat sees in Venice (II, p. 827; PIII, p. 634); and that Morel and Albertine are old friends (II, p. 803; PIII, p. 600). Two further parallels can show the extent of Proust's integration of the characters: Marcel's chauffeur at Balbec was also the chauffeur for Charlus (II, p. 288; PII, p. 1006), and Mme Putbus' chambermaid is the sister of Théodore Sanilon, whom Marcel knew at Combray (II, p. 593; PIII, p. 307).

Though Proust makes parallels, he does depict chance meetings that play an important role. If Mme de Villeparisis had not appeared at Balbec, Marcel would not have met the Guermantes so rapidly. And without the presence of his grandmother, the whole chain reaction would not have taken place. In fact, it is through Marcel's parents, his relatives, and their friends that the different characters in the book are brought together to make up Marcel's world. His attention, therefore, is devoted to comprehending his internal world view.

The significance of involuntary memory becomes evident. Those precious moments of felicity, atemporal since past and present are blurred, are moments when Marcel experiences the unity of his existence. The teacup may revive Combray, the cobblestones Venice, a napkin Balbec, but what they bring back are complete "subconscious" worlds of the past, ordered worlds which never existed outside the narrator, but only within his being: "for, during the instant that they last, these resurrections of the past are so complete that they do not merely oblige our eyes to become oblivious to the room before them and contemplate instead the rising tide or the railroad track edged with trees; they also force our nostrils to inhale the air of places . . . [and] constrain our will to choose between the various plans" (II, p. 998; PIII, p. 875).

The pleasure derived from involuntary memory is the same for all instances recalled and complete in all cases. Through his involuntary memory Marcel could make the past worlds of Combray, Balbec, and Venice exist again—not the mere external worlds of Combray, Balbec, or Venice, but the magic towns recreated from the dreams and unconscious impressions of the narrator's internal world. The external fragmented world functions as a stimulus to Marcel's mind. His imagination will transform it into a subjective vision which becomes, for the narrator, the real world. When resurrected, the worlds are living totalities, which, when placed one against the other on a linear path of time, form the ordered internal world of the narrator.

Unfortunately, these involuntary memories pass too quickly. They should be retained and fully understood. And they should be brought together to create the unity and continuity which the internal world view represents. There is only one way to unify, preserve, and understand those experiences: Art. "I must try to interpret the sensations as the indications of corresponding laws and ideas; I must try to think, that is to say, bring out of the obscurity what I had felt, and convert it into a spiritual equivalent. Now this method which seemed to me the only one, what was it other than to create a work of art?" (II, pp. 1000-1001; PIII, p. 879).

Marcel realized that art was the only valid means of preserving the resurrected life because he had discovered through Vinteuil's music and Elstir's paintings that both artists had successfully recreated by art their own distinct world views. In the Elstir painting of Carquethuit, the land is represented in terms of the sea and sea in terms of the land, so that they seem to flow into one another to compose a unity. This is, in microcosm, what Proust is trying to do in *Remembrance of Things Past*. When Marcel listens to the septet, he again finds elements uniting into a totality. "I began to realize that in the body of this septet, different elements presented themselves in turn, to combine at the close" (II, p. 555; PIII, p. 252). (M. Piroué, underlining the significance of this scene, states that it is "the height of Proust's spiritual evolution."[4] He then assures us that all scenes which follow are basically poorer *redites*.) No doubt the septet scene is essential, for it does show "a fusion and a trans-substantiation of opposites that brings peace."[5] But Marcel does not act upon his intuition and retrieve his true self directly after the musicale.

Since the septet takes place in *The Captive*—which means that the Albertine love affair, Marcel's last important attempt to find happiness in the external world, is still far from over—it would have been premature to conclude the book shortly after, for in terms of esthetics the structure would have been incomplete: the roles of art and time become effective only when the reader experiences, almost unconsciously, the mutations, metamorphoses, and revelations of these themes after many decades have elapsed. Nor for the same reason could the theme of social movement permit Mme Verdurin's apotheosis too soon after the septet. It would seem implausible. Besides, Proust wanted to develop the meaning of love; more important, he wanted to underline how blind we mortals are to the meaning of the symbols which surround us. It will take repeated involuntary memories and finally the name of a woman to bring about the fusion hinted at so broadly one thousand pages earlier.

The septet scene is significant, moreover, because it permits Proust to expose the structure of the novel, the world view, through the septet. As Marcel listens to the different themes in the piece, they make him think of the different themes in his life which might be united in art, as Vinteuil united his themes so effectively. The septet, therefore, reveals to his conscious being that art is the way to preserve and order life and to communicate meaningfully, and Proust brilliantly uses the work of an artist, another personal world, to exemplify how Marcel can now fulfill his own life. As Swann is Vergil to the hell of the external world, Vinteuil, and even Elstir, are guides back to the lost paradise of Marcel's internal world. Art, in short, offers more than order and meaning; great art permits communication between different worlds: "as many as there are original artists, just so many worlds have we at our disposal" (II, p. 1013, PIII, p. 896).

Involuntary memories, place names, dreams, and art works have been perfectly integrated into the novel, in a double symmetry—there are always two ways or worlds which are combining. The first involves the teacup scene and the last *François le Champi*; both evoke Combray. By calling forth Combray, the past is linked with the present, and in such a way that the circular movement of the novel is affirmed. Paradoxically, *François le Champi* is also a work of art, a novel. Involuntary memory is thus stirred by an artistic effort which recalls Elstir and Vinteuil and therefore obliquely indicates the future resolution of Marcel's life experiences through art. The necessary leap from the subconscious to the conscious is but the first step of art. The intellect must then bring the surfaced material together with metaphoric or analogical equivalents in the process of creating a work of art.

Leo Bersani is correct in emphasizing that Marcel can successfully recreate the world of his past when he has discovered metaphorical capacities. But Bersani exaggerates when he states that Marcel can only know success in discovering metaphorical capacities when they "are not dependent on involuntary memories." [6] The involuntary memory serves as one of the basic methods to resurrect the internal world order, but the function of the metaphor is to transcribe the experience effectively for the reader. This can be done only by the author's rational appreciation of the resurrection, so that the appropriate metaphor may be chosen. The involuntary memory, therefore, is quite often the basis for an analogy.

Thus Marcel realizes that he must describe his inner life, for that is where he has found happiness. "I realized that only superficial and defective observation attaches all importance to the object, when the mind is everything" (II, p. 1025, PIII, p. 912). The ordered world within is the *"moi personnel,"* the internal self which will be the basis of the work and not the party-going exterior, *"le moi extérieur,"* which has been created by others and is therefore a false mask (I, p. 15; PI, p. 19).

Germaine Brée conceives the Proustian world as "clearly deterministic, pessimistic of man and society, variable in social relations . . . condemning everything to degradation."[7] The Proustian world might be deterministic, but after Marcel discovers the order of his personal existence, the external world remains variable. The fact that there is so much change in the world permits Proust to say: "the creation of the world did not take place in the beginning, it takes place every day"—which places him with the pre-Socratic thinkers who saw life as a continual cycle of birth, life, and death. This may temper Mlle Brée's view of Proust's pessimism.

From the Princesse's house Proust returns to the beginning of the novel, to the dream of sleep, to the original chaos, "the shifting kalidoscope of the darkness" (I, p. 4; PI, p. 4), where time and space are meaningless, where names and places flow freely about. It is within this floating world that the dream can appear and seemingly order existence. "When a man is asleep, he has in a circle around him the chain of the hours, the sequence of the years, the order of the heavenly host" (I, p. 4; PI, p. 5). And Proust did dream, not a nightmare or yesterday's wish-fulfillment, but the world view of his temporal and spatial existence: "I used to spend the greater part of the night recalling our life in the old days at Combray with great-aunt, at Balbec, Paris, Doncières, Venice, and the rest; remembering again all the places and people that I had known, what I had actually seen of them, and what others had told me" (I, p. 7; PI, p. 9).

The indication of the unity of his life is already present in the dream. Thus dreams have an important place in the novel and add another dimension to the world view. They contain the reality of a past moment, the fantasies and hopes of a person, and the structure of the work. There is no doubt that for Marcel the happiest moments are passed in the dream world, in fantasy. "The real paradises are the paradises that we have lost" (PIII, p. 877). Proust emphasizes the social climber's dream world, from which the individual derives his only real satisfaction, for the external world could never live up to the dream. While the ordinary mondain writers ridicule the snob for his exterior acts, Proust first reveals the poetry of the snob's dream world and then describes the difficult exterior world in which he moves: two worlds are united by juxtaposition into a totality.

The whole novel is a search for unity and happiness, a lonely voyage through time and space within oneself and in the exterior world. One could almost say that the word "voyage" is a leitmotiv. It appears at the beginning of the book: "an invalid who has been obliged to start on a journey [voyage]" (I, p. 3; PI, p. 4). The goal of the great voyage of life should be to discover the meaning and unity of the self, but Marcel makes a fatal mistake: He attempts to find in the external world the world he saw in his dream, a world within himself. "People . . . set out on a journey to see with their own eyes some city that they have always longed to visit, and imagine that they can taste in reality what has charmed their fancy" (I, p. 4; PI, p. 5). Unfortunately, Marcel continued to do this until he entered the salon of the new Princesse de Guermantes, and became disillusioned when he realized that external life could never fulfill for him the richness of a dream. Travels to Balbec, Doncières, and Venice could never equal his expectations, as he repeats at the end: "the journey . . . was merely suggested to me once more by the illusion that these old impressions existed outside myself" (II, p. 999; PIII, p. 877).

Travel is important for Marcel: "But after all, the special attraction of the journey lies in its making the difference between departure and arrival not as imperceptible but as intense as possible, so that we are conscious of it in its totality, intact, . . . in a single sweep which seemed miraculous to us not so much because it covered a certain distance as because it united two distinct individualities of the world" (PI, p. 644). That is, travel itself acts as a catalyst which joins two distinct regions into a totality within the mind of Proust and echoes the role of Mlle de Saint-Loup in uniting two seemingly distinct worlds.

The vehicles become symbols. The train especially is the physical catalyst which links two points into a totality; it joins the past, the departure point, with the present, the arrival, and thereby serves as a symbol of passing time in the external world. It serves too as an invitation to seek the mysterious, the unknown. "I could hear the whistling of trains, which showed me in perspective the deserted countryside through which a traveler would be hurrying toward the nearest station: the path that he followed being fixed forever in his memory by the general excitement of being in a strange place, of doing unusual things, of the last words of conversation, of farewells" (I, p. 3; PI, pp. 3-4). This sentence, then, based on the symbol of the train contains the voyage of Marcel's life into the mysterious outside world. The train is even the symbol of the narrator's own life moving in time and space. Is it any wonder that Proust places Marcel and the *petit clan* and the members of the two ways in his travel on the "Transatlantique"? The clans of Verdurin and Cambremer (a lower-class parallel linked to the world of Swann and Guermantes), Albertine, Bloch, and the rest, all the seemingly fragmented parts of Marcel's external life, are united sitting in the train or standing at the station stops.

The train symbolizes Marcel's way, around which cluster many experiences. The different people may group and separate at the different station stops—which represent the external world—yet in their relationship to the train (Marcel) they are integrated into its world. Moreover, it is aboard the train from Venice to Paris that Marcel learns that the two worlds are finally joined: the Guermantes' and Swann's ways are united by the marriage of Gilberte and Saint-Loup.

The travel theme is constant. Long trips take Marcel to Balbec or Venice, yet in each little world, at Combray, Doncières, or Balbec, there are always promenades, walks, and rides. In Combray the walks delineate the physical limits of Combray and indicate symbolically the perimeters of Marcel's life. And the trip to Venice is a dream of *evasion,* an attempt to find the fabled city unaltered in reality. It is especially the moving vehicle which puts us in rapport with Marcel's inner life. In Dr. Percepied's carriage, Marcel watches the steeples of Martinville and Vieuxvicq which cause him to feel a swell of happiness because the steeples represent not only Guermantes' Way, Swann's Way, and Combray, the grouping and regrouping of fragments that compose Marcel's little worlds, but even his different past worlds (Balbec, Doncières, Venice, etc.) juxtaposed but united in the full world view. And he sees the sun, like the steeples, from one side of the train or the other as the train heads for Balbec. In the same way, the major characters, like the sun, pass back and forth between Guermantes' Way and Swann's Way so that they seem to belong to both ways and fuse into a unity, a totality around the life span of the narrator. At Balbec, Mme de Villeparisis takes Marcel for a ride in her open carriage. Suddenly he spies three trees which release a sense of felicity within him, just as the steeples did when he saw them from Dr. Percepied's carriage. The moving carriage, as all other forms of transportation, symbolizes not only passing time and the "voyage" theme in the novel but also Marcel's seemingly directionless life.

The automobile which Albertine and Marcel rent will instigate a change in Marcel's sense of what is unique and of spatial proportions. What seemed like quite isolated villages or worlds when he saw them from a carriage appear to be less isolated when he sees them from a rapidly moving car. The use of the automobile instead of the carriage emphasizes the movement of time, human progress, and the relative meaning of distance in human life.

The moving vehicles, then, functions like time to disrupt the placidity of one simple ordered world, and by its movement causes us to reevaluate the relationships between objects, persons, and places. Elements belonging to Swann's Way or Guermantes' Way eventually pass back and forth across Marcel's Way. From the multiplicity of worlds outside Marcel one world emerges, a unity along the time line of the narrator. Proust uses the carriage, automobile, and train to symbolize Marcel's path from Combray to the matinee; from a simple bedroom to one world, from childhood to maturity, and from geographic to temporal perception of experience. Through the movement of the vehicle, Marcel unwittingly glimpses his world view.

Proust compared Marcel's life to a train trip, and each new station is like another episode, another little world, of his life. The main stops are at Combray, Paris, and Balbec; less important are those at Doncières and Venice. All represent objective

Avenue des Acacias, 1911. Photograph courtesy of Lartigue—Rapho Guillumette.

Bois de Boulogne, 1911. Photograph courtesy of Lartigue—Rapho Guillumette.

Race Course at Auteuil, 1910. Photograph courtesy of Lartigue —Rapho Guillumette.

Avenue du Bois de Boulogne, 1910. Photograph courtesy of Lartigue—Rapho Guillumette.

geographical locations, as well as psychological states of the different *moi*. Each is generally physically subdivided into three parts: Marcel's residence and the two separate ways.

Combray is at the center of Marcel's life. It offers all the possibilities he needs for his development and it is the starting point of his world view. It is clearly a little community, a provincial town. Marcel describes it at first as "no more than a church epitomizing the town . . . seen from the railway" (I, p. 37; PI, p. 48) (note the train theme). The church, like the sun moving to either side of the train, or the dancing steeples, symbolizes unity and immortality, the center of life. Combray is self-contained; one knows where it begins and where it ends. Beyond is the unknown: "[the train] would . . . proceed across the viaduct, out of the lands of Christendom, of which Combray, to me, represented the farthest limit" (I, p. 98; PI, p. 114). The town consists of a few streets, the names of which echo the medieval origins of the community. The people live in cramped quarters and lead very ordered if not ritualistic lives—Aunt Léonie religiously eats an hour earlier on Saturday (I, p. 84; PI, p. 110), for example, and the townsfolk watch Sunday afternoon maneuvers (I, p. 66; PI, p. 88).

Above all, Aunt Léonie's house, in which Marcel resides, physically represents the starting point of Marcel's Way, which will terminate at the *Matinée*. Different roads lead out of Combray, but only two of them are meaningful to Marcel—Guermantes' Way and Swann's Way. Proust places great emphasis on their differences. "For there were, in the environs of Combray, two 'ways' which we used to take for our walks, and so diametrically opposed that we would actually leave the house by a different door" (I, p. 103; PI, p. 134). One leaves for Swann's Way by the door of Rue St. Esprit (I, p. 104; PI, p. 135) and for Guermantes' Way—which is more difficult to reach—by the garden door of the Rue des Perchamps (I, p. 127; PI, p. 165). The detail underlines the dichotomy in Marcel's mind between the two ways. They are conceived as two separate worlds. "Since my father used always to speak of the 'Méséglise Way' as comprising the finest view of a plain that he knew anywhere, and of the Guermantes' Way' as typical of river scenery, I had invested each of them, by conceiving them in this way as two distinct entities, with that cohesion, that unity which belongs only to the figments of the mind" (I, p. 103; PI, p. 134).

Swann's Way offered the road of love, Guermantes' Way was the route to high society. For Swann's Way, the plain is the earth symbol of a contained world of love, as well as a class symbol: the bourgeoisie. The symbol for Guermantes' Way, the river, is that of the aristocracy, of the mystery in life—the poetry of existence, as well as the symbol of a self-contained world. The two ways are the basis of Marcel's emotional and intellectual development. "So the 'Swann's Way' and the 'Guermantes' Way' remain for me linked with many of the little incidents of that one of all the diverse lives along whose parallel lines we are moved, which is the most abundant in sudden reverses of fortune, the richest in episodes; I mean the life of the mind" (I, p. 141; PI, p. 183).

Whereas Marcel meets Swann and knows something about him, the Guermantes are strange poetic demigods. In the name "Guermantes" Proust fuses the title, the persons, and the place name (never seen in *Swann's Way*) into an unreal topography which exists only in Marcel's mind but which contains so much poetry that he will seek to know it in the external world. Georges Poulet, especially, has brought out clearly Marcel's need to synthesize the real and the unknown in order to create the subjective reality and happiness he craves.[8]

The two ways during his youth are distinct. Méséglise, the symbol of unity, is too distant; the great joining must wait many years—for Gilberte and Mlle de Saint-Loup. The "voyage," as I mentioned above, begins at the doorsteps of the home at Combray, at Aunt Léonie's. "And, during the whole of my boyhood, if Méséglise was to me something as inaccessible as the horizon, which remained from sight, however far one went . . . Guermantes, on the other hand, meant no more than the ultimate goal, ideal rather than real, of the 'Guermantes Way,' a sort of abstract geographical term. . . . And so to 'take the Guermantes Way' in order to get to Méséglise, or vice versa, would have seemed to me as nonsensical as proceeding to turn to the east in order to reach the west" (I, p. 103; PI, p. 134).

Thus Marcel sets forth like a Dante with Swann as his guide, sinking into the hell of external life and eventually climbing back to Paradise—the comprehended interior world of the mind.

Having known his first love in Paris, Marcel sets off for his first fabled city, Balbec, which he will visit twice in his career. Balbec will disappoint him, for whoever has been to a French resort bordering the English Channel knows how tame the area appears. Just as the steeple of Combray attracted Marcel, so the first thing he must see in Balbec is the Persian church—and it is no Taj Mahal. External reality continues to erode the dream.

Marcel finally settles in the Grand Hotel of Balbec. This hotel parallels Aunt Léonie's house as a symbol. Marcel's life is spent coming and going from it, and the building serves as the social center of the resort. It contains every level of society, each member of which is trying either to climb or to fend off an *arriviste*. The building's very location is symbolic—like Balbec it is on the shore, where land meets sea as well as where bourgeoisie and aristocracy merge. Here Marcel meets Mme de Villeparisis and Saint-Loup. In Balbec Marcel enters into his first real love affair with Albertine and makes his first attempt at social climbing. But the trip to Balbec offers a third alternative: Art. The visit to the studio and home of Elstir is one of the great moments in the book. In Elstir's painting of Carquethuit Marcel learns how mistaken his view of life has been until then. There are no distinct separate worlds but a blending of elements into a totality: "no fixed boundary between earth and ocean" (I, p. 629; PI, p. 836).

The rides into the country in Mlle de Villeparisis' carriage extend the limits of the geographical world for Marcel. Proust also develops an interesting parallel between this carriage ride, with the sudden memory evoked by the three trees, and the ride in Dr. Percepied's carriage, when Marcel saw the steeples. He saw both at the extreme outskirts of the little worlds of Combray and Balbec, and both memories revealed to Marcel that seemingly distinct worlds can be combined into one. Proust had Marcel experience the two memories at the frontiers of these two worlds to symbolize the greater world which he must yet discover within himself.

During his second trip to Balbec Marcel expands the circumference of the subjective frontiers of the resort. Marcel again stays at the hotel, but his trips are longer. There are two seemingly distinct ways here, as at Combray: La Raspelière and Féterne. La Raspelière is occupied by Mme Verdurin, who is a less impressive representative of the upper bourgeoisie than Swann. She rents La Raspelière, the beautifully situated château in the area, on a high cliff set back on the land with a view of the sea. Féterne, less desirable, is owned by the Cambremers, a provincial noble family. Notice again how Marcel creates a subjective view of Féterne like that of Guermantes: "on seeing this name Féterne, which had been for me, since my stay at Balbec, the name of a country house, become, what I had never dreamed that it could possibly be, a family name, I felt that same astonishment as in reading a fairy-tale" (I, p. 1102, PII, p. 541).

The Féterne estate, not by chance, is set by the water, and it has a lovely garden. Actually, Proust was merging his nature symbols, water and earth. By placing the Verdurin clan on the cliff (earth symbol) overlooking the sea (aristocracy), one recognizes at this stage of the novel the growing ascendancy of the bourgeois over the aristocracy. The Cambremers not only rent La Raspelière to the Verdurins, they visit them. The money of the bourgeoisie can help their social rise, or at least allow them to mingle with local gentry, the Cambremers, who can use the income, though they deny it. "I would let La Raspelière for nothing so as to be obliged to live at Féterne," (II, p. 151; PII, p. 810) says the dowager Mme de Cambremer. Clearly two worlds are being drawn together. The land and the sea symbols are joining—as in the Carquethuit of Elstir—to create a unity.

The ways of those living at Féterne and La Raspelière reflect the ways of the Guermantes and Swann. The merging of bourgeois and local gentry at Féterne and La Raspelière also foreshadows the fusion of the bourgeois and the aristocracy in the world of the Guermantes and Swann. Renée de Cambremer, the sister of the snob Legrandin, by her marriage to M. de Cambremer actually joins the bourgeoisie to the aristocracy, just as Mme Verdurin and Gilberte do later. In short, there are no distinct worlds at Balbec, or anywhere else, but rather one world of different parts or elements which interact with one another: people, clans, classes, suburbs, nature, and art; and these same elements comprise the worlds of Combray and the other places in the novel.

Clearly Balbec is a distinct little world for Marcel because he has created it out of his intellectual, emotional, and physical states which have reacted to the external elements with which he has come in contact. Marcel's Balbec, like Combray, like Paris, Doncières, or Venice, is an exact microcosm of the macrocosm of Marcel's world view.

Doncières, the next stop in Marcel's travels, is usually bypassed by most critics as tangential to the work, or just not very interesting. Marcel's stay in Doncières, however, has an important function in the work because Proust depicts the life of the military stationed in a little town. France was gravely concerned about her military after 1870 because it was the only bulwark France had against the hated enemy, Germany, as well as the only force they could use for revenge. It was, however, both honored and feared, for the military could always instigate a coup d'état against the fledgling republic (witness the near attempt by Boulanger). It was the stronghold of the monarchists, whether Legitimists, Orleanists, or Bonapartists. (Marcel in fact offers nuanced comparisons between the imperial and legitimist nobilities in the army.) But Doncières is important to the work not only because Proust can give us glimpses of military life but also because he could present the various shades in the military concerning the Dreyfus Affair, the events of which were to cause such a social upheaval in Proust's fictional world.

Furthermore, Proust bathes Doncières in a poetic glow as he depicts Marcel's search for friendship during his stay there. Marcel felt he could find it in Saint-Loup, the image of the ideal nobleman and military officer. But even friendship could not equal his estimate of it.

Marcel's life at Doncières is also like his life at Combray in other ways. Doncières too is a small town. A regimental parade is held on Sunday just as one was in Combray. Marcel even enjoys the long walks to watch the regiment in the field (I, p. 778; PII, p. 91), since they bring back memories of the long walks at Combray. His hotel room at Doncières figures in his dream and causes him discomfort in a new place, just as he was affected by his room at Balbec, but the room comes to symbolize his inner world here, as at Balbec and elsewhere. It is a place of retreat, but primarily it serves as a departure point to the outside world.

At Doncières the outside world is the dining room at a hotel where Saint-Loup and others board. Here we get the first real glimpse of Marcel participating in society and it reveals his *esprit* at table, which understandably aids his swift rise in the Guermantes circle. Doncières, then, is important in the novel. It is an echo of Combray, a social study of the military and the nobility, a preparation for Marcel's social climb, an image of France divided over the Dreyfus Affair, and a study of the illusion of friendship.

Paris, however, is the central location in which Proust portrays the main activities in the external world: love and social climbing. The world of Paris does not seemingly have the order and harmony of Combray or even Balbec.

Life in Paris is not tranquil; society is not a stable, closed world but a rapidly fluctuating one. There is no clearly defined Guermantes' Way or Swann's Way in Paris. In the metropolis one has the greatest grouping and regrouping of fragments. The Blochs, Verdurins, Odettes, Jupiens, Swanns, and Guermantes are all swirling back and forth, all jumbled, yet all are contained in the psychological unity called Paris. Proust emphasizes the unity by grouping everyone in a single apartment building, the symbol of Paris, a complete world whose representatives make up the life of Paris: the aristocrats, Oriane de Guermantes; the petty nobility, Baron de Norpois; the middle class, Marcel's family; the lower middle class and workers, Jupien and the concierge; and finally the servants, such as Françoise, the peasant girl. What a brilliant organizational idea! Anyone who has lived in the Eighth Arrondissement knows that the grouping is quite possible though not common.

Thus Paris, like Combray, does have a unity; whereas Combray at first sight is divided into three distinct parts, the town and the two ways, Paris is seemingly divided between people and groups in time. Indeed, Paris is the mature world of Proust's internal world view; Paris is the truest microcosm of the macrocosm. It is in Paris that Marcel, following Swann, meets disappointment in love and in social advancement.

Marcel makes his last trip, to Venice, and shatters his last illusion, that of finding fulfillment in the empirical world. The Venice he hoped to see was the one he dreamed of at Combray in his youth (I, p. 300; PI, p. 393). Marcel had envisioned Venice as "the city of marble and gold, in which the building of the wall was of jasper and the foundation of the wall an emerald" (I, p. 299; PI, p. 392); "the clattering streets, reddened by the light from Giorgione's frescoes" (I, p. 300; PI, p. 393); "the city of St. Mark's, the Rialto, the Grand Canal, the palaces and Venetian air, that marine atmosphere, indescribable and peculiar as the atmosphere of the dreams which my imagination has secreted in the name of Venice" (I, p. 300; PI, p. 393). After many years he arrives and is disappointed. Venice only reminds him of Combray and his youth. Marcel has trapped himself once again by superimposing the Venice of his imagination upon the physical Venice. Is it any wonder that the Rialto should cause such despair? "It seemed to me . . . a bridge not merely inferior to but different from the idea that I possessed of it" (II, p. 838; PIII, p. 653). The beautiful marble and jasper palaces hardly compare to the "slates of St. Hilaire" (II, p. 821; PIII, p. 623). The sea air of Venice can only restore "the feeling of coolness that I had known long ago at Combray" (II, p. 823; PIII, p. 626). Thus, all the images of Venice are but keys to memories of Combray. By some subjective cultural reminiscences, Proust expresses the same nostalgia, disappointment, and local patriotism found in the celebrated verse by Joachim du Bellay, a sixteenth-century compatriot who longed to escape Italy.

> When shall I resee, alas, the smoking chimney
> Of my little village, and in what time
> Shall I see the door of my poor house
> Which is a province to me and so much more?
> I prefer the cottage which my ancestors built
> To Roman palaces with their haughty facades;
> Rather than tough marble I prefer fine slate,
> My Gallic Loire to the Latin Tiber,
> My little Liré to the Palatine Hill,
> And rather than the sea air, the flavor of Anjou.

Marcel's departure from Venice closes forever the chapter of the love affair with Albertine and presages the final unity of the social world in which the aristocracy joins the bourgeoisie, when Gilberte Swann marries Saint-Loup, the nephew of Oriane de Guermantes. How beautifully Venice reflects this! The city perfectly integrates the water and the land, and becomes one psychological unit, a contained world. Marcel's experiences in Venice serve to hint at the coming unity of his full world view which will become apparent in *Time Recaptured.*

Like the Vinteuil theme for Swann, the parting song, *Sole Mio,* "was my distress . . . rising like a dirge for the Venice that I had known" (II, p. 838; PIII, p. 653). This simple folksong hints —like the Venetian masterpieces of Bellini, Giorgione, Tintoretto, and Tiepolo, which had fired Marcel's youthful fancy to visit the fabled city, like the septet or "Carquethuit" of Elstir— at Marcel's ultimate goal: the creation of a work of art.

At the end of the matinee, Marcel grasps at last his entire world view. He must leave the salon and recreate, deepen and filter what he dimly saw: the unity of his own existence. In his world view, the external world will remain hopelessly fragmented, and only the internal existence, the life of the mind, can have order. With the aid of involuntary memories, and rational interpretations of them, determined inquiry into the meaning of his dreams, together with memories of art and journeys, Marcel can unify the different psychological moments of his existence (made up of persons, places, and things integrated about Marcel). Swann's Way and Guermantes' Way, therefore, are symbolic perimeters of his internal world view; from Combray to the matinee they anchor the many events of Marcel's life.

What seemed to be outside worlds—Guermantes' Way and Swann's Way and all the other people and places—have meaning only as part of Marcel's internal world order. What Marcel had considered as fragments are actually all in contact with himself and with one another, though they interchange their positions like the steeples as he moves; actually all the fragments (parts of himself) make up the larger internal world order which Marcel at last comprehended, ordered, and made the basis of *Remembrance of Things Past.*[9]

Art is the sole means of presenting the internal world view to the external world, of preserving the world view from the decay of the body in which it is trapped. But the artist must fully understand the personal interior world before it can be translated effectively. Then art will preserve the internal world view from the corrosion of time "in the necessary rings of a beautiful style" (II, p. 1008; PIII, p. 889). Thus the Proustian world view places man in the center of his universe, around which circle, rationally understood, his life's journeys and experiences—all interrelated and fused into an ordered totality which is preserved by a band of art like a magnetic ring around the earth. Meanwhile the external world remains in fragmentation—millions of worlds—awaiting the sole means of authentic communication from one world to another: Art. Proust, therefore, despairs—which seems paradoxical to the reader—of ever understanding the external world, but he delights in knowing and recreating through art his own internal world view.

Democracy, by breaking down all distinctions, has done away with the barriers which for centuries had guarded the old social hierarchy, and today our salons at their best have little individual character, and at their worst are all exactly alike.

—*Arthur Meyer,* 40 Years of Parisian Society *(1912)*

The Grand-Hotel of Cabourg will open its doors on June 16; all of the staff of Noël and Pattard have arrived from Monte-Carlo. . . .

—Le Gaulois, *June 7, 1898*

Elegant society at Cabourg very lively this season. Seen at the restaurant or on the terrace of the Grand Hotel, social center of this beautiful seaside resort: Duc and Duchesse d'Uzès, Marquis de Moustier, Comte and Comtesse de Mortemart, Comte de Clermont-Tonnerre, Mme Archdeacon, Comte Léon de Montesquiou. . . .

—Le Gaulois, *July 28, 1898*

Wherever one went one always met the same people at the same hours in order to say the same things to one another.

Comtesse J. de Pange née de Broglie, Comment J'ai Vu 1900

The Duke and Duchess of Windsor, just back from the south of France, are enjoying their beautiful moulin outside Paris, these lovely Indian summer days. The Windsors' new pug, Black Diamond, acquired on their last trip to New York, is a huge success and a real treasure. Everyone adores him.

—San Francisco Chronicle, *October 5, 1969*

Chapter IV

THE SOCIAL INSTITUTIONS

INTRODUCTION

In as complex a society as the French during the Belle Epoque, social institutions were varied and highly developed, and played an essential role in *A la Recherche.* Proust very carefully chose particular institutions comprised of specifically selected people in order to capture and convey the spirit of the age. A study of these institutions will give us, therefore, an interesting cross-section of individuals, the reasons for their presence, and will reveal the structure and significance of the institutions themselves. We can also demonstrate how Proust uses the social institutions as basic building blocks in the structure of the novel: each institution plays a distinct role in the disjointed worlds which, when brought together, form the ordered inner world of Marcel. By considering the institution Proust can study the gestures, manners, dress, and speech of people, and also their attitudes toward politics, society, culture, and economics. Above all, Proust can demonstrate man's interrelationship with man, and gain insight into the individual characters as well as a great deal of society itself.

Social institutions are the meeting places of society. They are the foundation which supports the concerns and values of the age by which society judges the individual. In this chapter we shall place particular emphasis on the salon and the resort, for the narrator spends much time describing these two mainstays of social life. But there are many other important institutions, too, which we shall review first: the spiritual meeting place, the church; a "physical" meeting place, the brothel; the social parade grounds, the Bois de Boulogne, the Champs-Elysées, the cafés and restaurants; and the entertainment centers, the theater, the opera, the salons. The lack of any comment on political or economic institutions may be surprising, but it reveals that the leisured bourgeois and the aristocrat were no longer actively interested in pursuit of greater wealth or governmental power. (The novel concentrates on the life of the upper classes; references to the lower classes are only in terms of their relationship to the bourgeoisie or the aristocracy.) An examination of the social institutions described by Proust also will probe the esthetic structure of the novel and its contribution to social history; it will afford a view of the effects of leisure on humanity, a subject of some importance for our own society.

It is at Combray that we encounter the first salon scene, Swann's visit to Aunt Léonie's house. But Combray also offers the church, St. Hilaire, the spiritual meeting place for the town and surrounding countryside. The spiritual function however, has mostly been replaced by a more worldly one; for although the church of Combray offers the timeless rites of the Church, the people have gathered primarily for a social occasion. Take, for example, the wedding of Dr. Percepied's daughter. Present are Marcel's family, the Sazerats, and a special honor: The Duchesse de Guermantes (I, p. 134; PI, p. 174). The church ceremony is forgotten by people glimpsing at who is present and what they are wearing. And even Sunday mass, though a basic part of the religion, is really a social rite in Combray, a communal meeting place which serves as a prelude for the wonderful dinners which follow. The stained glass windows introduce Guermantes' Way and permit a comparison between the Guermantes of dreams and the living Oriane.

I am convinced that the emphasis on the stained glass windows and church architecture throughout the book is intended to do more than offer material reinforcement to the time theme. It is very much an expression (conscious or unconscious) of the interest of the leisured classes in "esthetic Catholicism—specifically, the interest in medieval church architecture. This was the age of great pride in things French, especially if they brought back glory and grandeur (the French were still smarting from the 1870 fiasco). Medieval art had been popularized by the brilliant works of Ruskin and Emile Mâle, and leisure provided the time for excursions, especially during Eastertime. The French church provided both a patriotic rallying point for French xenophobism and a fashionable cultural experience which became the "thing to do." Barrès, a darling of the age, made France and medieval cathedrals almost synonymous in his work. Even Marcel's dream worlds are centered around the churches at Balbec and St. Mark's in Venice (I, p. 300; PI, p. 393). Swann, the esthete who was always *à la page,* mentions the beautiful churches at Beauvais and St. Loup-de-Naud (I, p. 224; PI, p. 292). Mme Verdurin takes her flock for historical outings, including trips to churches and châteaux —at Dreux, Compiègne, and Pierrefonds (I, p. 225; PI, p. 293), which Swann correctly mocks as second-rate Louis-Philippe and Viollet-le-Duc. And even Oriane wants to visit historic sites and churches, such as the two Saint-Georges de Venise, on her next trip to Italy (I, p. 1138; PII, p. 593). The church, in short, has been despiritualized; it has been turned into an esthetic showpiece, a salon in which the original symbolic trappings have become the ornaments of a worldly society. Only the steeples seem to maintain their spiritual purity—albeit esthetically—as they dance an immortal *pas de trois* upon the horizons of Martinville and Vieuxvicq.

But if man is spirit, he is also flesh. As the church cares for the spirit, the brothel attempts to satisfy man's more earthly desires. Most of us, raised in an age of proclaimed moral rectitude, cannot conceive of the house of prostitution as an accepted part of society, sanctioned even by the government. (The image of a *fin de siècle* brothel can be most vividly seen in the paintings of Toulouse-Lautrec.) Proust, however, was well aware of physical drives and more than adequately describes three exotic brothels of his time.

The first brothel is rather nondescript except for the *"belle juive,"* Rachel (a Balzacian reminiscence?). The *"belle juive"* theme, almost an archetype in European literature and folk myth, is not unlike the fantasies of white American males about Negro women being more sensuous. In Europe the "Jewess," like the "Negress," is the untamed tigress; thus skilled "innkeepers" pamper to exotic, escapist, and racist drives of their clientele.

The bordello of Balbec is typical of our usual preconception of the Gay Nineties. In its own building, the brothel of Balbec is large and noisy: "A gathering more clamorous than the stock exchange or a sale room" (II, p. 340; PII, p. 1097). Men of every class and taste are present: Jupien, Morel, Charlus, the Prince de Guermantes, soldiers, gentlemen. The boredom of a correct salon is overcome by the garish search for satisfaction: "Take this gentleman to twenty-eight, the Spanish room." "Open the door again, these gentlemen want Mademoiselle Noémie. She's expecting them in the Persian parlor" (II, p. 340-341; PII, p. 1079). Again the escapist needs of this society are evidenced by the existence of a Spanish room, a Persian salon, or even the name Noémie, evoking the Orient. The divans and walls are covered with magic symbols; false mirrors and peepholes add to the general mystery of enclosed rooms (II, p. 341-342; PII, p. 1080). The prostitutes, of course, are efficient and try to force high-priced bottles of champagne on the "guests," for the brothel is a business.

Proust spares us no aspect of bordello life, and we are also led into a male brothel. Once again the appearance is that of a hotel with Jupien, the madame, as director and receiver of accounts. The rooms are less ornate but contain "Pompeian paintings" which are clearly more gross than the magic symbols in the high society brothel. Foreigners, aristocrats, bourgeois, soldiers, and even a priest frequent the hotel, where homosexuality is presented as a universal occurrence. There are scenes of flagellation, of pitiful clients seeking murderers and thieves to relieve their boredom, although they know they can never be satiated by the poor amoral types playing their roles for a fee.

In these scenes the whole fabric of high society is ripped open to reveal the decadence of too many members of good society. "At the same moment a young man in a dinner jacket came in and with an air of authority asked the manager, 'Can I have Léon tomorrow morning at a quarter to eleven, instead of eleven o'clock, because I'm lunching downtown' " (II, p. 965; PIII, p. 829). The bordello, initially an institution for satisfying physical drives, becomes an institution for escapism, exoticism, and finally a place of delusion and perversion, of total moral and ethical degradation. As Jupien rings out "Something to help defray the costs of the faith, M. l'abbé" (III, p. 964-965; PIII, p. 829), the bombs of

World War I begin to drop overhead, and the physical decay of European society, as well as its spiritual chaos, is clearly exposed. The priest's presence in the brothel symbolizes the fall of the old moral order: as the church became a worldly social center, so the once innocent, lusty brothel leads to social degeneration.

The period between the two wars of 1870 and 1914, misnamed the Belle Epoque, was a great parade, be it the troops marching on Sunday afternoons at Combray or Doncières, or the social parade taking place every day along the Champs-Elysées, l'Avenue de l'Impératrice, and l'Avenue du Bois (formerly l'Avenue de l'Impératrice [1854-1870], today Avenue Foch [1929-]), and along the Allée des Acacias of the Bois de Boulogne. The Champs-Elysées and its little parks, especially near Avenue Gabriel, were the strolling grounds of nannies with their charges. Here the children of the rich played and were occasionally visited by their parents returning from or going to some social event. While the Champs-Elysées was primarily for the children of the "élite" or women *déclassées* like the old lady of the *Débats* (I, p. 310; PI, p. 405), the Bois was the real parade ground of snobbish adults. It may seem hard for us to believe that every day, especially during spring, it was essential to take a constitutional in the park. But the leisured classes needed to display themselves; it was the one activity to which they gave themselves wholeheartedly. And the Bois had provided the ideal setting for it, since the Second Empire, when the Empress Eugénie used to leave the Tuilleries every afternoon for her ride in the Bois.[1] It is thus not surprising that Proust also places the Princesse Mathilde, cousin of Louis-Napoleon and niece of Napoleon, in this park setting (I, p. 413; PI, p. 543), and mentions all the important chic places in the Bois: the Allée des Acacias, the Allée de la Reine-Marguerite (I, p. 318; PI, p. 417), the lake (I, p. 243), the Jardin d'Acclimation (I, p. 322; PI, p. 423). A visit to the Bois usually began in the late afternoon, before six. Odette generally came at five (I, p. 186; PI, p. 243) and Charlus at six o'clock (II, p. 4; PII, p. 602). The hour or so spent strolling or riding in carriages successfully filled the time between the matinee and evening activity.

By seven o'clock, the allées become less crowded. It is time for the evening entertainment. "And as a matter of fact, almost immediately, the Acacias are deserted: carriages rapidly return to Paris, or scatter towards the Madrid, the Armenonville, or the Chinois,"[2] restaurants in the Bois which often serve as meeting places for rich lovers like a Marcel, who wishes to court Mlle de Stermaria at the Ile du Bois restaurant (I, p. 993; PII, p. 383). There also were summer restaurants for the upper bourgeoisie, such as for the Verdurin.

The Bois is primarily a place for women to display themselves, "le Jardin des femmes" (I, p. 318; PI, p. 417). The use of the park for this purpose is first indicated by Proust at Combray, where by the river Vivonne is a house surrounded by woods in which a seemingly elegant woman, apparently abandoned, walks about hoping for her lover's return. "And I watched her, as she returned from some walk along a road where she had known that he would not appear, drawing from her submissive fingers long gloves of precious, useless charm" (I, p. 131; PI, p. 171).

Proust notes, "the Allée des Acacias was thronged by the famous beauties of the day" (I, p. 318; PI, p. 417). The beautiful Mme Swann, the former Odette, constantly appears here either in her carriage or walking. She usually begins with the Allée des Acacias and then proceeds to the Allée de la Reine-Marguerite (I, p. 318; PI, p. 418). "On certain days when I had missed her in the Allée des Acacias I would be so fortunate as to meet her in the Allée de la Reine-Marguerite, where women went who wished to be alone, or to appear to be wishing to be alone; she would not be alone for long, being soon overtaken by some man or other, often in a grey 'tile' hat, whom I did not know, and who would talk to her for some time, while their two carriages crawled behind" (I, p. 321; PI, p. 421). This little scene describes the life of a demi-mondaine in the park. And Proust places Mme de Montmorency (I, p. 412; PI, p. 541), another successful demi-mondaine, in the same promenade so that the demi-mondaines can greet one another and permit Proust this sharp observation: "I had been told that I should see in the alley certain women of fashion, who in spite of their not all having husbands, were constantly mentioned in conjunction with Mme Swann, but most often by their professional names—their new names when they had any, being but a sort of incognito, a veil which those who would speak of them were careful to draw aside, so as to make themselves understood" (I, p. 318; PI, p. 418).

Thus Proust placed people, like these cocottes, in settings corresponding to our memory of them: "this or that woman, this or that scene." (I, p. 993; PIII, p. 383) By brilliant "intuition," both the site and person are historically accurate. The demi-mondaines have, in short, taken over the promenades in the Bois de Boulogne.[3] In fact, neither the Duchesse nor the Princesse de Guermantes, women so conscious of where to be at the right time, ever go to the allées. What was "chic" among the aristocracy under the Second Empire is *démodé* in the Third Republic. Thus a social institution like the stroll in the Bois reveals the class differences between Odette and an Oriane, at least circa 1890. The presence of Princesse Mathilde at the Jardin d'Acclimation, at this same time, further underscores the fact that a visit to the Bois is out of style, for the Princesse herself is an anachronism.

The Bois also is the sinister pleasure haunt of a Charlus, who invites Marcel to join him there (I, p. 1117; PII, p. 383). It hosts the visit of Albertine with Marcel (I, p. 993; PII, p. 562), and even the social-climbing Bloch goes into the "Elysian Garden of Woman" (I, p. 325; PI, p. 427), for "adventures" (I, p. 414; PI, p. 543), as well as "little shopgirls, midinettes, prostitutes . . . strolling in the Bois" (II, p. 488; PIII, p. 157). Proust has brought together the different social worlds which make up society in the novel, although each class is present for different reasons and in different places in the Bois. The Bois, then, is a totality, a world unto itself much like Marcel's own inner world. "The Bois de Boulogne displays more separate characteristics, assembles more distinct elements in a composite whole" (I, p. 322; PI, 432). It exists as a geographical entity and represents that "romantic world" because the people fused to the different parts of the Bois in Marcel's mind give it a subjective existence as well. In this way Proust uses the Bois to reveal class differences, as well as to capture an age, and also to represent in the external world one further example of the inner world order.

However, the Bois and its elements, being in the external world, are subject to time and to changes, including changes in custom and fashion. We learn that by 1913 even the famous "cocottes" are gone from the Allée and that the clothing and elegance of old have passed on (I, p. 324; PI, p. 426). Mme Swann, almost the living essence of the Bois, is no longer present, and automobiles replace carriages (I, p. 324; PI, p. 425). Marcel is aware of time passing and records changes in social customs. "The reality that I had known no longer existed" (I, p. 325; PI, p. 427). But it will take many years for him to discover this truth: "The places that we have known belong now only to the little world of space on which we map them for our own convenience. None of them was ever more than a thin slice, held between the contiguous impressions that composed our life at that time" (I, p. 325; I, p. 427).

The world of the theater received great attention from the "beautiful people" of the time. It was an extension of the great parade—this time, however, in the gilded grottos of theaters. Everyone who could go to the theater went. Mme Verdurin (the haute bourgeoise) could be seen following a score at a concert (II, p. 193; PII, p. 870) or attending the Ballets Russes with the Princess Sherbatoff; Odette (a demi-mondaine) is at a play when she meets Swann (I, p. 149; PI, p. 195); Marcel (from a good bourgeois family) goes to hear La Berma. Everyone is present to observe and be observed in their latest outfits. But the real social event is a night at the opera every Monday. (Proust seems to have had a lapse of memory because the first description he gives is of the Opera [I, p. 756; PII, p. 60] but later of the opéra-comique [I, p. 1022; PII, p. 426]. However, this slip is not very important, since Proust was more concerned with revealing the social significance of the opera gathering than describing the institution itself.)

In the novel, the Princesse de Parme has taken over the theater for her guests, thus transforming it into a salon. But for Marcel it is essentially an aquarium in which beautiful creatures float back and forth: "their brilliant faces appeared behind the gaily breaking foam of the feather fans they unfurled and lightly waved, beneath their hyacinthine locks begemmed with pearls, which the flow of time seemed to have caught and drawn with it" (I, p. 741-742; PII, p. 40). This is a poetic description which perfectly corroborates Renoir's or Degas' paintings of theater life.

Marcel's aquarium, rather than being a single large fishbowl, is instead divided along social lines. The balcony and boxes are filled by the Princesse de Parme with guests who are not all members of the highest aristocratic society—witness Mme de Cambremer (I, p. 752; PII, p. 55). But the "baignoires" or boxes around the orchestra do contain the highest society. In the right-hand side box is seated the Princesse de Guermantes and the Duchesse de Guermantes as well as the Prince de Saxe. (Supposedly Comtesse Greffülhe always held this box in the Opera on Monday nights.) The highest member of the aristocracy present is the Duc d'Aumale, the last son of Louis-Philippe, who is seated like a monarch. Mme d'Ambresac helps him take off his overcoat; she "was envied by all the rest her being thus honored" (I, p. 741; PII, p. 40). This little scene reveals how the aristocrats maintained the form of serving the king or a member of the royal family and the ridiculous excitement it caused—not unlike the time Louis XIV stopped to talk to Mme de Sévigné after a Racine play and made the other courtiers jealous. It also shows that the reigning social queens like Oriane de Guermantes, of the purest and highest nobility, have gained their supreme social position in part by their own popularity and in part by the continued absence of the true political and social head of aristocratic society, the Pretender exiled at Twickenham. The Guermantes may be resplendent but the Duc d'Aumale is still "Monseigneur" and they are, so to speak, his vassals. Thus Proust cleverly distinguishes the aristocratic hierarchy and the social hierarchy. The Duc d'Aumale is the head of the legitimate aristocracy in France, and the Duchesse de Guermantes is the social head of the aristocracy. However, an Oriane would always need the kind graces of a Duc d'Aumale, whereas he, of royal blood, is socially secure so long as the aristocratic society believes in its myth of aristocratic hierarchy.

We come now to the last rank of guests, the mortals, the bourgeois, who are seated in the orchestra. In this social group are the extremely wealthy, the *nouveaux riches* of finance and industry (I, p. 739; PII, p. 37), and several rich snobs: " A certain number of orchestra stalls had been offered for sale at the box office and bought, out of snobbishness or curiosity, by such as wished to study the appearance of people whom they might not have another opportunity of seeing at close quarters. And it was indeed a fragment of their true social life, ordinarily kept secret, that one could examine here in public" (I, p. 740; PII, p. 38).

The social snob in the theater is not the same as the dreamy, underwater character of Marcel's image. Whereas Marcel, in the springtime of his snobbery, admires this seemingly unattainable world of the Guermantes, the frustrated snobs seated next to him, "some common people" (I, p. 741; PII, p. 39), attack the outfits and people they recognize and cannot join. Thus Marcel sees the Princesse de Guermantes as "a mighty goddess who presides from far aloft over the sports of lesser deities" (I, p. 742; PII, p. 41) while neighbors completely reject his envy: " 'That's the Princesse de Guermantes,' said my neighbour to the gentleman beside her, taking care to begin the 'Princesse' with a string of P's, to show that a title like that was absurd. 'She hasn't been sparing with her pearls. I'm sure, if I had as many as that, I wouldn't make such a display of them; it doesn't look at all well, not to my mind' " (I, p. 743; PII, p. 41).

Proust also distinguishes the captains of industry and finance from the social élite. While a nouveau riche appears with "a sharp, haughty tone in speaking to an inferior, the great gentleman, affable, pleasant, smiling, had the air of considering, practicing an affectation of humility and patience . . . as a privilege of his good breeding" (I, p. 739; PII, p. 37). Thus Proust places the aristocrats above the bourgeois in the physical setting of the theater and he underlines their differences by describing their manners and dress.

Lost amid this glittering society is the art to which the theater is supposedly dedicated. Everyone is supposed to be anxiously awaiting the great interpretations of La Berma, but the "budding genius who had taken a stall in order to hear La Berma thinks only of not soiling his gloves" (I, p. 741; PII, p. 39); the bourgeois neighbors are airing their frustrations in caustic comment; La Berma's enemy has come to boo her (I, p. 749; PII, p. 50); Mme de Cambremer and other unprominent aristocrats are too concerned with the impression they are making on their benefactor, the Princesse de Parme; and the great mondains, who are perfectly comfortable in this setting and have no material or social preoccupations, are too lazy or too stupid to cultivate a taste for music. So much for dedication to culture.

It is not without purpose that Proust has Marcel discover the great beauty of La Berma's art at this juncture. As Marcel's snobbery develops, the true world of art is also revealed. Thus the false external world at its most brilliant is placed directly against the immortal world of art, reminding us of the stay at Balbec. While Marcel is excited to make the acquaintance of Mme de Villeparisis, Charlus, and Saint-Loup as his social climbing begins, the visit to Elstir's studio reveals how art can be the fullest expression of existence. Once again Proust has made a typical social institution of the age, the theater, an integral part of the novel: should Marcel go toward the world of art or climb into the world of high society?

THE SALON

The salon was the social institution par excellence in Proust's society, as well as in the novel. Everyone from the Marquise of the Public Restrooms to the most pretentious duchess operates a salon. Descriptions of salon scenes account for more pages than are devoted to any institution in the work. The salon scenes, which last at most an evening, permit great concentration on individuals and allow further commentary on the past and future and on individuals, groups, and institutions. The salon reception, like a ride in the Bois, or an appearance at the opera, is another prancing ground for vanity.

Proust records the changing relations of man, the passing of time, and the changes in social structure as well as in social customs through his portraits of various salons. Events in the world affect the makeup of the salon as well as its traditions, yet the salon retains a certain structural unity: it is a defined pattern of manners and etiquette. Proust is especially interested in individual mannerisms because they reveal inner thought or lack of it. Though many salons exist on different class levels, the purpose and construction of all of them remain more or less the same, as in a theme and variations. People are brought together from common backgrounds, common points of view or interests. Each salon is a distinct entity with its heroes and enemies, likes and dislikes, realities and pretensions.

A salon scene, big or little, always maintains a formal nature; that is, there is always a guest and host relationship. (Few scenes of ordinary friendly meetings exist in the novel, except when Albertine visits Marcel and perhaps when Charlus happens to visit Jupien.) The salon scenes in the work can be divided into the following types: the dinner reception, the formal reception, the recital reception, and various combinations of these three. Proust describes eight major social occasions and more than eight minor ones. (1) The first social occasion is rather simple, but essential for the development of the novel: Swann's visit and dinner at Aunt Léonie's house, a purely bourgeois affair. (2) Mme Verdurin's dinner and recital in *Un Amour de Swann* (a pretentious bourgeois salon). (3) The recital reception of Mme de Saint-Euverte (a lower aristocratic affair). (4) The dinner given by Marcel's father to honor Norpois at Marcel's home (showing the world of the diplomat). (5) The receptions of Mme Swann, *"le jour"* d'Odette (exhibiting the "professional" bourgeois). (6) Elstir's studio at Balbec, where the student Marcel meets the artist and is introduced to Albertine. (7) The Bloch family dinner (which presents a Jewish world). (8) The afternoon reception of Mme de Villeparisis, which is mainly a family reception of the Guermantes (though not a prominent social salon) and in which the Dreyfus Affair is treated. (9) The soirée given by Mme de Villeparisis, at which Marcel is invited to dinner by the Duchesse de Guermantes. (10) The dinner given by the Duchesse de Guermantes (in the most socially prominent salon) during which a description of the Princesse de Parme's salon is given (highly aristocratic and socially prominent) and descriptions of Courvoisier salon life. (11) The reception of the Marquise of the Public Restrooms is ironically placed between receptions in the two most important salons to underline the pretensions of the aristocratic hostesses as well as to display the universality of snobbery. (12) The grand reception given by the Princesse de Guermantes (attended by the highest aristocratic society). (13) The dinner-

At a Ball (1900), Learning the Cakewalk. From *Illustration*.

Comtesse Greffülhe nee Caraman-Chimay (1860-1952). Painting by P. A. de László, 1909. Courtesy of the Duc de Gramont.

Comtesse Anna de Noailles in her salon, about 1912. From *Illustration.*

recital of Mme Verdurin at La Raspelière (attended by the upper bourgeoisie and provincial nobility). (14) The recital reception given by Mme Verdurin at Paris (for the bourgeois "clan" and high aristocratic society). (15) The short visit to Oriane in *La Fugitive,* where Marcel encounters Gilberte de Forcheville. (16) The Verdurin reception as described in the Goncourt pastiche (attended by bourgeois), which is placed just before the last salon scene to contrast with the change in the Verdurin salon. (17) The poetic recital reception, the matinee of the Princesse de Guermantes nee des Baux, alias Mme Verdurin (the queen of the most socially prominent salon); and an interpolation, the farewell scene of La Berma.

Though all these receptions are similar, one distinguishing feature is the music constantly offered in Mme Verdurin's salon —typical of the upper bourgeoisie, who have cultural pretensions à la Mmes Caillavet et Aubernon. Mme Verdurin is always looking for "great talent" to be fêted (and fettered) in her salon. Odette, in fact, imitates Mme Verdurin and consciously endears herself to Bergotte, who frequents her salon. The music offered at the minor aristocratic salon of Mme de Saint-Euverte tends to be placed in the background—musicians are "hired help." The great aristocratic salons of the Duchesse and Princesse de Guermantes, one may notice, attempt to follow in the grand tradition of the Marquise de Rambouillet, Mme de Tencin, Mme Récamier: displays of wit, sparkle, banalities; one talks, plays cards, and pays respect to the hostess. There is no pretension that this is a literary or cultural salon; being a gathering of aristocrats it already is one.

The Physical Characteristics of a Salon

Proust wastes little time on the physical or visual aspects of the salon scene, and the reason is simple: they are the same in all salons. Proust does, however, give a most detailed physical description of a salon scene, at Mme de Saint-Euverte's house, to make a savage attack on the physical accoutrements of a salon. We follow Swann's entrance into the main reception room as we would "a series of pictures" (I, p. 248; PI, p. 323). We are first met by grooms at the entrance way; we enter, and in the lobby we are relieved of our coats or capes and hats by a footman. Then, as we begin the climb up the monumental stairway lined by footmen in livery—cold, detached, and bored as statues—we notice a servant following behind us. At the top, more valets scurry about to inscribe our names in the guest book. Then we pass a small room decorated with a single work of art and come upon an usher who bows and opens the door into the main salon.

This is formalized, frozen etiquette, like a dream from the court of Versailles, although, even in 1900, few could afford such daily luxury; all these footmen, servants, and valets are hired only for the evening. Yet every hostess did this—it was obligatory; even today one can hire the "garde républicaine" for a reception. Clearly Proust has recorded Swann's entrance not only to capture the form but also to display that this pretentious ceremony in which society turns servants into statues and guests into demigods is even more ridiculous because it is only a "one night stand." Like the *Arabian Nights,* the salon is an escape from reality by its participants. Proust does not condemn the salon itself, but rather the people who, by rushing daily to this "make-believe" world of liveried servants and men in formal dress, accept this world as reality. And as if Proust has not sufficiently stripped away the mask of this dream world by telling us that the servants are from Potel and Chabot, caterers, he "dots his i's," as the French say, by underlining that they "dined at home like small shopkeepers, and might tomorrow lapse into the plebian service of some successful doctor or industrial magnate" (I, p. 249; PI, p. 325). Thus Proust exposes the false exterior of the salon, releasing us from an imposing *trompe l'oeil* effect.

We finally enter the salon—on our guard. In a panoramic vision we watch different types of people standing or walking to and fro "talking of Michelangelo." There is a vase, some flowers, a portrait, a chair as an obstacle, a piano, and perhaps a fashionable easel in a corner (I, p. 803-804; PII, p. 124). Proust, however, is not now as interested in objects as in people: their background, speech, dress, and mannerisms, but especially their social behavior and function. He watches people forming little groups, then breaking up and starting new ones. We see the Marquis de Bréauté talking to General de Froberville (I, p. 250; PI, p. 326) while on the other side of the salon Mme de Franquetot is listening to music with Mme de Cambremer (I, p. 251-252; PI, p. 329); then the General is seen conversing with the Princesse des Laumes (I, p. 251; PI, p. 340), who soon after joins Swann. Finally Swann introduces General de Froberville to Mme de Cambremer (I, p. 263; PI, p. 343), thus completing a great circle and bringing together disparate groups of people. Proust considers the mingling of the people at the salon as similar to his world view: people go back and forth across the room as from Guermantes' Way to Swann's Way and back again, forming little worlds which fuse and diffuse within the larger world of Mme de Saint-Euverte's salon.

Sometimes Proust will shift his attention from one room to another, as at Mme de Villeparisis', or from different rooms in the mansion to the garden outside, as at the Princesse de Guermantes' reception. These changes continue the symbolism. The different physical spaces of the salon, though separate, are juxtaposed to form the unity of the salon world just as the fusion and diffusion of groups of people within the physical space of the rooms do the same on a human level. Thus there is no difference in the basic structure of a bourgeois or aristocratic salon. Each is conducted in exactly the same way as microcosms of the Proustian world view.

Dinners

The social gatherings organized around a dinner also provide an interesting study of people. Proust describes six dinners in the novel, both bourgeois and aristocratic: Swann's visit, the first Verdurin reception, the dinner for Norpois, the Bloch dinner, the Duchesse de Guermantes' dinner, and the dinner at La Raspelière. Though it would be difficult to speak of a "dinner theme" in the style of thematic critics, the dining table is nevertheless essential. People of all classes will sit for hours and discuss art, literature, other people, politics, genealogy, and so forth over a grand banquet too rich and too long for our diet-conscious age. Formality and observation of etiquette is strict. The guests first assemble in the salon before entering the dining room, but only go in when the formal "Madame is served" is announced by the maître d'hôtel or by the offering of a hand by Mme Verdurin to M. de Cambremer (II, p. 227, PII, p. 918) or by the dinner bell, as at Combray (I, p. 21; PI, p. 27). In all cases, the dining room doors swing open like drawn curtains and the "subservient and sumptuous clockwork, mechanical and human" (I, p. 1029; PII, p. 435), of the dinner scene begins.

The different courses, though following a classic order, reveal the passing of time within the salon just as a reference to a play or a political event clues us to the chronological time and setting within the overall plan of the work. In fact, the courses reveal not only the passing of time but they permit one to see, once again, that the same foods and order of sequence are followed universally, whether in a formal aristocratic salon or at a tiny bourgeois dinner, such as that in honor of M. de Norpois. Everyone follows the same social conventions. At the Duchesse's party the dinner begins with soup (I, p. 1028; PII, p. 434); by page 1073/500 and 1076/503 Marcel is being reoffered the "asparagus and Mousseline sauce," having just finished the "financière chicken." Dessert, vanilla ice cream, follows (page 1085/516).

Although many different discussions are taking place and we, the readers, feel that Proust may have lost control of his structure, he has subtly built the scene on the movement of time as represented by the formal order of the meal, which stretches over one hundred pages! We can observe this structural device at the first Verdurin dinner reception beginning on pages I, 193/PI, p. 251; later Mme Verdurin says: "Give M. Biche some more sole" (I, p. 196; PI, p. 255); on pages 200/260 she says, "Finish your sweets," and by pages 202/263 dinner has concluded and liqueurs are being offered. This clever technique can also be seen at the short Norpois dinner, where the meal begins on pages 349/455 with the main course, "cold beef, spiced with carrots" (I, p. 351; PI, p. 458), then "pineapple and truffle salad" (I, p. 352; PI, p. 459), and finally "pudding à la Nesselrode" (I, p. 357; PI, p. 466) concludes the dinner.

The time it takes to reach the different courses approximates the actual amount of time that has passed, as in a classical play when the unities are followed explicitly. The courses announced at the different moments are like chimes of a clock giving time a physical dimension and permitting time, through the courses, to serve as the structural backbone of the scene. The structure also underlines the hollowness of these people who place such great value on formal, ordered, social conventions, so that they are stultified in an existence exterior to themselves, trapped in time and space without hope of escape.

Probably the most organized example of this type of structure is the virtuoso dinner-recital-reception at La Raspelière. For fifty pages (II, p. 190-225; PII, p. 866-917) we watch the arrival of the guests starting with the "faithful" of Mme Verdurin, then Morel and Charlus (II, p. 218; PII, p. 906), and finally the special guests, the Cambremer (II, p. 222; PII, p. 911). The actors are assembled, and everyone is united in the salon exchanging witticisms until Mme Verdurin gives the signal for dinner (II, p. 226; PII, p. 918), a dinner punctuated by discussions of art and etymologies. Dessert, "strawberry mousse," is served (II, p. 241; PII, p. 939), and "château-Margaux, château-Lafitte, port wine" are drunk. (Bordeaux wines were favored by 1900 high society; fine Burgundies, such as La Romanée-Conti, became more acceptable only after World War I.) Finally Mme Verdurin announces, "We could rise from the table" (II, p. 242; PII, p. 941). Clearly the length of time (twenty-one pages) to reach the dessert and then the short space after, two pages, to end the dinner scene reveal Proust's conscious use of announcements to imitate the actual passage of time. Then, as is typical of a formal evening, the guests retire into the salon and side rooms and prepare to listen to a few pieces by Morel (II, p. 251-252; PII, p. 953-955). After the little performance, people chat or continue to play whist (II, p. 258; PII, p. 964). A bit later, it is time for a little refreshment (orangeade, of course) (II, p. 260; PII, p. 966), and by pages 268/978 the last guests are leaving. The structure of the soirée is as solid and tight as can be. The conversations may seem to go in all directions, and there are no doubt repetitions, but Proust's whole attempt is to convey the atmosphere and flavor of the evening: the floating, meaningless parade of people, words, and convention. Yet by treating the event in terms of the formal conventions of such an evening, and by making quick references to the particular episodes—the mousse, the recital, the orangeade—we have a steady progression of time accentuated almost every twenty pages to enclose the ebb and flow of this false world within the structure of the scene, which paradoxically uses outward social conventions as the pillars of the structure. Thus we can observe typical salon scenes of the age or watch the great theme of time revealed, for both themes are brilliantly combined in the structure of the scene.

The Evolution of Salons

The evolution of the salons is the final means by which Proust follows the transformation of society as well as revealing the passage of time. From this point of view, the Verdurin salon is the most important because it offers five long scenes covering the years 1880-1922. The Verdurin salon evolves from a small bourgeois meeting place to the most aristocratic and socially prominent salon in Paris. This successful evolution has been accomplished by Mme Verdurin's concentration on presenting musical recitals and cultivating various artists, which attracted certain cultivated and socially prominent aristocrats; by the correct attitude toward the Dreyfus Affair; by a successful offensive to ensnare and exploit important "mondains" (like Mme Molé or Charlus); and above all by a felicitous marriage to the Prince de Guermantes. Within the salon itself, Mme Verdurin knew how to weed out the old faithful and bring in the aristocrats. Furthermore, she seems never to die (she must be nearly eighty years old in the final salon scene), as we see one generation disappear and the generation of Marcel, Bloch, and Morel reach maturity. We can graphically represent the change in the salon by watching and cataloguing the movements of its members. (See the chart showing the evolution of the Verdurin salon in Appendix I, p. 237).

The years 1880 to 1902 show little advancement. Mme Verdurin has at best gained a foothold in provincial nobility through the Cambremer, but Charlus will become valuable only years later. The great change occurs between 1902 and 1912. Mme Verdurin's pretensions are quite clear. She has developed new aristocratic friends like Mme Molé and Princesse Yourbeletieff; her salon has become the official salon for the visiting Ballets

Russes and the meeting place for visiting artists (II, p. 544; PIII, p. 236) like Igor Stravinsky or Richard Strauss and at which "the greatest ladies in Paris and foreign royalties were not too proud to gather" (II, p. 545; PIII, p. 237). Besides, by playing both sides of the Dreyfus Affair, she has made valuable friends in both camps, which has helped her rise through the social hierarchy. The 1912 recital, however, is a failure because she has moved too quickly to consolidate her rising status. It is also that the old aristocracy was still the social elite and was not yielding quickly or easily to the purely bourgeois advance. Between 1912 and 1922 the two major events for the salon were World War I and the death of M. Verdurin. The World War permitted Mme Verdurin to become one of the social queens because of her contacts in the ministry of war information, her increasing wealth which permitted the old luxuries, her musicales, and her willingness to admit the "bores," being no longer afraid to have them. Furthermore, after the death of M. Verdurin, her marriage to the Duc de Duras gave her the necessary title and the security of being an official member of the socially privileged class. Her final marriage to the Prince raised her position and permitted her to draw guests from the pure aristocratic society of the former princess, which she mixed with her own favorites. Thus the matinee of 1922 is interesting because the great socially prominent aristocrats, the Duchesse de Guermantes, Princesse de Nassau, Duc de Chatellerault, and so on, mix with people they would never have deigned to know even ten years earlier, including not only the new Princesse but her friends, Odette, Ski, Morel, and those who have finally reached the highest rung of society, Legrandin, Mme de Cambremer, Bloch, and Rachel. Thus an enormous evolution has taken place in which the ascending bourgeois has successfully invaded the old aristocratic haunts but, instead of remaining bourgeois, had usurped the titles which give the final touch of respectability and preserved the aristocracy even while injecting more bourgeois into the salon. What remains of the old "clan"? Nothing. They are all dead or conveniently exiled. The Verdurin salon indeed reveals the social evolution of an age.

The Hostess

Throughout French history women have been thought to perform the role of "civilizing agents," and following this tradition, a salon is formed and dominated by its hostess. Each woman chooses her guests and gives the tone to her salon. (That Charlus is so knowledgeable about salon rites and traditions only underlines the feminine aspect of his being, since the role of salon-keeper has through the centuries been considered a purely feminine duty.) The women, then, have tremendous power in selecting and in casting aside people they consider to be not "proper" for their salon or their social world. Thus Elstir is acceptable to Oriane and her salon not because he is a great artist—this is unimportant since he would not even be mentioned unless the art world had already acknowledged his talent—but rather "he is more than intelligent, he is really quite clever" (I, p. 1075; PII, p. 501).

The man's real value in the salon is never important; rather, how his presence might improve the hostess' salon and bring *her* the honors is the important consideration. The success of a hostess depends primarily on her own abilities (wit, leadership qualities, style, and recruiting techniques) and social position. In France at the turn of the century it was most advantageous to have a title, an authentic one, and of course illustrious quarters. But if ancestry counted greatly, elegance, liveliness, wit, and especially *savoir-faire* were prerequisites to reaching the pinnacle as a social queen of the age.

Oriane de Guermantes elegantly fulfills all these qualifications. Speaking of her salon Proust says "Oriane's own wit . . . formed its chief attraction" (I, p. 1042; PII, p. 453). As the ironic but "delicious" hostess she amuses her guests by commenting on the other guests of her salon.

> —Poor General, he's been defeated again at the elections, said the Princesse [de Parme]. . . .
>
> —He has consoled himself by giving his wife another baby.

—What! Is that poor Mme de Monserfeuil in an interesting condition again, cried the Princesse.
—Why, of course, replied the Duchess, that's the one division where the poor General has never failed to get in. (I, p. 1082; PII, p. 512)

As we can see, the wit is nimble, slightly vulgar, elegant, spiteful. This is the clever hostess in action. Everyone and everything is clearly more important than the individual. Furthermore, a certain social daring is necessary as well. Since the society is so stultified, even the slightest deviation in behavior is cause for shock, surprise and appreciation. In fact, Oriane's genius for bringing about the unexpected is part of her enormous appeal. "Oriane's latest," is the key word to her charm and spirited independence which hardly shies from banality. For example:

> To start people on the topic of an "Oriane's latest" it was sufficient that at a performance at which all Paris was present and a most charming play was being given, when they looked for Mme de Guermantes in the boxes of the Princesse de Parme, the Princesse de Guermantes, countless other ladies who had invited her, they discovered her sitting by herself, in black, with a tiny hat on her head [contrary to all social conventions of how to dress for the theater], in a stall in which she had arrived before the curtain rose [it was fashionable to arrive late]. "You hear better, when it's a play that's worth listening to," she explained, to the scandal of the Courvoisiers [old school nobles] and the admiring bewilderment of the Guermantes and the Princesse de Parme, who suddenly discovered that the "fashion" of hearing the beginning of a play was more up to date, was a proof of greater originality and intelligence (which need not astonish them, coming from Oriane) than that of arriving for the last act after a big dinner-party and "going on" somewhere first. (I, p. 1059; PII, pp. 478-479)

By breaking some of high society's sacrosanct conventions—not only is she dressed simply and seated in the orchestra, but she even arrived on time—Oriane has breathed a bit of novelty into the lifelessness of society.

Inevitably a social queen becomes the social arbiter of the age. When Oriane decides not to go to the masked ball of the Greek minister, the other "correct" ladies will not attend either (I, p. 1058; PII, p. 476). In the same way, she will dispose of the garden party of Mme de Saint-Euverte (II, p. 52; PII, p. 669). Eventually her excessive "originality" will contribute to her downfall, yet for the moment let us leave her on top of the wheel of Fortune, the image of a social queen circa 1900.

Oriane was established, seemingly invincible, and her doors were tightly shut; this was her means of fighting back the crush. But she knew how to recruit people as efficiently as those ladies ascending the rungs of society. "Oriane . . . had the art of attracting men who were in the public eye to her house, in a ratio that of course never exceeded one per cent, otherwise she would have lowered its tone" (I, p. 1026; PII, p. 430). Elstir, Bergotte, Saint-Saëns, Pailleron, and Forain were accepted. Recruiting was the main concern for a woman whose salon was on the rise or who wanted her salon to retain its importance. There were two methods, active and passive. Mme Verdurin represents a person who relied on the passive method to recruit followers, setting up a specialized salon. Mme de Saint-Euverte relied on the active method, attending the parties of others to choose guests for her own soirée. "As a matter of fact, Mme de Saint-Euverte had come this evening, less for the pleasure of not missing another person's party than in order to ensure the success of her own, recruit the latest additions to her list, and, so to speak, hold an eleventh-hour review of the troops" (II, p. 52; PII, p. 669). Mme de Mortemart is even worse. After listening to Morel at Mme Verdurin's musicale, Mme de Mortmart decides to steal him away for a party she is giving. "She regarded it only as an opportunity for giving a particularly smart party and was calculating already whom she would invite and whom she would reject . . . before she has even thought of what Morel was to play (which she regarded, and rightly, as a secondary consideration, for even if everybody this evening, from fear of M. de Charlus, had observed a polite silence during the music, it would never have occurred to anyone to listen to it" (II, p. 567; PIII, p. 269). Of course Mme Verdurin, through charity concerts and other such proper activities, meets people who are valuable for her salon, but when she attempts a great move she lets Charlus handle the salon, which is an error. (Mme Verdurin's rise is an evolution.) "The Verdurin salon was understood to be a temple of music" (II, p. 193; PII, p. 870). This specialization attracts the most intellectual part of the aristocracy and eventually others. Odette imitates Mme Swann by sequestering Bergotte, and thus begins an intellectual literary salon. "In Odette's case, at the start, a few men of the highest society, anxious to meet Bergotte, had gone to dine, quite quietly, at her house. She had had the tact, recently acquired, not to advertise their presence . . . Odette took them with Bergotte . . . to interesting first nights. They spoke of her to various women of their own world who were capable of taking an interest in such novelty" (II, p. 105; PII, p. 745). Both methods are effective and are used interchangeably. The most important danger to be suffered from the application of either is the ravages of time, which destroys the novelty craved by a bored society and thus requires fresh changes which must be accepted if the salon is to survive, even though altered. The problem is how to be in step with time and still preserve the elegance of a salon. Oriane was a master at this effort for years, and in her way Mme Verdurin was also.

Obviously, exclusiveness is the main concern of the hostess. If you are climbing, as in the case of Mme Verdurin, the persons you want are above you, but the socially superior would not deign to enter her abode. She had to protect herself and the world of her salon, which she made subservient to her, becoming a restless semi-benevolent tyrant. We never sense the freedom of an Oriane who is laughing and joking, for Mme Verdurin is too busy supervising the discussion to be witty. While she took the defensive cleverly to preserve her salon, she also took the offensive to improve it: she claimed that the socially superior were "dullards" and thereby proclaimed herself and her guests the truly enlightened beings, the true elite. This tack, of course, could freeze the position of the salon, but the genius of Mme

Verdurin was to allow into her salon aristocrats who somehow were not "bores." She therefore tolerated homosexuals and other types undesirable to polite society if they could help improve the salon's standing. Thus when a "faithful" wishes to warn the "patronne" that the Baron de Charlus and Morel were infamous, Mme Verdurin turns on the sculptor furiously. "Certain that the Verdurins were making a grave mistake in allowing an individual of tarnished reputation to be admitted to so 'select' a household as theirs, the sculptor [Ski] felt it his duty to take the Mistress aside. 'You are entirely mistaken, besides I never pay any attention to those tales, and even if it were true, I may be allowed to point out that it could hardly compromise me!' replied Mme Verdurin, furious, for Morel being the principal feature of the Wednesdays, the chief thing for her was not to give any offense to him" (II, p. 216; PII, p. 904). To insure the success of her salon she will sacrifice her code of ethics; above all, the salon must be protected. Even Mme de Villeparisis is concerned about the success of her salon. Bloch, for instance, is not introduced by Mme de Villeparisis to a rival hostess friend "for fear of his being asked to produce the same play that he was arranging for her drawing-room of the Quai Malaquais" (I, p. 856; PII, p. 197).

Oriane de Guermantes, of course, has her own phrase by which she avoids recognizing new people who would not be valuable for the standing of her salon: "I don't know her." This is Oriane's key response, similar to the oft-quoted *"les ennuyeux"* of Mme Verdurin.

—Who is the woman, and why does she bow to me?
—But you know her perfectly, she's Mme de Charleval's daughter, Henriette Montmorency.
—Oh, but I knew her mother quite well, she was charming, extremely intelligent. What made her go and marry all these people I never heard of? (II, p. 55; PII, p. 673)

—Have you been invited to Lady Israels'? Mme de Villeparisis asked the Duchesse. . . .

> —Why, thank heaven, I don't know the woman. (I, p. 897; PII, p. 253)

> If I don't go . . . to see this Princesse d'Iena . . . it's simply because I don't know them. (I, p. 259; PI, p. 338)

Like all the hostesses, Oriane must maintain the exclusivity of her salon; Proust bluntly states, "One pretended not to know that the body of one's hostess was at the disposal of all comers, provided that her visiting list showed no gaps" (I, p. 1021; PII, p. 423).

Oriane de Guermantes has the most chic salon because she has managed to bring new faces into her drawing rooms. She has let Empire nobles mix with *ancien régime* titles, a daring move (I, p. 1053; PII, p. 468-469). It is at her salon that the bonapartist Princesse Mathilde meets the Orleans Duc d'Aumale. (I, p. 252-253; PI, p. 329) And of course M. Detaille, a French military artist and author, is invited. In fact the artist causes more excitement than the presence of the King of England, which emphasizes the importance of novelty.

> The Faubourg Saint-Germain had not yet recovered from the shock of learning that, to the reception which she had given to meet the King and Queen of England, the Duchess had not been afraid to invite M. Detaille. The clever women of the faubourg who had not been invited were inconsolable, so deliciously thrilling would it have been to come into contact with that strange genius. . . . Finally, a last straw of scandal, M. de Guermantes . . . had repaired to the green-room of the Comédie Française, and had begged Mlle Reichenberg to come and recite before the King, which having come to pass constituted an event without precedent in the annals of routs. (I, p. 1025; PII, p. 430)

These petty innovations bring glory to Oriane.

The Courvoisier family, which is as well pedigreed as the Guermantes, lacks the initiative or adventuresome spirit to turn their salon into the "chic" center of social life. They are more like the Guermantes-Bavière, who maintain a pure upper aristocratic salon, whose lack of surprises makes it dull. Mme Verdurin, on the contrary, successfully mixes different types, only bourgeois at the beginning, but eventually artists, bourgeois, and aristocrats. Thus her salon offers, besides her music, a variety of people, which provides the novelty essential to a rising social queen.

When Oriane searched for new people, especially non-aristocrats, it was always some "celebrity who had recently come into prominence by the discovery of a new cure for something or the production of a masterpiece" (I, p. 1025; PII, pp. 429-430). However, they had to be witty and proper for the tone of the salon. Oriane capitalizes on the fame of the scientist or artist, not on his work, which reveals that in spite of her pretensions she cares little for talent and mainly for her own work—the salon.

It is the conduct of the hostess within the salon which individualizes her social gathering. Oriane (I, p. 864; PII, p. 208) and Mme Leroi (I, p. 854-855; PII, p. 195) both take pleasure in discussing banal generalities and in exchanging witticisms with their guests, especially with artists and musicians. They both enjoy watching the artists play poker and avoid any discussions of art—"this reserve was simply a matter of good form" (I, p. 861; PII, p. 208). For Proust, this destroys in one blow the validity of a salon and the cultural pretensions of the "elite." In fact, these hostesses attempt to erase the real value of the guests by making them subservient. Thus they destroy all professional, political, or artistic accomplishments, which are valueless to the hostess (I, p. 1046; PII, p. 459). Mme Verdurin, in contrast, forces her artists and musicians to show their paintings and to play for her, in order to display the artistic nature of her salon. She treats her professionals, Cottard and Brichot, with a certain admiration which she will lose as she climbs. But for Proust she is limited, too, since Wagner gives her a migraine: he is too sublime, and thus cannot be performed. Thus the hostess' affectations and hinted inability to appreciate great music is mocked.

Her only concern is to keep her position in her own social

world. "But it was pre-eminently from the negative point of view that intellectuality made itself felt. If the necessary coefficient of cleverness and charm declined steadily as the rank of the person who sought an invitation from the Princesse des Laumes became more exalted, vanishing into zero when he or she was one of the principal Crowned Heads of Europe, conversely the farther they fell below this royal level the higher the coefficient rose" (I, p. 1041; PII, p. 452). Thus both Mme Verdurin and Oriane are liars. Mme Verdurin wants the "bores" but cannot have them, while Oriane wants to give the impression of running a great urbane salon but in reality is mainly concerned with keeping an aristocratic salon with a dash of paprika—artists and intellectuals —for variety. This social snobbery, this need to protect and maintain the exclusiveness of the salon reaches the greatest absurdity when the toilet attendant dubbed "la marquise" announces that her public comfort station is like a salon. "And besides, she went on, I choose my customers, I don't let everyone into my little parlors, as I call them. And doesn't the place just look like a parlor with all my flowers?" (I, p. 937; PII, p. 310). (Odette, Mme Verdurin, and Oriane all have flowers galore in their salons.) Proust even depicts how a woman who desperately needs a stall is told that there is nothing available (though we know that one is free) because the attendant does not like her! This comic scene points out that there are no class differences where social snobbery is concerned, and that a hostess will do anything in her power to maintain her salon no matter what her social level.

If, God forbid, someone slips through the fine nets into a salon and proves dangerous, a rapid execution is performed. Every hostess performs this task with a certain relish, for it secures the salon and makes the hostess a "grande dame" in the eyes of her guests. Mme Verdurin performs the most executions in the novel (Swann, I, p. 222 and PI, p. 289; Saniette, I, p. 204 and PI, p. 266; and Charlus), but her style leaves something to be desired. She is brutal, especially in the case of Charlus, who is denounced in front of all as a homosexual by his "lover" through the machinations of Mme Verdurin. Mme de Villeparisis has much more finesse (Proust believed the aristocrats had better form because their whole life centered on exterior actions). Whereas

Mme Verdurin sneakily sets Morel against Charlus, Mme de Villeparisis executes Bloch by total silence. It is a stage play with the courtiers milling around the queen. The following quotation is one of the finest bits of social observation and satire that Proust creates in the novel:

> She decided, therefore, to make it plain to Bloch that he need not come to the house again, and had no difficulty in finding, among her social repertory, the scene by which a great lady shows anyone her door, a scene which does not in any way involve the raised finger and blazing eyes that people imagine [which is in the bourgeois Verdurin style]. As Bloch came up to her to say goodbye, buried in her deep armchair, she seemed only half-awakened from a vague somnolence. Her sunken eyes gleamed with only the feeble though charming light of a pair of pearls. Bloch's farewell, barely pencilling on the Marquise's face a languid smile, drew from her not a word, nor did she offer him her hand. This scene left Bloch in utter bewilderment, but as he was surrounded by a circle of spectators he felt that it could not be prolonged without disadvantage to himself, and, to force the Marquise, the hand which she had made no effort to take he himself thrust out to her.* Mme de Villeparisis was startled. But doubtless, while still bent upon giving an immediate satisfaction to the librarian and the anti-Dreyfusard clan, she wished at the same time to provide for the future, and so contented herself with letting her eyelids droop over her closing eyes. "I believe she's asleep," said Bloch to the librarian who, feeling that he had the support of the Marquise, assumed an indignant air.† "Good-by, madame," shouted Bloch.

* This improper act of etiquette is underlined not only to show how it is used to destroy someone but to emphasize as well how exterior gestures have been so internalized that they are the basis of existence.

† This addition has two purposes: to oppose dramatically the enemies, the anti-semite and the Jew; and to underline the cowardice of the salonnards who always seek protection from their hostess.

> The old lady made the slight movement with her lips of a dying woman who wants to open her mouth but whose eye can no longer recognize people.* Then she turned, overflowing with a restored vitality, to M. d'Argencourt. . . . (I, p. 893-894; PII, p. 248)

One could analyze minutely the language of the theater, the emphasis placed on parts of the face, the brilliant use of words which hint and suggest the languid ebbings of studied half-hearted intentions, but let us move on to the final irony of the scene. "She had acted once and for all the little scene of the indignant lady that she had wished to act, a scene that had been universally admired and discussed the same evening in various drawing-rooms, but in a version which had already ceased to bear any resemblance to the truth" (I, p. 894; PII, p. 249).

An execution is not only a salon recreation, and a means of getting rid of undesirables, but the promptest means by which a hostess can assert herself.

Proust offers a further panorama of the different hostesses and how they receive. The Princesse de Guermantes, seated in a chair flanked by two Highnesses and the ambassadress, thanks the guest for coming—and curtly sends him off to the prince. "To some indeed she said nothing, showing them her admirable onyx eyes, as though they had come merely to visit an exhibition of precious stones" (II, p. 29; PII, p. 636). Yet after the dinner she visited all the little groups the guests had formed in less than three-quarters of an hour "but had the paramount object of making it apparent how naturally 'a great lady knows how to entertain' " (II, p. 29; PII, p. 635). The Princesse de Parme also receives while seated on a sofa surrounded by her two most important dinner guests ostensibly playing cards ("a practice of the German court"). The guests enter and each "sank before the upright presence in a curtsy which was tantamount to a genuflexion. . . . But at that moment the Princesse . . . raised the kneeling figure

* What a marvellous actress! Indeed this only emphasizes Proust's attitude that people at social gatherings are not honest but acting, wearing masks.

. . . with incomparable grace and sweetness, and kissed her on both cheeks. A grace and sweetness that were conditional, you may say, upon the meekness with which the arriving guest inclined her knee" (I, p. 1043; PII, p. 454-455).

Afterwards, Mme Verdurin likes to sit in her large chair placed so that she can see all the movement in the salon as well as be near enough to the center of activity to make her dogmatic pronouncements. Mme de Villeparisis, however, plays the artist and sits and paints a little at her easel as her guests look on (I, p. 868-869; PII, p. 214). Proust actually satirizes Madeleine Lemaire, a contemporary, who maintained a popular salon in her artistic studio. In short, each hostess has her own style which is none too original and highly unnatural. That Proust made such an effort to individualize each salon hostess, however, and that we can identify them historically, supports the argument that he went to such detail in order to capture the image of the social life of his age. Indeed this wealth of detail opens him to the criticism of not distinguishing the forest from the trees—an attack which is not always unwarranted.

The hostesses considered the guest at best as chattel. The Princesse de Guermantes even refers to the Highnesses in her salon as "my little dogs" (II, p. 45; PII, p. 659). Mme Verdurin possessively talks of *her* "faithfuls" and Oriane makes fun of her own behind their backs. If a regular guest should die, there is no mourning. The salon must continue to shine; the old faithful are quickly forgotten.

> Mme Verdurin, like most people who move in society, simply because she needed the society of other people, never thought of them again for a single day, as soon as, being dead they could no longer come to the Wednesdays, not to the Saturdays, nor dine without dressing. And one could not say of the little clan, a type in this respect of all salons, that it was composed of more dead than living members, seeing that, as soon as one was dead, it was as though one had never existed. (II, p. 211; PII, p. 896)

Thus Mme Verdurin disposes of the deaths of Dechambre (II, p. 211; PII, p. 896) and Princesse Sherbatoff (II, p. 536; PIII, p. 228). And the Duchesse de Guermantes at the matinee can hardly remember Swann. As I have said, guests exist only to improve a salon's standing; friendship and warmth have no place. Only pettiness and vindicativeness abound. Mme Verdurin warns Marcel not to go to her rival Mme Cambremer, for "Féterne is starvation corner. . . . I'm sure, when I go there, I shall have my dinner before I start" (II, p. 263; PII, p. 972). Aunt Léonie protects her little world by counseling the sisters of Marcel's grandmother not to ask Swann about his name in the *Figaro*. "Whenever she saw in others an advantage, however trivial, which she herself lacked, she would pity so as not to have to envy them" (I, p. 17; PI, p. 22). And Oriane unnecessarily needles Mme de Villeparisis by stating that she is dining chez Mme Leroi, the bane of Mme de Villeparisis, because Mme Leroi considers the Villeparisis salon second-rate and refuses to visit or to extend to Mme de Villeparisis an invitation to her own "smart" salon (I, p. 904; PII, p. 263). A merry-go-round of artificiality, vindictiveness, sterility: it exists on all levels of society when people attempt to be more than they are.

But the salons eventually fall, that of the Duchesse of Guermantes for example. What has happened? "She did not think she needed to buttress a position she considered impregnable" (II, p. 1091; PIII, p. 1004), so she grew lazy; like all society people she needed new excitement. "She made advances to women with whom in former years she would not have been willing to exchange calling cards" (II, p. 1091; PIII, p. 1004). Oriane had already challenged society by her ever so minor, yet daring departures which made her a success. But by bringing in so many outsiders of such low station—especially actresses—her salon lost its tone and her social position was challenged by the newcomers. She had forgotten that high society is entrapped in the movement of time, which destroys what it creates. Even if Oriane were not losing her position by associating excessively with the wrong people, nor by not allowing the new "stars" of high society into her salon, nor by taking her position for granted, her social power would still diminish because time was against her. Society wanted a fresh face for its reigning queen. She had her decades of glory; now time demanded that a new goddess be anointed, and Oriane's salon became second-rate. "She had herself become a Mme de Villeparisis, at whose house women solicitous of their social standing dreaded meeting certain men and women whom the younger generation, taking note of the situation as it was without knowing what had gone before, believed to be a Guermantes of an inferior vintage, of a poorer harvest, a déclassée Guermantes" (II, p. 1092; PIII, p. 1004).

Oriane was a bit more intelligent than the average hostesses, but her downfall nevertheless was hastened by that very intelligence, which made her crave new adventure. She was also caught in a life struggle with one woman who was at least as intelligent as she was, Mme Verdurin, who brought the same bourgeois determination to conquer society as did the previous bourgeois generations which had created the industrial revolution. Poor Oriane could not stem the tide of social transformation nor the passing of time nor the intransigeance of her own weak nature.

If I have emphasized the role of the hostess, it is because she is the physical representative of the salon and its image. She creates it, directs it, and eventually destroys it. Proust clearly realized this, as we can see from the tremendous amount of detail he collected to individualize each hostess and her salon; yet in the end he concludes that the fine distinctions were of no real importance. Every hostess, no matter of what caste, falls into the same pattern. She is crass, ignorant, and pretentious, and places personal glory through social position above everything else. She will destroy everything, even beauty, if it will aid her salon; she will lie, cheat, and even break the moral codes which outwardly she so fiercely defends. She has no friends, no real relationships. She is a lonely woman looking for an escape from a world she has created around her, which in itself is as void of meaning as her own life. She floats continually in an aura of total material comfort, sterile, waiting for snobs to be ensnared by her glitter and for poets and historians to immortalize her.

The Salonnard

If the hostess is the prima donna of the ball, the guests or "*salonnards*" (a wonderful term coined by Léon Daudet) are the corps de ballet. Indeed, they are a real troupe carefully selected and constantly reviewed. The *salonnard* gives support to the prima donna; a *mondain* must never attempt to usurp the star's position. If he does, it is a challenge, and eventually someone must suffer a social death. But who are these *salonnards?* They are aristocrats, rich businessmen now living on "revenues," former professionals; they are "brilliant men, fitted for a career to which, whether it were in the arts, diplomacy, parliamentary eloquence or the army, they had preferred the life of a small and intimate group. Possibly this preference could be explained by a certain want of originality, of initiative, of will power, of health or of luck, or possibly by snobbishness" (I, p. 1045; PII, p. 458). In any case, they are all failures, social climbers, snobs fascinated by a life they have dreamed of and attempted to find in their external existence. Here they are presented in their natural habitat:

> Along gilt chairs lay resplendent a host of bare shoulders. The varied crests of feminine hairdoes, studded with scintillating glimmers were undulating under an imperceptible breeze of well-being, fanning flurries of vanity. A voluptuous aroma mixed with a nerve-racking hubbub with glints of satin, jewelry, silk, flesh, velvet and gold rose from these forty long rows where, in a marvelous discipline, so many diverse specimens of the feminine beast were rigidly posed encased within their festive trappings.
>
> The herd of "white ties and tails" who were parked behind numbered only men distinguished by birth or refined manners, almost all bearing the names of bygone courtiers or of modern battles, of saints or great estates, only a small number possessed any personal glory, some bedecking themselves with decorations, others with a sense

> of "tradition" in their remarks, always placing their ascendance in one corner of an escutcheon.
>
> And above all else there rose from the gathering a particular atmosphere which characterizes high society's most elegant occasions: a vaporized aura of being among one's kind, among people very solidly unified by nothing at all. . . .

A colorful description, though smelling of midnight oil. Here the *salonnards* are frozen in a panorama of conspicuous consumption, and the author appeals to all our senses and teases our intellect with irony. It is an ensemble view, detached and precise, written not by Proust but by Paul Hervieu (*L'Armature,* 1895).[4] Proust, of course, was a great synthesizer and drew from many predecessors who were keen social observers such as Hervieu and Abel Hermant. The major difference between Proust and other writers of social novels is that Proust uses a non-omniscient narrator who describes the society he reflects in the first person singular, peppering it liberally with subjunctive verbs. Writers like Hervieu, Donnay, Pailleron, and others usually reflect what they observe in the third person singular and generally use the imperfect indicative tense, always remaining objective and removed.

Proust was ingenious also because he avoided making a sweeping description of a group, such as the one just quoted from Hervieu, in favor of giving a psychological description of a person, who serves as a representative of the group. Proust did this not only because he believed in the fragmentation of external existence, which makes each person a small floating world in the larger one of the salon, but also because it permitted him to make a closer analysis of a type and allowed him to look for laws of social behavior *in flagrante delicto.* By way of comparing the two styles, let us examine one of Proust's descriptions of a salon, but an atypical one in which the first person narrative is *not* used, for then the differences between Hervieu and Proust would be too readily apparent at the start. We turn to *L'Amour de Swann,* in which the narrator *is* omniscient and writes in the third person. The Hervieu passage describes the *salonnards* watching a salon comedy; Proust's scene takes place at Mme de Saint-Euverte's salon while the guests are listening to a recital:

> Swann had gone forward into the room, under pressure from Mme de Saint-Euverte and in order to listen to an aria from *Orfeo* which was being rendered on the flute, and had taken up a position in a corner from which, unfortunately, his horizon was bounded by two ladies of "uncertain" age, seated side by side, the Marquise de Cambremer and the Vicomtesse de Franquetot, who, because they were cousins, used to spend their time at parties in wandering through the rooms, each clutching her bag and followed by her daughter, hunting for one another like people at a railway station, and could never be at rest until they had reserved, by marking them with their fans or handkerchiefs, two adjacent chairs; Mme de Cambremer, since she knew scarcely anyone, being all the more glad of a companion, while Mme de Franquetot, who, on the contrary, was extremely popular, thought it effective and original to show all her fine friends that she preferred to their company that of an obscure country cousin with whom she had childish memories in common. Filled with ironical melancholy, Swann watched them as they listened to the pianoforte intermezzo. (I, p. 251; PI, p. 328)

The focal point is Swann, the hero. Through him we observe the ladies, and we always return to him for some emotional response to the scene. The narrator, then, is not peering down at the group, as in the Hervieu scene, but stands directly behind Swann and describes what Swann sees.

Proust does individualize the guests: first he names them, and then he gives their salient characteristics, especially in terms of social standing. Whereas Hervieu is excited to describe with bitter irony the exterior accoutrements of the guests, which *does* effectively create an atmosphere, Proust mentions only a fan and a handkerchief to insist not only on the wealth and ease of these people but on the psychological dependence of the individual upon the object. In short, Hervieu has a more limited objective: to create the image and atmosphere of a salon through a panoramic view interstitched with social comment—much as John O'Hara, John Updike, or Philip Roth might do. Proust, on the other hand, goes beyond describing the image of the *salonnard* to reveal his psychological state by individualizing him and then exploring his gestures and remarks—the external signs which expose hidden thoughts. In this way he captures the attitudes of a given *"race, moment, et milieu"* and uses it to offer insights into the ways of humanity in social relationships. Proust's originality in social observation thus extends beyond the technical innovation of the first person, non-omniscient narrative. Hervieu, however, remains useful only to the social historian, whereas Proust interests the social historian, the literary scholar, the critic, and—let us hope—above all, the educated reader.

We can continue the study of the *salonnard* by examining a classic type—the Marquise de Gallardon. She is a typical aristocratic snob, and excellent for our purposes because she also reveals Proust's technique of salon observation. She happens to be present at the recital at Mme de Sainte-Euverte's as well:

> On the other side (and a little way in front) of Mme de Franquetot, was the Marquise de Gallardon, absorbed in her favorite meditation, namely upon her own kinship with the Guermantes family, from which she derived both publicly and in private a good deal of glory not unmingled with shame, the most brilliant ornaments of that house remaining somewhat aloof from her, perhaps because she was just a tiresome old woman, or because she was a scandalous old woman, or because she came of an inferior branch of the family, or very possibly for no reason at all. (I, p. 252; PI, pp. 328-29)

There is no physical description, but we are made aware of her presence in the salon, her social standing, her psychological attitude toward her surroundings, and the impression she gives to others. Her desire, as a snob, is to be received by her prominent young cousin Oriane who has not invited the Marquise for six years. She does not listen to the music but rationalizes to herself why she has not been invited. "It was because of the risk of meeting the Princesse Mathilde there—a degradation which her own family, the truest and bluest of Legitimists, would never have forgiven her; she had come gradually to believe that this was the reason for her not visiting her young cousin" (I, p. 252; PI, p. 329). But, prodded by the desire to climb, we watch her then place the blame on her cousin for not inviting her: "After all, it isn't for me to take the first step; I am at least twenty years older than she is" (I, p. 252; PI, p. 329). Proust then shows how her snobbery affects her physical appearance (I, p. 253; PI, p. 329) and finally how even her language is touched by her inner pride and frustration: she repeats constantly " 'at my cousins the Guermantes,' " " 'at my aunt Guermantes' " (I, p. 253; PI, p. 330).

Having presented the Marquise psychologically and physically, Proust continues his study of the *salonnard* in action. Oriane arrives. How will Mme de Gallardon react? At first she plans not to answer Oriane's bow—a vindictive outgrowth of her frustrations—but, on seeing her, the Marquise "dashed towards her, upsetting all her neighbors" (I, p. 255; PI, p. 333). Clearly snobbery has triumphed over pride. With exquisite precision Proust follows the conflicting desires on the physical plane of the character and leads us into the direct encounter through dialogue and an *explication de texte:*

> She felt bound to modify this air of dignity and reserve by some noncommittal remark which would justify her overture and would force the Princess to engage in conversation; and so, when she reached her cousin, Mme de Gallardon, with a stern countenance and one hand thrust out as though she were trying to "force" a card, began with: "How is your husband?" in the same anxious tone that she would have used if the Prince had been seriously ill. The Princess, breaking into a laugh which was one of

> her characteristics, and was intended at once to show the rest of an assembly that she was making fun of someone and also to enhance her own beauty by concentrating her features around her animated lips and sparkling eyes, answered: "Why, he's never been better in his life!" And she went on laughing.

The Marquise had several reasons for speaking to Oriane: first, she wanted to show the others her Guermantes relationship; second, she wanted to glean an invitation; and finally, as we shall see, she wished to ensnare Oriane for her own party. Notice, however, that Oriane is on her guard, and above all wishes to shine for all at the expense of her second-rate cousin. Her laughter is a double-edged sword. But let us continue this social ballet:

> "Oriane (at once Mme des Laumes looked with amused astonishment towards an invisible third, whom she seemed to call to witness that she had never authorized Mme de Gallardon to use her Christian name), I should be so pleased if you would look in, just for a minute, tomorrow evening, to hear a quintet, with the clarinet, by Mozart. I should like to have your opinion of it."
>
> She seemed not so much to be issuing an invitation as to be asking a favor, and to want the Princess's opinion of the Mozart quintet just as though it had been a dish invented by a new cook, whose talent it was most important that an epicure should come to judge.
>
> "But I know that quintet quite well. I can tell you now . . . that I adore it."
>
> "You know, my husband isn't at all well; it's his liver. He would like so much to see you," Mme de Gallardon resumed, making it now a corporal work of charity for the Princess to appear at her party. (I, p. 256; PI, pp. 333-34)

Proust's commentary here is at least as biting as Hervieu's. He exposes the façade of culture placed before the most vulgar social climbing and shows the depths to which a typical *salonnard* will stoop to gain social acceptance. But Oriane is not trapped and leaves the Marquise with a "perhaps"—more polite, but just as firm in the salon as a "No."

Another writer might have ended the study of a *salonnard*'s conversation at this point and commented on the vulgarity of snobs. But Proust is not content simply to amuse the reader with an example of how to rebuff a social climber. He wishes to show all sides of the *salonnard* in action. A supercilious Marquise to her neighbors, a frustrated Marquise within herself, an obsequious Marquise to her social superiors, Mme de Gallardon's inner frustrations now create a vindictive Marquise who attacks an innocent bystander, Swann, a converted Jew, who has entered Oriane's world while she, an older cousin, is left out. (Social antisemitism, then, is due in part to the frustration of aristocrats who have not fared well in their own social climb and who use the newcomers, the Jews, as scapegoats. By attacking Swann, a friend of Oriane's, the Marquise releases her aggressions towards Oriane.)

> "Oriane, don't be angry with me," resumed Mme de Gallardon, who could never restrain herself from sacrificing her highest social ambitions, and the hope that she might one day emerge into a light that would dazzle the world, to the immediate and secret satisfaction of saying something disagreeable, "people do say about your M. Swann that he's the sort of man one can't have in the house; is that true?"
>
> "Why, you of all people, ought to know that it's true," replied the Princess des Laumes, "for you must have asked him a hundred times, and he's never been to your house once."
>
> And leaving her cousin mortified afresh, she broke out again into a laugh." (I, p. 257; PI, p. 335)

Unable to retire graciously, the Marquise attacks Oriane directly.

But again, she is no match for her social superior and is left revealing only her own hypocrisy and the inferiority of her salon. And so Oriane turns away with a laugh which is the final stinging rebuff.

Proust shows us how snobbery, this social malady, can mentally and emotionally cripple a person as terribly as any physical disease. Paul Hervieu describes for us the outward splendor of a *salonnard;* Proust shows us what the social institution does to an individual, internally *and* externally, and further reveals the false premises upon which the institution is built. Under all the fans and jewels and make-up is a jungle, but it is a false jungle since the ones who dominate reign only by the delusions of the snobs and the evident continued complicity of the ennobled.

Marcel, Legrandin, and Bloch are examples of male *salonnards,* while on the distaff side, Mlle Legrandin is an example of a woman, who would gladly abandon a brilliant education at the Sorbonne for the pleasure of saying "my aunt d'Uzai" (II, p. 157; PII, p. 819); and Oriane could always depend on the Princesse de Parme, who found that everything "at the Duchesse de Guermantes', people and things alike, was of a quality superior to that of anything that she had at home" (I, p. 1030; PII, p. 437). Another typical female *salonnard* is the Turkish ambassador's wife (who, by the way, did exist, for Proust mixes real names and incidents within the novel). In 1898 the Turkish ambassador was quite the social "hit," as recorded in this *mondanité* of the *Figaro,* June 11, 1898: "At the Turkish embassy. The salons of the Turkish embassy have become, as we see it, one of the most elegant social rendezvous. It is a personal success for S. Exc. Munir-Bey, who knew how to create an exceptional position in Parisian high society."

We can hardly imagine a more powerful indictment against the *salonnards* than when the dying La Berma is abandoned by her own daughter to hear Rachel, her arch-rival, at the Princesse's matinee, because that is the chic place for *salonnards* to be at that moment.

Proust, like the writers of *Ars Amandi* in the Middle Ages, not only attacks the *salonnards* but offers a course on how to succeed as a *salonnard* as well. Proust does not believe that it is difficult to penetrate high society. (All those who do enter, like Odette, Bloch, or Legrandin, are actually of rather obscure backgrounds.) Of course the most effective way to enter Belle Epoque society is through marriage, but failing this and lacking a title, one must be able to create an aura of mystery around oneself (II, p. 192; PII, p. 869). He also should take advantage of the latest economic, social, and especially political changes (like a General de Froberville, II, p. 57; PII, p. 676) and hold the right opinions as well as break with former acquaintances whose opinions might place him in a poor light. Above all, one must be charming and witty, always ready to oblige the host or hostess.

We must not forget that the *salonnard* almost never works at any business. This frees his mind to worry about the petty: "why wasn't I invited to the Guermantes' party?" And even when he is in the desired salon he only fishes for more invitations (Mme de Saint-Euverte is the finest representative of this kind of activity). And almost naturally his interpersonal relations are pervaded with intrigue, because the salon does not unite friends but rather brings together people deemed socially worthy for the moment; therefore they are all in competition: "They envied Mme Cottard, whom the 'Mistress' called by her Christian name" (I, pp. 457-58; PI, p. 601). No one will help anyone else; on the contrary, the *salonnard* will quickly disassociate himself from someone out of favor as I pointed out earlier. The *salonnard* desperately needs to "keep up," and thus he will mock something like Brichot's articles publicly (even though he reads them with pleasure in private) "in order not to seem less intelligent than the others" (II, p. 939; PIII, p. 793). In the end, of course, "there are very few things that they remember" (II, p. 404; PIII, p. 39).

Proust abhors *salonnards,* especially because of their bad upbringing, bad taste in personal relations, and lack of artistic appreciation. As has been said, whether they are looking at paintings or listening to a recital of music or verse, they are not only ignorant but really do not care. Thus Proust describes the vulgarity of the aristocratic *salonnards* who visit Mme Verdurin's salon:

> Having come there partly out of friendship for M. de Charlus and also out of curiosity to explore these novel surroundings, each Duchesse made straight for the Baron as though it were he who was giving the party [first error] and said, within a yard of the Verdurins, who could hear every word: "Show me which is mother Verdurin; do you think I really need speak to her? [second error] I do hope at least that she won't put my name in the paper tomorrow, nobody would ever speak to me again. What! That woman with the white hair, but she looks quite presentable." (II, p. 550; PIII, p. 245)

The salon serves Proust as the ideal place in which to strip the masks from these crass beings, whose mechanical existence can affect them horribly: "Certain forms of existence are so abnormal that they are bound to produce certain characteristic faults; such as the life led by the King at Versailles among his courtiers . . . and, far more even than his, the life of her courtiers" (I, p. 759; PIII, p. 64). Who are the present *salonnards* if not the courtiers of yesteryear? But the courtier in Louis XIV's time knew who was the head of society and could therefore go and ingratiate himself with the king if he were clever; the modern *salonnard,* however, has no one social leader or any valuable recompense, be it political, social, or economic. The modern *salonnard,* ineffective and without purpose, performs rituals he does not question, like the courtier of old, but he remains unsatisfied and frustrated, with a gloomy face which reveals "all those nervous conditions which may make them end in suicide" (I, p. 1106; PII, p. 548).

Etiquette and Deportment

We have thus far insisted upon the constraints of form imposed upon *salonnards;* a study of the etiquette and external mechanisms of society would seem to follow logically. Proust relies heavily on the formulas for etiquette and deportment as invaluable means of capturing an age or a particular society as well as for revealing psychological laws of behavior. "Even the human beings most stupid as to gestures, remarks, and spontaneously expressed sentiments demonstrate laws that they are not aware of but which the artist unexpectedly discovers in them" (II, p. 1017; PIII, p. 901). The gesture is also the means by which Proust expresses his humor, and he loves to caricature the unconscious mannerisms of the *salonnard.*

Of all the gestures he records, Proust's favorite seems to be the handshake. The handshake is the culmination of an introduction, a physical sign of recognition and amiability, and he describes each handshake ironically or humorously, and differently each time. The following detailed description reveals the conceit of the Guermantes while amusing the reader with its hyperbolic compilation of small gestures:

> When the Guermantes, after a rapid twisting thrust that explored the most intimate secrets of your soul and laid bare your title to honor, had deemed you worthy to associate with him thereafter, his hand, directed toward you at the end of an arm stretched out to its fullest extent, appeared to be presenting a rapier at you for single combat, and that hand was in fact placed so far in advance of the Guermantes himself at that moment that when he afterwards bowed his head it was difficult to distinguish whether it was yourself or his own hand that he was saluting. (I, p. 1035; PII, p. 444)

Naturally the Baron de Charlus has the most distinctive handshakes. The first time he offers only his fourth and fifth fingers to young Marcel—obviously a sign of disdain (I, p. 570; PI, p. 753). To Mme Cottard, the Baron "held out his hand as though to a housemaid, without rising from his chair" (II, p. 336; PII, p. 1073), which is a direct insult. Mme de Gallardon extends her hand as if to "force a card" (I, p. 225; PI, p. 353); Mme de Vaugoubert shakes hands with Marcel without knowing his name (II, p. 35; PII, p. 645); Swann gives an "affectionate handclasp"

(I, p. 1129; PII, p. 579); the Guermantes and Courvoisier women have a distinct means of greeting too long to quote (I, p. 1036; PII, p. 445). Proust uses gestures to reveal character, and it is clear that he enjoys his task.

But Proust would rather fill us with moral outrage than really amuse us with his ironic descriptions, whereas a Molière or a Thackeray wished first to amuse while serving a didactic cause. Proust took art too seriously; he would never accept himself as simply a purveyor of entertainment.

Etiquette and protocol, the art of performing symbolic acts which permit effective communication between two people, became for an effete society its *raison d'être*. Society internalized what was at best an arbitrarily agreed-upon set of rules for social conduct. Proust saw this as the major tragedy of high society, because it entrapped people—especially those with some talent, like Saint-Loup—and prevented them from ever finding an individually significant existence. Moreover, etiquette in this society becomes an instrument of separation and thereby denies its original purpose by refusing people the right of access, be it by refusing to introduce one person to another or by refusing to acknowledge a bow or salute which would normally permit further social intercourse. Etiquette was also turned into a razor-sharp weapon of insult. A good example of this is when Mme Molé, a young rival of Oriane, left an envelope at Oriane's house instead of the usual calling card, ostensibly because she had forgotten her own. Oriane, aware of the slight, but wishing to be correct by acknowledging receipt of the letter, instead of sending her own (no doubt beautifully engraved) calling card, retaliates by sending Mme Molé an enormous envelope which had contained some photographic reproductions.

Etiquette is also very time-consuming, and such rituals, as Veblen points out, could only be performed by the leisured. They therefore revealed class distinctions, for only those who had leisure could learn them and only those in high society had the chance to practice and perfect them to the point that these rituals became a natural part of life. The ascending leisured bourgeoisie accepted, however, the aristocratic rules of etiquette and were learning them quickly. Marcel is a good example of one who did. For example, at the Duchesse de Montmorency's party in honor of the Queen of England, the Duc de Guermantes made a friendly "come here" sign to Marcel to introduce him to the Queen:

> But I, who was becoming word-perfect in the language of the court, instead of going even one step nearer, keeping my fifty yards' interval, made a deep bow, but without smiling . . . then proceeded in the opposite direction. . . . the Duchess . . . told her [Marcel's mother] of it, and . . . said that her husband had been lost in admiration of my bow. . . . They never ceased to find in that bow every possible merit, without however mentioning that which had seemed the most priceless of all, to wit that it had been discreet [a key word for high society], nor did they cease either to pay me compliments which I understood to be even less a reward for the past than a hint for the future." (II, p. 48; PII, p. 663)

Marcel's success in the salon clearly demonstrates how central to the Guermantes type correct form is; it is the entire life of the *salonnards.*

The observation of the mechanical is basic. The proper use of calling cards, particularly as a weapon, also is important, as I have indicated above. An elegant lady, even when traveling abroad, will be certain to leave her card bent in the upper right-hand corner at every important palace she visits—though she will avoid seeing its inhabitants (II, p. 824; PIII, p. 629). The Duchesse advises Marcel to leave cards to all the friends to whom she introduced him: "I beg that you will be polite" (II, p. 90; PII, p. 724). Saint-Loup, too, wants to see as many people as possible on his furlough or he would have to "leave cards on" (II, p. 72; PII, p. 697). In short, a calling card is as good as a visit, and the *salonnards* spend hours of each day delivering their cards to people they have met and who might be valuable to cultivate.

The proper introduction at a party, still with us today, concerned Proust because many of those invited to the salons became acquainted with no one, unless they performed a real social gaffe by introducing themselves—which would have brought their ouster or something equally unpleasant. The case of M. d'Herweck, the musician, also reveals poor taste, for he asked a lady, the Duchesse, to introduce him to her husband (II, p. 61; PII, p. 683). This problem also troubled Marcel, who wished to meet the prince. "In any case I should have to find somebody to introduce me" (II, p. 31; PII, p. 638). The result is that many people float about the salon, bowing now and then, waiting to be recognized or hoping for some kind person to introduce them properly to other people.

Another major concern of high society was title and precedence. Though the royal court no longer existed, the *salonnards* insisted upon preserving its ways, especially in terms of precedence (exactly as in the *Memoirs* of Saint-Simon). Whether upon entering a house or room, sitting at a dining table, or in any other social activity, protocol had to be observed. It went to such an extent that "Prince Gilbert, the husband with antiquated ideas . . . made his wife sit on his left when they drove out together because her blood, though royal, was inferior to his own" (I, p. 1032; PII, p. 439). Even dull M. de Cambremer, the guest of honor at La Raspelière, hesitates before entering the dining room with Mme Verdurin. "I can't, really, go in before M. de Charlus" (II, p. 227; PII, p. 918). He has been correctly trained to know that Charlus precedes by virtue of a higher title. The Verdurins, still ignorant in the aristocratic pastime of genealogy, seat their guests with only a rudimentary knowledge of precedence (a sure sign that their salon is quite insignificant) and learn to their embarrassment that though a baronet is lower than a marquis, one must bear in mind all a guest's titles:

> "But, don't you see, since we happened to have M. de Cambremer here, and he is a Marquis, while you are only a Baron . . ." "Pardon me," M. de Charlus replied with an arrogant air to the astonished Verdurin, "I am also Duc de Brabant, Damoiseau de Montargis, Prince d'Oloron, de Carency, de Viareggio, and de Dunes. However, it is not of

> the slightest importance. Please do not distress yourself. . . . I could see at a glance that you were not accustomed to society." (II, p. 243; PII, p. 942)

Charlus reveals more than his names; he is clearly annoyed at being slighted in terms of the precedence from which he draws such evident vanity. "I fully expect one of these days to find myself seated at table below a Russian revolutionist" (II, p. 942; PIII, p. 798). Precedence is also observed even after the dinner party, for no one can leave before a Highness (I, p. 1104; PII, p. 544).

Proust does not think anything is wrong with etiquette itself; he even admires it. Precedence in the aristocratic sense, though basically effete and silly, is harmless. However, when an arbitrary code of external behavior supersedes one's ethical obligations to friends, if not to humanity, and has pure self-interest as its motivating factor, then we agree that the society which condones such a code is amoral and decadent. The red shoe scene conveys the crux of Proust's feeling. It is the final dramatic confrontation in which the *salonnard* is put to the test: Will she go to the party because she has been invited there first and would like to go, or will she cancel the party engagement to console Swann who is dying? Are one's worldly obligations more important than one's ethical principles?

> Placed for the first time in her life between two duties as incompatible as getting into her carriage to go out to dinner and showing pity for a man who was about to die, she could find nothing in the code of convention that indicated the right line to follow, and, not knowing which to choose, felt it better to make a show of not believing that the latter alternative need be seriously considered, so as to follow the first, which demanded of her at the moment less effort, and thought that the best way of settling the conflict would be to deny that any existed. "You're joking," she said to Swann. (I, p. 1139; PII, p. 595)

There is no need to relate how in her rush to get to the party Oriane makes the mistake of wearing black shoes which her husband insists must be changed. We know that the extra minute spent changing from black shoes to red shoes reveals that visible "correctness" was more important than giving a moment of her time to sympathize with a fellow human being. That Oriane could have even doubted which action to take already condemns her and her society. All the proper etiquette, the polish and grace which glitters down through the ages, is dimmed before our eyes. The red shoes "anecdote," is a parable (and also reveals Marcel's total disillusionment with social aristocratic life). The red shoes are symbols of frivolity, the passing caprices of life, the external attractions which consume our time and corrupt our nature. They symbolize a social life which has become morally decadent and leaves us outraged, especially as the marionettes of a duke and duchess—now correctly shod—set off shouting to poor Swann, "You'll bury us all." What is their good education? The knowledge of genealogies, the conceits of precedence, the art of insult? Poor Oriane, she had no one to guide her; was she wrong? Proust seems to give her the free will to choose, yet her habits permitted but one action, and thus she remains condemned forever, along with her whole society.

Language

Even the language which the *salonnards* speak reveals how "high" they have ascended from their origins. The florid language of a Legrandin, an esthete from the time of 1880 (I, p. 100; PI, p. 130), the anglicisms of Odette, the Parnassian language of Bloch, reveal at the beginning of the novel their low estate, yet by the time they have been admitted to the matinee their language has been purified so that they appear to have always belonged to the select caste. Rachel, who has no doubt had the longest and hardest climb is a perfect example of this interesting change in language. "Rachel, who was now acquainted with ladies of high society and unconsciously imitated them, replied, 'I am greatly flattered and honored by your appreciation' " (II, p. 1090; PIII, p. 1002). Thus as M. LeBidois observed correctly in his article on the language of Proust's characters: "We express ourselves like those of our mental caste and not our birth caste."[5] Language fascinated Proust as a guardian of the past, hidden away but glimpsed in surprising places (Françoise's speech, for example) (II, p. 99; PII, p. 736). But language, from the point of view of a *salonnard,* is a skillfully cultivated weapon of aggression and defense.

> "I never had the honor of knowing Monsieur Taine," M. de Charlus continued, with that irritating habit of inserting an otiose " 'Monsieur' " to which people in society are addicted, as though they imagine that by styling a great writer "Monsieur" they are doing him an honor, perhaps keeping him at his proper distance, and making it evident that they do not know him personally. " 'I never knew Monsieur Taine, but I felt myself greatly honored by being of the same opinion as he.' " (II, p. 321; PII, pp. 1052-53).

If gesture reveals character, so does language, for the pompous character of Charlus is clearly suggested by Proust in the passage above. Moreover, language for the *salonnard* is a mode, like a dress. He loves to use slang to give a tone of intimacy and an air of the chic. Also everyone must have a nickname. Hannibal de Bréauté-Consalvi is Babal; Charlus, Mémé; Prince Von Faffenheim, Von; La Rochefoucauld, Coco; Jacques Bonami, Talondebois. The nickname is very important because it gives one "a social identity, a prime element indispensable in the formation of a 'personality' " (J.S. III, p. 35). And Marcel discovered that it was necessary to know some English because everyone knew it (I, p. 415; PI, p. 544). Proust, in short, used language to reveal character, to record a change in caste, and to show the passage of time through the changing popularity of words.

Dress

Let us now turn to the external manifestation of the manners, etiquette, and language of the *salonnards:* clothing. The importance of the current style in dress dominates the life of a *salonnard.* As the contemporary sociologist Goblot, said: "How many women would be more ashamed to wear 'last year's hat' than to be found guilty of lying." [6] Oriane, after all, sacrificed Swann for the red shoes. And yet years later when Marcel asked her to describe her outfit on the day of Swann's farewell, she could only repeat "You are sure they were red shoes? I thought they were gold ones" (II, p. 1097; PIII, p. 1011). This revival of the red shoes scene some thousand pages later reveals not only the passage of time but re-emphasizes the superficiality of a society which placed external appearance above moral duty.

Newspapers regaled their readers with reports of high society and its dress. The *salonnard* women eagerly awaited their copy of the *Gaulois* or the *Figaro* (for snob appeal some even read the *Herald-Tribune*) to see if they were listed among the elegantly attired. Here, for example, is a typical *mondanité* about the *soirée de gala du Cirque Molier,* a "chic" spot captured by both Seurat and Toulouse-Lautrec in their extraordinary paintings. A "beautiful and honorable closing of the great social season last night at M. Molier's. . . . What a ravishing hubbub of silks, tulle, swishing muslin amidst black coats! Marvelous wardrobes of exquisite taste worn with elegance by the prettiest women of Parisian high society. What an incomparable atmosphere (*Le Gaulois,* June 12, 1898, p. 2). The style of writing is pure *fin de siècle,* elegant and effervescent. And Proust was not beyond some preciosity himself (though he sprinkled it with irony) when he described the dresses of the Princesse and Duchesse de Guermantes:

> Instead of the wonderful downy plumage which, from the crown of the Princess's head, fell and swept her throat, instead of her net of shells and pearls, the Duchess wore in her hair only a simple aigrette, which, rising above her

> arched nose and level eyes, reminded one of the crest on the head of a bird. Her neck and shoulders emerged from a drift of snow-white muslin, against which fluttered a swandown fan, but below this her gown, the bodice of which had for its sole ornament innumerable spangles (either little sticks and beads of metal, or possibly brilliants), moulded her figure with a precision that was positively British. (I, p. 751; PII, p. 53-54)

The comparative simplicity of the Duchesse's dress is her chic; she displays her social-queen qualities not only in her "incomparable" wit but in her dress as well. Proust is trying to detail what was considered the proper mode of the age so that we will realize the frivolity of constantly changing taste, which in turn further underlines the theme of time.

One can observe a person's dress and determine his social caste rather quickly. Françoise is obviously lower class because of the style and material of her dress even though her taste is sure (I, p. 493; PI, p. 649). But when we reach the level of the *salonnards,* where everyone, it is assumed, can afford to dress well, then the differences of social class are not so easily observable. Odette as a demi-mondaine has rather loud gowns, yet when she ascends she quickly adopts the proper sobriety. "But women know how to adapt themselves. After three or four times, these ladies realized that the very gowns they had thought chic were taboo among really chic people; they laid aside their golden gowns and resigned themselves to simplicity" (II, p. 899; PIII, p. 733). I mention Odette because she is one of the women who learned to dress properly rather rapidly. (Even Brichot, our philosophic dandy, is a specialist in dress and gives impromptu lessons on smart dress to his colleagues [II, p. 192; PII, p. 869].) It is the really skilled dressers like Oriane and Odette who can make a Mme de Cambremer jealous, because the Marquise cannot add that extra little touch which can make dress itself a weapon of social combat, like a well-aimed remark.

Dress can also personalize an individual. For example, Proust lavishes all his skill to dress Charlus so that he is exquisite (and suggests his homosexuality): "A dark green thread harmonized, in the stuff of his trousers, with a clock on his socks, with a refinement which betrayed the vivacity of a taste that was everywhere else conquered, to which this single concession had been made out of tolerance for such a weakness, while a spot of red on his necktie was imperceptible, like a liberty which one dares not take" (I, p. 570; PI, p. 753). Charlus, the arbiter of society, is the impeccable "correct gentleman" in this outfit—truly an image of France in 1900.

Clothing becomes an expression of love for Marcel. And Proust observes that Albertine, because she is poor, "took a far keener interest in all these pretty things than the Duchess, because . . . poverty . . . gives to women what is better than the garments that they cannot afford to buy, the desire for those garments which is the genuine, detailed, profound knowledge of them" (II, p. 421; PIII, p. 63). It is realistic that a poor girl suddenly free to buy whatever she likes is obviously going to take full advantage of the opportunity, but Albertine has an instinctive taste whereas Oriane has a sure taste—and that makes a great difference in the salon.

Clothing is a favorite salon topic; the subject represents not only the interests of the *salonnards,* but the constant reference to the dresses by Fortuny, Callot, Doucet, and Paquin is a distinct contribution to social history. These men created the taste of the time by their "originals," and naturally encouraged yearly changes of mode. In no earlier period did dress designers write about their age.[7] We must remember that both men and women changed clothing five to ten times a day. Charlus changes twice in the afternoon at the beach, wears his evening dress for evening reception, and receives Marcel in a Chinese lounging robe!

Proust castigates the frivolity, vanity, and hollowness of this society as he reveals the concern over dress. Mme de Marsantes, for example, does not really mourn the death of her cousin or parents, but she would never give up her black dress of mourning, especially if she could wear it to parties, because it enhanced the image of her as a woman of "piety," "devotion," and "good taste," yet preserved her social life (I, p. 895; PII, p. 250). During the war, when the life of the country is at stake, these *salonnard* women, now patriotic, wear new outfits which revolt Proust with their vulgarity.

> Young women were going about all day long in high-cylindrical turbans, such as a contemporary of Mme Tallien might have worn. Showing their civic spirit by their straight, Egyptian jackets of dark color, very military looking, over extremely short skirts, they wore leather puttees resembling the buskin à la Talma, or high leggings like those worn by our men at the front; it was, they explained, because they were mindful of their duty to rejoice at the sight of those warriors that they still dressed up, not only in soft, clinging gowns, but in jewelry suggesting the army by its decorative theme, if, indeed, the material itself did not come from the army. (II, p. 893; PIII, p. 723)

Proust describes how the handling of the hat serves to reveal the characters of the different types in the salon (particularly in the salon of Mme de Villeparisis): those who are old-fashioned, those who are up-to-date, and those who do not worry about such matters. Proust just indicates the etiquette involved in holding one's hat when he depicts Bloch inadvertently mocking the habit of holding a hat in one's hand in the house. He is quickly rebuked by the hostess who teaches this naïve social climber that one holds a hat in his hand if the king is in the house, for at that moment one is a guest in his own house (I, p. 852-53; PII, p. 192-93). Shortly after, Comte d'Argencourt, Baron de Guermantes and the Duc de Châtellerault enter and "following a custom which was the fashion at that time they laid their silk hats on the floor, by their feet" (I, p. 867; PII, p. 212). Mme de Villeparisis makes fun of this new fad and lauds the reasonable Robert de Saint-Loup, who simply leaves his hat in the antechamber. M. de Norpois, Mme de Villeparisis' lover, is the image of a past world; he enters, hat in hand (I, p. 874; PII, p. 222), to pay his compliments to the Marquise. The Duc de Guermantes, always a slave to convention, places his hat on the floor next to him (I, p. 881;

PII, p. 231). And finally Marcel, who at this point in his social career is but a few steps ahead of Bloch, completes the hat theme by revealing an ignorance of aristocratic customs almost as great as Bloch's: when Charlus takes a hat marked with a ducal crown and a "G," Marcel remarks, "You'd better take care, sir, you have picked up the wrong hat by mistake." Charlus: "Do you want to stop me taking my own hat?" (I, p. 915; PII, p. 278) Thus Marcel learns—as Mme Verdurin will later—that Charlus is a member of the House of Guermantes. The innocent little hat, then, like the courses of the meal, is constantly though unobtrusively mentioned and plays a vital role in the structure of this salon scene. The hat also further distinguishes those who were slaves to convention, and more interestingly, those who were now ignorant but would soon change.

Proust also relies on changes in dress to record the passage of time. The change of dress in the Verdurin salon marks an end of a period. At first "evening dress was barred, because you were all 'good pals,' and didn't want to look like the 'boring people' " (I, p. 145; PI, p. 189). At La Raspelière, a little later, "they became most anxious that people should now come to dine with them in evening dress" (II, p. 194; PII, p. 871). By the time of the great Vinteuil recital, evening dress is taken for granted. The external appearance of the clan changed, showing the growth of the salon, and it also showed how time had passed. This obsession of Proust's is brought out directly when Marcel notes the change in attire as he passes through the Bois. "All the hats now were immense, covered with fruits and flowers and all manners of birds. In place of the lovely gowns in which Mme Swann walked like a Queen, appeared Greco-Saxon tunics, with Tanagra folds, or sometimes, in the Directoire style, 'Liberty chiffons' sprinkled with flowers like sheets of wallpaper. On the heads of the gentlemen who might have been eligible to stroll with Mme Swann in the Allée de la Reine Marguerite, I found not the grey 'tile' hats of old, nor any other kind. They walked the Bois bareheaded" (I, p. 323-24; PI, p. 425). Proust describes changes in the taste in clothing to indicate the passing of time; he also relies on it extensively to describe the external world.

While the dress and the hat are basic, it is the accessories which give the glamor if not the essential dash to the *salonnards'* costumes. The best, the rarest of material goods are used—feathers in the hair, pearls on the neck, diamonds on the wrists, such are the accessories of women; for men, there is but one, the monocle. Every man wears one: Saint-Loup (I, p. 552; PI, p. 729), the men at the Saint-Euverte party, at the Opera, the Duke, even Bloch (II, p. 385; PIII, p. 12), and naturally Swann (I, p. 429; PI, p. 563). The *honnête homme* has his wig, the *homme comme il faut* wears his monocle. Indeed, French society can be dated by the painting or photograph with some eyeball staring through a black-rimmed circle of glass. Proust comments on the use of a monocle to make many sarcastic observations, of which the following is a typical example: The Count Hannibal de Bréauté-Consalvi "installed his monocle beneath the groined arch of his eyebrow, thinking that this would be a great help to him in discovering what manner of man I was" (I, p. 1025; PII, p. 429).

The Newspaper in Salon Life

Another symbol that the *salonnard* was a success was his mention in the social column of the morning *Figaro* or *Gaulois,* the two papers catering to upper class and snobbish tastes. (The Guermantes read the *Figaro.* II, p. 784; PIII, p. 572.) Yet Proust notes that the names mentioned do not include all of those well-received in the highest circles. In fact, many of the finest salon-keepers did not send their guest lists to the newspapers. "And so these hostesses, ignorant or contemptuous of the power that publicity has acquired today, are considered fashionable by the Queen of Spain but are overlooked by the crowd, because the former knows and the latter does not know who they are" (II, p. 53; PII, p. 671). However, Saint-Euverte, after collecting a fine crop of guests for her garden party, will be certain to place the names in the newspaper; she is aware of the illusion the press can create of her party, which in turn could aid her social climbing. The listing of duchesses does in fact give her salon a brilliant glitter, though for those "in the know" "it was one of the lowest." The only people who are really fooled, says Proust, are "these worldlings who see the world only as reflected in the newspapers"

(II, p. 53; PII, p. 670). Nevertheless, a Duc de Guermantes is not above having his name listed first at a typical mondain meeting place—a funeral (II, p. 50; PII, p. 667).

It is to a *salonnard's* credit, naturally, if his name is mentioned at a truly chic salon, but he is also fearful of being reported at a party below his station, for instance, at Mme Verdurin's (ante-bellum, of course): "I do hope at least, that she won't put my name in the paper tomorrow, nobody would ever speak to me again" (II, p. 550; PIII, p. 245). The newspaper therefore serves as a medium through which a member of society can be harmed or benefitted according to how he is mentioned in the social column. A knowledgeable reader can glance at the lists of those attending various salons published in the social news, as a businessman at the stock quotations, and can quickly interpret the value of the salon as well as the worth of the individual.

The newspaper report offered a sense of security that high society existed and had meaning. The typical *salonnard* actually could not realize that the *mondanités* were but the printed recordings of a mass delusion (Proust attacks Arthur Meyer, the editor of the *Gaulois,* for abetting the deification of aristocratic French families [II, p. 982; PIII, p. 853].) The *mondanités* were essential to the *salonnard* because they marked his presence in a world to which he wished to belong; the printed word fulfilled the delusion of the snob that the beautiful social world which, according to Proust, could only exist in his mind, was an actuality in the exterior world: Could he not read that he was one of the *nec plus ultra* of the Duchesse de Guermantes' salon?

Salon Conversation

The salon was originally organized and maintained to carry on enjoyable but worthwhile conversation, and not to degenerate conversation into discussions without purpose: conversation for conversation's sake. Proust's sarcastic comments leave no doubt about his attitude toward contemporary salon intercourse: "Now in society, there is nothing but conversation. It may be stupid, but it has the faculty of suppressing women who are nothing more than questions and answers" (II, p. 507; PIII, p. 183-184). Salon conversation usually was dull, unintellectual, banal. However, the social chatter does have a certain charm or wit in some salons, especially at the Guermantes (I, p. 1047; PII, p. 460). In the Guermantes salon wit was more important than intelligence whereas in the bourgeois salon of Mme Verdurin the reverse was true. Through conversation, we can see the differences in tone of the two castes. Swann and Oriane are speaking:

> "But surely these Cambremers have rather a startling name. It ends just in time, but it ends badly!" she said with a laugh.
>
> "It begins no better," Swann took the point.
>
> "Yes; that double abbreviation!"
>
> "Some one very angry and very proper who didn't dare to finish the first word."
>
> "But since he couldn't stop himself beginning the second, he'd have done better to finish the first and be done with it. We are indulging in the most refined form of humor, my dear Charles, in the very best of taste—but how tiresome it is that I never see you now," she went on in a coaxing tone, "I do so love talking to you. . . . Do agree that life is a dreadful business." (I, p. 262; PI, p. 341)

First of all, the play on the words *cambronne* and *merde* is fairly witty, trite, and vulgar, but elegantly so.

Moreover, this witty exchange on the name Cambremer is actually an attack on an innocent woman sitting hardly a few feet away. This is typical of the Guermantes wit of which Proust speaks. Second, although the conversation takes place in Mme de Saint-Euverte's salon, Proust confronts us with Swann and Oriane at this moment to bring our attention to the spirited life of the Guermantes set, and to contrast its high tone with the boredom of the other conversations in the salon Saint-Euverte. The last remark, however, is the most interesting since it reveals that even this banter does not really satisfy the boredom of *salonnard* existence.

When we compare the quotation given above with a bit of humor from the Verdurin salon, the differences between the two worlds of aristocracy and bourgeoisie are blatantly exposed. Brichot picks up an inane remark of Cottard who shouted "Blanche de Castille" when Forcheville complimented Mme Verdurin on her original "white gown" *(robe blanche).*

> "I think I heard the Doctor speak of that wicked old humbug, Blanche of Castille, if I may so express myself. Am I not right, Madame?" Brichot appealed to Mme Verdurin, who, swooning with merriment, her eyes tightly closed, had buried her face in her two hands, from between which, now and then, escaped a muffled scream.
>
> "Good gracious, Madame, I would not dream of shocking the reverent-minded, if there are any such around this table, *sub rosa. . . .* I recognize, moreover, that our ineffable and Athenian—oh, how infinitely Athenian—Republic is capable of honoring, in the person of that obscurantist old she-Capet, the first of our chiefs of police. Yes, indeed, my dear host, yes, indeed!" he repeated in his ringing voice, which sounded a separate note for each syllable, in reply to a protest by M. Verdurin. "The *Chronicle of Saint Denis,* and the authenticity of its information is beyond question, leaves us no room for doubt on that point. No one could be more fitly chosen as Patron by a secularizing proletariat than that mother of a Saint, who let him see some pretty fishy saints besides, as Suger says, and other great St. Bernards of the sort; for with her it was a case of taking just what you pleased."
>
> "Who is that gentleman?" Forcheville asked Mme Verdurin. "He seems to speak with great authority." I, p. 194; PI, p. 252)

We are immediately struck by Cottard's stupidity and the vain humorless remarks of Brichot. If one can laugh at these words, it is only at the expense of Brichot. The attempted humor is heavy-handed, a university professor's erudite joke which is even footnoted: Suger, *La Chronique,* see also Saint Bernard. Clearly only a person who has spent many hours studying Blanche de Castille or who knows her personality extremely well would have said "that humbug Blanche of Castile"—from regret of all the time lost studying, or for sheer excitement, not unlike an impatient scholar who mocks an unfinished work on which he has spent too much time. And those pedantic affectations: *"sub rosa* . . . I recognize, . . . oh how infinitely Athenian—Republic. . . . Whereas Swann and even Oriane are discreetly witty, Brichot works hard at shining brilliantly at standing out (a vulgar *mondain* sin); there is no real or pleasant give and take. Mme Verdurin's reactions are expectedly in poor taste—one never hides his face in his hands. The Forcheville remark points out the ignorant *salonnard.* Proust does not deny Brichot's intelligence, but the level of his humor, and its success, reveals this salon's immaturity compared to the world of Oriane.

In an aristocratic salon like Oriane's, genealogical discussions were very popular. Each noble could boast of his ancestry and compare his own with that of others. The Duc de Guermantes was a specialist and expounded continuously: "However," went on M. de Guermantes, "his mother, I believe, was the sister of the Duc de Montmorency, and had originally been married to a La Tour d'Auvergne. But as those Montmorencys are barely Montmorencys, while those La Tour d'Auvergnes are not La Tour d'Auvergnes at all, I cannot see that it gives him any very great position. He says—and this should be more to the point—that he's descended from Saintrailles, and as we ourselves are in a direct line of descent" (I, p. 1095; PII, p. 531). Charlus is another specialist and at the drop of a hat will gladly give a detailed explanation of his family tree (II, p. 247; PII, p. 946-47), which, if one were not listening carefully, would seem to be grafted to the tree of Jesse! The aristocrats constantly discuss genealogy because that is all they still possess, and from it they gain ephemeral positions of power: the rising bourgeois, ignorant of the possessors, accept the titles as undisputable proofs of the individual's social prestige.

But if genealogical discussions characterize aristocratic salons, the etymologies of Brichot distinguish the bourgeois Verdurin salon. Brichot assaults our patience with detailed explanations of place names and churches until we feel that we are in the presence of Meyer-Lübke: "As for Saint-Mars, formerly (save the mark) Saint-Merd, it is Saint-Medardus, which appears variously as Saint-Médard, Saint-Mard, Saint-Marc, Cinq-Mars, and even Dammas. Nor must we forget that quite close to here, places bearing the name of Mars are proof simply of a pagan origin [the god Mars] which has remained alive in this country but which the holy man refuses to see" (II, p. 206; PII, p. 888-889). This display of erudition, knowledge, and intellectual curiosity is the keynote of Mme Verdurin's salon, and the professional group which gathered there could appreciate Brichot's remarks; the members of the Guermantes' salon would have been outraged by this display of vain learning. Genealogies were sometimes discussed at the Verdurin salon, but only by visiting aristocrats like Forcheville or Charlus, and were not appreciated by Madame for obvious reasons.

The discussion of politics was forbidden in Oriane's elegant salon (I, p. 883-4; PII, p. 235) as well as in that of La Trémoïlle (II, p. 406; PIII, p. 41), for it can disrupt the salon with arguments and thereby destroy the ambiance if not the salon itself. From this point of view the Dreyfus Affair absolutely could not be discussed, for it did shake the *salonnards* deeply. " 'I think you're all equally tiresome about this wretched case,' said the Duchesse de Guermantes, who, in the social sphere, was always anxious to show that she did not allow herself to be led by anyone" (I, p. 886; PII, p. 238). And yet to assure everyone in her circle that she is on the right side, she clearly states that her salon is free of Jews—which could ruin a fashionable aristocratic salon during the Affair—and thereby underlines the continued purity and elegance of her social creation. " 'It can't make any difference to me, so far as the Jews are concerned, for the simple reason that I don't know any of them, and I intend to remain in that state of blissful ignorance' " (I, p. 886; PII, p. 238).

One might add that the aristocratic anti-Dreyfusard salons were antisemitic, which, as we know, was not a rare phenomenon in Europe. The charming Mme de Marsantes, the idol of the Faubourg, summed up the salon discussions concerning Jews and their "proper" exclusion: " 'I shall never go near anyone of that race again. While we had old friends, country cousins, people of our own flesh and blood on who we shut our doors, we threw them open to Jews. And now we see what thanks we get from them' " (I, p. 897; PII, p. 253). The remarks of Saint-Loup's mother are also important not only because they capture a social phenomenon of the age but also because they reveal that the salon functions by purely arbitrary exclusion; one year the Jews are out, the next year they are in.

Meanwhile, Mme Swann has Bergotte writing clever novelettes about the Affair and the latest intellectual currents, and Mme Verdurin has turned her salon over to the Dreyfusard cause entirely. Her salon is the intellectual center of the Affair, where Picquart, Clemenceau, Zola, Reinach, and Labori meet to discuss strategy (II, p. 106; PII, p. 747).

Salon conversation really did not vary greatly from one salon to another. Certainly the most common element in all discussions is malice and endless sarcasm of voice. Listen to Oriane talking to General de Froberville about Mme de Saint-Euverte's guests:

> "By the way, I don't know whether you're particularly 'well up' in the brilliant society which we see before us, because I've no idea who all these astonishing people can be. What do you suppose they do with themselves when they're not at Mme de Saint-Euverte's parties? She must have ordered them in with the musicians and the chairs, and the food. 'Universal providers,' you know. You must admit, they're rather splendid, General." (I, p. 258; PI, p. 337)

This remark attacks Froberville ("I don't know whether you're particularly 'well up' "); the guests ("astonishing people"); and in particular Mme de Saint-Euverte, who has such a second-rate salon. Mme Verdurin likewise attacks M. Cambremer to his face by mocking the furniture of La Raspelière: "Mme Verdurin was annoyed that M. de Cambremer should pretend to feel so much at home at La Raspelière. 'You must notice a good many changes, all the same,' she replied. 'For one thing there were those big bronze Barbedienne devils and some horrid little plush chairs which I packed off at once to the attic, though even that is too good a place for them' " (II, p. 226-227; PII, p. 918). This continual need to be nasty has at its base boredom and the drive to impress others with one's social position.

Traditionally, one of the supposed purposes of most salons was to foster the arts. Oriane and Verdurin, Saint-Euverte and Odette, Mme de Villeparisis and Mme Bontemps all subscribe to the importance of culture. Proust shows that some discussion of cultural topics, be it music, art, or literature, takes place even though we may be shocked by the ignorance, bad taste, and superficiality the mondains reveal despite the fact that they are surrounded by the best authors, composers, and painters of the day.

> Instead of Franck she [Mme. Cambremer] asked for Debussy's *Fêtes,* which made her exclaim: "Ah! How sublime!" from the first note. But Morel discovered that he remembered the opening bars only, and in a spirit of mischief, without any intention to deceive, began a March by Meyerbeer. Unfortunately, as he left little interval and made no announcement, everybody supposed that he was still playing Debussy, and continued to exclaim "Sublime!" Morel, by revealing that the composer was that not of Pelléas but of Robert le Diable created a certain chill. (II, p. 251; PII, p. 954)

More interesting than the *salonnard's* ignorance is his hypocrisy —if only Morel hadn't revealed the truth! Everyone present would have preferred being mistaken to having their ignorance demonstrated. At the musicale of Mme Verdurin "a duke, in order to show that he knew [Proust is ironic here] what he was talking about, declared: 'It is a difficult thing to play well' " (II, p. 559; PIII, p. 258). And we know how Wagner gives Mme Verdurin migraines.

Painting is not appreciated. The Duc de Guermantes has never heard of Vermeer's *View of Delft* (I, p. 1090; PII, p. 523-24), and members of the Verdurin salon make fun of a decent artist, a recently deceased ex-faithful, by attacking his work as "made with excrement" (I, p. 196; PI, p. 255). The *salonnard's* taste in literature is appalling. Oriane has a penchant for Mérimée, Meilhac, and Dumas fils. "[Oriane] never seemed to me so stupidly Faubourg Saint-Germain as when she was talking literature" (I, p. 1071; PII, p. 496). And the Princesse de Parme asks, " 'Victor Hugo is not as realistic as Zola though, surely?' " (I, p. 1072; PII, p. 497). Yet, what is the Princesse's remark compared to Mme Cottard's developed literary taste: " 'Now, *Serge Panine!* But then, it's like everything that comes from the pen of M. Georges Ohnet, [a popular contemporary writer whom Proust detested] it's so well written' " (I, p. 197; PI, p. 257). Proust has unmistakably revealed that bad taste and ignorance do not belong solely to aristocratic *mondains;* they belong to all *salonnards,* regardless of social origins.

Another popular subject in all the salons centers on where to buy things, especially clothing, which is mainly discussed by women. Even Elstir talks about the best dress designers (I, p. 675; PI, p. 900). Where to buy food is another concern. One buys "the grapes from Crapote, whose specialty they were, the strawberries from Jauret, the pears from Chevet" (I, p. 238; PI, p. 309). Odette buy flowers from Lemaître; "Besides, Lachaume is really becoming too dear" (I, p. 458-9; PI, p. 603). And, more out of snobbery than knowledge, they will insist that their shops are the best.

Another subject which is discussed in all of the salons is homosexuality. The Duchesse d'Ayen spent five hours talking about it (II, p. 594; PIII, p. 308), and we know how Mme Verdurin not only tolerates homosexuals but will use homosexuality as a weapon against Charlus. One would have expected such a topic to be taboo, but the need for novelty, it appears, permits almost any topic which will keep the salon lively.

The salon emphasized conversation and the hostesses did their best to make it flow—each according to her image. The hope was to keep the conversation pleasurable and enlightening, but the salon conversations Proust writes about are anything but that. Purely intellectual conversation is generally forbidden in favor of maliciousness and gossip, which is evidence of the decline of the salons in 1900 from the heights they attained in the 17th and 18th centuries under the Marquise de Rambouillet and Mme de Tencin. The salons and their members had become decadent; they had lost their original function and survived like the present American fraternity: for snobbery, for social exclusiveness, for protecting an effete way of life.

Food and Entertainment

The ritual of the salon dictated even the food and beverages that should be consumed during the evening. At Oriane's there were two distinct drinks, "in winter a cup of Linden tea" and "in summer a glass of orangeade" (I, p. 1082; PII, p. 513). "There was no record of anything else, among the Guermantes, in these evenings in the garden, but orangeade. It had a sort of ritual meaning. To have added other refreshments would have seemed to be falsifying the tradition, just as a big at-home in the Faubourg Saint-Germain ceases to be an at-home if there is a play also, or music" (I, p. 1082; PII, p. 513). The institutionalization of the orangeade seems to have been widespread and typical of the age. Morel drinks orangeade at the brothel (II, p. 341; PII, p. 1079); Mme Verdurin serves orangeade (II, p. 260; PII, p. 966/II, p. 571; PIII, p. 276); Marcel quaffs orangeade at the hotel during the war (II, p. 993; PIII, p. 868); Odette makes orangeade for Swann (I, p. 229; PI, p. 298), and later in the salon she serves orangeade and petits fours (II, p. 105; PII, p. 745).

Petits fours usually were served with the orangeade, but Marcel causes a pleasant sensation when he introduces some variation at the salon of the Guermantes. "People marveled at my influence because I was able to procure the addition to this orangeade of a jug containing the juice of stewed cherries or stewed pears. I was disliked on this account by the Prince of d'Agrigente" (II, p. 1082; PII, p. 513). That Proust should have insisted on the ritualization of the orangeade appears to be not only a historian's look at the typical "social dish" (I, p. 1083; PII, p. 514), but an indictment of a frozen society: merely varying the orangeade provokes surprise, envy, a new excitement.

The hostesses knew how to provide entertainment in addition to conversation and refreshments; they always attempted to turn the entertainment into the chief attraction of the evening. One of the most popular entertainments was the musicale. Poetry recitals were popular, too. Mme Verdurin has Rachel read at the matinee and the Duc de Guermantes had Mlle Reichenberg recite at a rout "an event without precedent in the annals of routs" (I, p. 1025; PII, p. 430). Plays also were popular. Bergotte performed novelettes at Mme Swann's salon, and Bloch wrote sketches for Mme de Villeparisis. The Verdurins played charades (I, p. 145; PI, p. 189), and the ducal Guermantes did ironic imitations of people they knew (I, p. 1047-8; PII, p. 461). These cultural entertainments, which should have provided moments of happiness, became merely rituals, and the ignorant and disinterested guests mistook the Kreutzer Sonata for Ravel (II, p. 1108; PIII, p. 1026) and La Fontaine's poem "Les Deux Pigeons" as "but an adaptation, of which at most one-fourth was from La Fontaine" (II, p. 1090; PIII, p. 1002). (The *mondains* were enthusiastic over card playing. Members of every salon played cards, be it at the Verdurins' [II, p. 258; PII, p. 964] or at the Princesse de Guermantes' [II, p. 40; PII, p. 652].)

The Decline of the Salon

The salon as a social institution was originally created to mix people of common interests for social pleasure. It was to serve as a focal point for cultural endeavors and to develop the arts of comfort and grace. But like any human institution it had a rise and a fall. Proust recorded the fall. He shows that by the time of the Belle Epoque salon members were concerned only with social snobbery, exclusiveness, and outmoded protocol. The salon had become a damper to any creativity: "a worldly and frivolous life paralyses our sensibility and robs us of the power to resuscitate the dead" (II, p. 788; PIII, p. 578). Arbitrary laws of social behavior have become all-important. "Values are so reversed that anyone who does not come, after accepting the invitation, or does not arrive until roast is being served commits a more reprehensible act than the immoral conduct discussed so lightly in the course of the dinner along with recent deaths," for "death or serious illness are the only excuses for not coming (and then only provided you notify your hostess of your dying condition in time for her to invite a fourteenth person") (II, p. 1117-8; PIII, p. 1039-40).

The hostess, who was concerned only with the brilliance of her salon, was mainly responsible for the decline of the salon. Oriane complains that Swann, who visited her every day for twenty-five years, has the "cheek" to wish to introduce Odette and Gilberte to her. "There would be no more entertaining if one was obliged to make friends with all" (II, p. 60; PII, p. 680). (Though we know that years later Odette and Oriane become friends.) The hostess is simply inhuman. "I moved away from her [Princesse de Guermantes] and did not venture to approach her again, feeling that she had absolutely nothing to say to me" (II, p. 30; PII, p. 638).

The *salonnards,* of course, are but sheep following the arbitrary rules of what is *comme il faut,* and Proust has attempted by studying habits, gestures, and remarks, to show "the vacuity of that form of life" (I, p. 1015; PII, p. 416). He notes the tie or the handshake which, though trivial in itself, begins to gain importance as we read and collects more and more incidents that create the individual, the salon, and the sterile, lonely atmosphere of this world. The effect is similar to that of a pointillist painting, in which the seemingly randomly spaced dots of color take on shape and meaning when the canvas is viewed as a whole.

Everything must adapt or be swept away in time. And change is caused not only by exterior events, like the Dreyfus Affair or World War I, but also by an interior principle of which the *salonnards* take little heed:

> Thus, in the Faubourg Saint-Germain those three apparently impregnable positions of the Duc and Duchesse de Guermantes and the Baron de Charlus had lost their inviolability, just as all things in this world change through

> the action of an inner principle no one had given thought to—in M. de Charlus, his love for Charlie, which had made him a slave of the Verdurins and then induced his senility; in Mme. de Guermantes, a love of novelty and art; in M. de Guermantes, a despotic love like others he had experienced in his life but which the feebleness of old age made still more tyrannical, a love whose weaknesses were no longer controverted and socially atoned for by the austerity of the Duchess's salon, where the Duke no longer appeared and which, for that matter, had virtually ceased to function. (II, p. 1102; PIII, p. 1018-19)

The salon, as the major social institution in the novel, serves many functions. It places the characters in the foreground; it reflects the interests and manners of the age; it is the chief means by which time is shown in movement; it is the dream world of the narrator, who discovers its meaninglessness and then escapes from it to record its meaning in his life.

THE RESORT

Balbec, supposedly Cabourg, on the English Channel, is a resort where the notables and less noted assemble, mix freely, and enjoy the summer holiday in a more relaxed atmosphere than that which prevails in Paris. We have already discussed the importance of Balbec in the world view of Marcel Proust; now let us look at Balbec in terms of its inhabitants and at the resort as a social institution.

The seaside resort is actually a novelty to Western man. The rich Romans had summer villas at Tivoli, Capri, and Lake Como, but the descendants of Tacitus' Germans—the English, Germans, and French—knew little of resorts and villas until the coming of the railroad. Then the resorts sprang up: Baden-Baden for the waters, Monte Carlo for winter, Deauville-Trouville for the summer horse races. Monet has beautifully captured this world of the seaside resort with its Grand Hotel, its boardwalk glittering with parasols and tricolors fluttering from *fin de siècle* parapets. The sand and hills all blend together to create a world in which the social classes, too, are juxtaposed and united. In our century only Matisse and Dufy (especially in water colors) have captured the wonderful frivolity and lightness of life at the resort.

The social season on the coast began after the Grand Prix at Paris; the height of the season was marked by the horse races, and concluded around August 26.[8] Contemporary accounts in *Le Gaulois* convey the excitement a vacation provoked in France in those days:

> The seaside resorts are in full effervescence . . . The extreme ease of communications, the universal taste for traveling, the practice of returning to Paris later and later, has assured them an immense clientele . . . For several days now, trains have been bringing in numerous tourists: practically all, familiar faces of Parisians.
>
> —*Le Gaulois,* August 10, 1898

Similar interest was shown in the American summer resorts of Newport and Southampton. The resort of Balbec obviously had its physical attractions, but it was more a state of mind.

A typical day at a resort began, obviously, when one arose, at a decent hour in the morning, no later than ten o'clock, and emerged after breakfast from the hotel for a promenade. Around one o'clock the vacationer had lunch on the terrace of the hotel and then prepared for a sea bath, a ride in the country, or bicycled, played tennis, both of which were much in fashion, visited friends in villas, or went yachting. In the evening he ate at the Grand Hotel, "exquisite fare" (I, p. 504; PI, p. 664) or at one of the farm restaurants in the area. Then everyone returned to the casino for dancing and perhaps a little *chemin de fer*. Proust recorded the social institution of the resort with almost as much detail as the salon, for it was truly quite indicative of the age.

The Grand Hotel is the focal point for most of the activity at the seashore. Proust used the hotel, of course, to symbolize the

The Beach of Villerville, 1908. Photograph courtesy of Lartigue —Rapho Guillumette.

The Beach at Trouville, 1905. Photograph courtesy of Lartigue —Rapho Guillumette.

The Hotel at Cabourg.

external. From the beginning of the novel the hotel is foreign to the narrator; he mentions the unpleasantness of sleeping in "a strange hotel" (I, p. 3; PI, p. 4). Foreign, too, was the hotel at Doncières, "And I knew beforehand that I was doomed to find sorrow there (I, p. 772; PII, p. 82). It serves as the emblem of the external world which leaves him lonely.

The hotel is a little world unto itself in which every social class is represented. It is run, however, like a great salon. In fact, the description of Marcel's entrance into the hotel is not unlike that of Swann's entrance to the Saint-Euverte mansion. Both buildings have a "monumental staircase" (I, p. 249; PI, p. 324; I, p. 503; PI, p. 662); both have the cold, liveried servants and major-domo (I, p. 249; PI, p. 325; I, p. 504; PI, p. 664); in both places the guests must sign in (I, p. 250; PI, p. 325; I, p. 503; PI, p. 663); both Swann and Marcel must pass through a vestibule or the "lift" to attain their final objective (I, p. 249-50; PI, p. 325; I, p. 505; PI, p. 666). Marcel sees the hotel as simply one more salon scene, a series of tableaux, a play (II, p. 126; PII, p. 773-74).

There is no doubt that Proust was also fascinated with the help who make the hotel function smoothly, from Aimé, the director, down through the receptionists, waiters, messenger boys, bellhops, floor servants, elevator boys, bus boys, and *putzfräu* (Proust points out that even the world of domestics was riddled with levels of distinction and individual snobbery.) The servants had a distinct understanding of the social hierarchy of the other classes. Aimé, the director, is as snobbish about the clientele as the Marquise of W.C., or Oriane de Guermantes, or even the notary's wife. But Aimé's judgments are based on what kind of cigar a guest smokes or the attire he wears, which obviously is as faulty a method of evaluating people as that of the other snobs; he "stood there . . . classifying, whenever the 'omnibus' discharged a fresh load, the 'nobility and gentry' as 'geesers' and the 'hotel crooks' as nobility and gentry" (I, p. 503; PI, p. 662). The servant world of the hotel also has the task, so much a part of the resort scene, of supplying wenches, male or female, to the clientele. Nissim Bernard had his favorite Ganymedes (II, p. 174; PII, p. 843), and so did Charlus (II, p. 274; PII, p. 986) and others.

In streets near the hotel are the little boutiques (I, p. 504;

PI, p. 664) so popular with tourists, especially the nouveau riche variety. The hotel terrace even receives the local gentry or those who rent summer villas, like M. de Stermaria or M. de Cambremer or Bloch, who visit their vacationing friends at the resort. The hotel also serves as a point of departure for little excursions to the villas or countryside. The constant movement of people creates a sense of evanescence and artificiality, which is further expressed by the hotel stairway "that *looked* like marble" (I, p. 503; PI, p. 662), the director who is a *naturalized* Monacan citizen of Rumanian origin (I, p. 505; PI, p. 666), or the "artificial voice" of the beloved authentic grandmother asking about room rates (I, p. 504; PI, p. 663). But the world of the resort is unreal because a vacation is an attempted escape from daily reality. The hotel caters to our fantasy and Proust makes it, itself, the enchanted palace of the *Thousand and One Nights.*

The villa or chateau outside town is important, too, and Proust describes Bloch's La Commanderie, the Verdurins' La Raspelière and the Cambremers' Féterne. The extremely rich all have villas. Mme de Pange nee Broglie (of the highest aristocracy) wrote in her *Mémoirs,* "It was fitting to have a villa," [9] as do the social climbers Verdurin and Bloch. They are all very hospitable; the Cambremers, for example, give a weekly Sunday party which depopulates the hotel by half (I, p. 518; PI, p. 682). In fact, according to *Le Gaulois* of August 15, 1898, "one of the characteristic facts of existence here is the great hospitality of those who own villas; if one is slightly known and sufficiently likable, one is assured, men above all, to have two or three invitations a day to lunch or dinner, to say nothing of five o'clock teas."

The greatest pleasure of resort lovers is food. "At night, intimate dinners in villas or at restaurants are always in style. Then, the rest of the evening is generally spent at the Casino, or better yet at the Eden [Casino] where one can applaud the inimitable Loie Fuller, etc." (*Le Gaulois,* August 26, 1898). The restaurants of the resort are "terribly" active, but the best food is prepared in the hotel itself. Proust describes the hotel restaurant once again as populated with a tiny cosmos of people: M. de Stermaria, the provincial lawyers and notaries, the actress and her lover, Marcel and his grandmother, Nissim Bernard, and others. All eat in the same room and have no rapport with one another except through the eyes of Marcel, the narrator, who has brought them together in the restaurant. He compares the restaurant and its members to an aquarium (reminding us of the Opera in Paris), and Proust depicts how Balbec society appears to the peasant peering in: "hidden springs of electricity flooding the great dining room with light, it became as it were an immense and wonderful aquarium against whose wall of glass the working population of Balbec, the fishermen and also the tradesmen's families, clustering invisibly in the outer darkness, pressed their faces to watch, gently floating upon the golden eddies within, the luxurious life of its occupants, a thing as extraordinary to the poor as the life of strange fishes or mollusks" (I, p. 517; PI, p. 681). Proust, in recording the age of vast opulent restaurants, where banqueting in elegant attire was the vogue, again reveals the ease and security of this society.

While the hotel restaurant was the center of haute cuisine, the farm restaurants were also quite popular to the vacationers. Always looking for something a little different, Marcel and his friends dined at these, too: "Ecorres, Marie-Thérèse, de la Croix d'Herland, de Bagatelle, de Californie, de Marie-Antoinette" (I, p. 677; PI, p. 903).

Proust presents one of the most important scenes of the book at Rivebelle, a former farm (I, p. 622; PI, p. 826). "This restaurant was the resort not only of demi-mondaines; it was frequented also by people in the very best society, who came there for afternoon tea or gave big dinner-parties" (I, p. 612; PI, pp. 812-813). It is here that Proust reveals Marcel's greatest concerns with the social world, but it is also important because the author gives some indication of Marcel's world view, which he does not make fully apparent until Marcel meets Mlle de Saint-Loup many years later. The dining-room scene is symbolized as another aquarium (I, p. 613; PI, p. 813), but the diners and waiters are, for the most part, compared to the planets and stars:

> I looked at the round tables whose innumerable assemblage filled the restaurant like so many planets as planets are represented in old allegorical pictures. More-

> over, there seemed to be some irresistibly attractive force at work among these diverse stars, and at each table the diners had eyes only for the tables at which they were not sitting, except perhaps some wealthy amphitryon who, having managed to secure a famous author, was endeavoring to extract from him, thanks to the magic properties of the turning table, a few unimportant remarks at which the ladies marveled. The harmony of these astral tables did not prevent the incessant revolution of the countless servants who, because instead of being seated like the diners they were on their feet, performed their evolutions in a more exalted sphere . . . their perpetual course among the round tables yielded, after a time, to the observer the law of its dizzy but ordered circulation. (I, p. 611; PI, pp. 810-11)

The different diners, waiters and bus boys are each performing their pre-established functions. Confusion exists only for the uninitiated—the fishermen staring in. Without realizing it fully, Marcel has struck upon one of the great laws of *A La Recherche:* behind any external fragmentation lies a unifying principle. Order is imposed by rationally fusing the parts into a larger unit. The Rivebelle restaurant scene is a metaphoric presentation of Marcel's inner world view in which fragments are fused into a meaningful whole.

A thousand pages later, Proust repeats the meaning of the Rivebelle experience, unity in disparity: "Thus I once saw at Rivebelle a big dinner party of ten women, all of whom I happened to know—at least by name—women as unlike one another as possible, perfectly united nevertheless, so much so that I never saw a party so homogeneous, albeit so composite" (II, p. 440; PIII, p. 90).

The Rivebelle restaurant is also the focal point of love, social climbing, and art. Marcel goes to the restaurant with Saint-Loup, his new friend and first real social conquest, with the hope of again seeing "some woman whom I had noticed, last time, at Rivebelle" (I, p. 608; PI, p. 806). He is also very careful to pay his respects to the Princesse de Luxembourg. "I raised my hat without stopping. She remembered me, and bowed her head with a smile" (I, p. 613; PII, p. 814). Thus Proust has placed before us the two roads of his external life: social climbing and love of a woman. While we are primarily concerned with the former, the love theme can be viewed as another aspect of Marcel's relationship to the empirical world, to society. Marcel will resort to love once again when he discovers that social climbing permits no authentic human contact. Albertine becomes the microcosm of the outside world, the Other, and the means by which Marcel desires to achieve involvement and communication. But for Proust love is really a delusion of the mind and art is the only means of communicating with others in the outside world.

As Marcel becomes inebriated at Rivebelle, his mind is freed. Extremely lucid, he decides that the most essential task in life is to discover one's being. Vacations, adventures, are simply evasions from the discovery of reality which can be realized in the quiet of one's own home. "They face, unnecessarily, the dangers of a sea voyage, of a trip in an airplane or motor car, when there is waiting for them at home the creature whose life their death would shatter, or when there is still stored in the fragile receptacle of their brain that book the approaching publication of which is their one object, now, in life" (I, p. 614; PI, p. 815).

Marcel's revelation at Rivebelle is similar to the dream sequence described on the first page of the book, where Marcel feels "the subject of my book would separate itself from me" (I, p. 3; PI, p. 3). In fact, he returns home from Rivebelle and has a wild dream which in its elemental chaos resembles the dream on the first pages, where the past, present, and future are confused. The work of art that will result from Marcel's introspection has its first manifestation in a physical representative: Elstir. The great artist dines from time to time at Rivebelle (I, p. 622; PI, p. 826), and meeting him places Marcel on the road of salvation through art.

Proust's use of the restaurant is important not only at Balbec, where its function is to echo the structure of the novel, but at Doncières (I, pp. 782-789; PII, pp. 96-119), where Proust presents a restaurant scene to give us a view of the world of the military, and where it permits the introduction and discussion of the Dreyfus Affair.

The restaurant is clearly important for the novel from the point of view of structure, symbolism, and social history. There is no more democratic social institution than the restaurant, which admits all who can pay. After dinner, the Casino is a favorite spot; Saint-Loup, for example, goes there after the grand dinner at Rivebelle (I, p. 613; PI, p. 814). The Casino was operated with much the same policy as the restaurant: whoever could pay could enter. The main attractions were gambling at the baccarat tables (I, p. 514; PI, p. 677) and dancing (there were always contests in the latest dance steps) (I, p. 660; PI, p. 879). The first inklings of Albertine's distorted tastes appear at the Casino, where she is seen dancing a little too closely with her girl friend (II, p. 140; PII, p. 794). Once again Proust gives us a historically correct setting: dancing in a casino—typical of the age—particularly with women often dancing together. Thus Proust uses the Casino to convey social history and as the setting for one of the more sensational developments in the novel—lesbianism.

The possibility of society mixing at a resort was enhanced by the many activities offered. Certainly, the hotel, beach, and boardwalk provided a large area in which the different social classes could meet more easily than they could in Paris. Thus Marcel's grandmother can introduce her grandson to Mme de Villeparisis, who in turn introduces Marcel to Saint-Loup and Charlus. Charlus even invites Marcel and his grandmother for tea (I, p. 573; PI, p. 758). But while meeting people might be easier, the significance was less also. "Life by the seaside robbed an introduction of the ulterior consequences which might be feared in Paris" (II, p. 315; PII, p. 1044).

Marcel's grandmother accepts Mme de Villeparisis' attentions for summer amiability "typical of life at a watering-place" (I, p. 549; PI, p. 724). Since there is so much movement it is hard to discern the class system of Paris; in dress and interest there is hardly a recognizable difference. Marcel mistakes excellent horse-back riders for socially important people when they are only "the sons of the questionably solvent proprietor of a linen-drapery to whom my father would never have dreamed of speaking" (I, p. 518; PI, p. 683). He makes similar mistakes with other petty bourgeois: "I gazed at them with a passionate curiosity, in that blinding light of the beach by which social distinctions are altered" (I, p. 512; PI, pp. 674-75).

On the beach Marcel meets Bloch and his sister, and Bloch meets Marcel's new-found friend Saint-Loup (I, p. 558-9; PI, p. 738). The beach is first of all a *public* playground, a typical scene of resort activity, and, as Proust uses the symbolism of land and sea as representing bourgeois and aristocrat, he uses the beach, the neutral zone between land and sea, for the encounter of bourgeois and aristocrat, Marcel and Saint-Loup. Bloch's being on the beach also underlines the divided character of his being neither all Jewish nor all French, but like the beach, neither earth nor water. Bloch, as well, is an unassimilated mixture, peripheral to both worlds—and certainly to the French social classes, aristocratic or bourgeois.

For those who are bored on the beach, there is always the promenade. It was good form to take a walk along the breakwater; Marcel's grandmother, the clique, the provincials were always strolling along it (I, p. 595; PI, p. 788). This walk, of course, is merely a transference of the Parisian social parade in the Bois. The jetty, the symbol of where one physical world ends and a new one begins, Proust also uses as the setting for the place where Marcel encounters love for Albertine. The symbolism is clear: sea and land are uniting. Male and female, Marcel and Albertine; the force of nature is drawing opposites together. Perhaps the man-made sea wall which keeps the water from reaching the soil represents the basic uncommunicability of people as well, but let us not push symbolism too far. Proust's reasons for using the promenade on the pier are obvious enough: it was a typical resort activity affording further opportunity for social observation, and it provided a dramatic setting in which nature could be used to reflect the human condition.

The need to travel, to move, is part of the great need for novelty, for an escape from boredom. The guests could always hire a buggy or a car to visit the countryside. The *Gaulois* of August

28, 1898, supports Proust's description of these rides in the country: "It's very stylish to take rides out to the countryside. Many carriages and motor cars line the highways." Sports activities also served as a means of diversion. Horse races, polo, and yachting are extremely popular and elegant (I, p. 674; PI, p. 898); when we meet Albertine and her friends for the first time, they are engaged in sporting activities. "One of these strangers was pushing as she came, with one hand, her bicycle; two others carried golf clubs; and their attire generally was in contrast to that of the other girls at Balbec, some of whom, it was true, went in for games, but without adopting any special outfit" (I, p. 595; PI, p. 788). "As for those who lead the 'high life,' sport in all its forms is the basis and the goal. Morning, even for women, begins very early; the bicycle continues to be very popular, although the progress of the latest comer, the motor car, is giving it tremendous competition. . . . The prospect of beginning the new game of golf . . . was it owing to the English crowd?" (*Le Gaulois,* August 10, 1898).

Proust's historical accuracy is reflected once more when Marcel's grandmother becomes very flattered when Saint-Loup wants to photograph her despite Marcel's impatience (I, p. 593; PI, p. 786). To Marcel's chagrin, he learns a thousand pages later that she had asked Saint-Loup to photograph her as a farewell gift to Marcel before she died (II, p. 127; PII, p. 776). The photograph is like a work of art: it captures a given moment, it can be immortal, and it suggests what Marcel himself must do one day. The photograph, therefore, becomes the exterior symbol of the voyage he must make into himself in order to free his past self or selves and to translate them into a work of art which will remain his being forever. But this whole scene is not merely an esthetic contrivance of the author. In the *Gaulois* of August 28, 1898, we read the following words about life at the resorts: "Photography is the latest rage. Everywhere cameras are quickly taken out and aimed at a pretty view and above all on a picturesque group of friends and acquaintances. And in the evening, the amateur photographer develops in a dark room *ad hoc* the scenes of pretty women leaning on an umbrella and looking out to sea, or simply sitting at a pastry shop nibbling some eclairs." Proust's use of photography and Saint-Loup, who is always in style, was therefore not arbitrary. This talent for recording a hobby in vogue, photography, and then making it an essential element within the development of the narrative again reveals the genius of Proust as a social historian as well as an artist.

The relaxation of class distinctions even permits that unpleasant snob Mme de Cambremer nee Legrandin nonchalantly to allow the Verdurin to visit Féterne. "I don't see why we shouldn't invite that woman, in the country one meets anybody, it needn't involve one in anything" (II, p. 347; PII, p. 1088). One is on vacation and different social types permit new adventures which could always make good salon conversation back in Paris. The resort spirit continues the world of the Parisian salon but in a much less demanding way, and the difference is marked even in clothing: Marcel wears a "dinner jacket" (I, p. 608; PI, p. 806), which is more informal than evening dress. The resort, a distinct nineteenth-century creation, is clearly an important social institution made up of many varied but ultimately harmonious parts.

In terms of the social novel, Proust's is the first great study of a resort and its composition. Today the "package deals" offered in the *New York Times* every Sunday, to Europe or the Antilles, permit all ranges of society to travel and holiday together in places once limited to the idle rich. Proust's work not only records many aspects of the resort, but it reveals that Proust understood the importance of this new social institution as a leveler of social distinctions.

The church, brothel, opera, salon, and resort serve many functions within the novel. Proust uses the social institutions as a building block, a setting, if not a world, for the characters. The particular people present in each social institution and the specifically chosen institutions themselves form the basic distinguishing elements of French social history from 1870 to 1920. The very evolution of the characters and the institutions reinforce the theme of time. Moreover, we are presented with the extreme superficiality of this society as expressed in its interpersonal relations, gestures, and physical appearances. Marcel's disgust with the society people and their ways has been made quite evident.

Proust followed the positivist tradition in treating persons and institutions by using Taine's trilogy of "race, moment, milieu" with great fidelity. Thus the social institutions are essential to the Proustian community and to an understanding of the novel, for the external life to Proust is but a series of vain social institutions appealing to delusions fleeting through time.

Anti-Jewish works and volumes sent free of charge to all our readers.
May 20, 1899, La Libre Parole

It is impossible for us Jews to accept conditions of life incompatible with our dignity as men. We have the right to develop ourselves in every fashion, this right must be guaranteed to us in an effective way.
—Bernard Lazare (1898)

The delicious Charles Haas, the most sympathetic and most brilliant of society people, the most excellent of friends, had nothing Jewish about him except his origins, and was not afflicted, to my knowledge —a unique exception—by any of the faults of his race.
—Gustave Schlumberger

[The Jews] . . . an elite people . . . sure of itself . . . and dominating.
—General de Gaulle, Press Conference, November 11, 1967

One cannot study the condition of Jews in France without stumbling on antisemitism at almost every step.
—Pierre Aubéry, Milieux Juifs De La France Contemporaine

CHAPTER V

THE BIOGRAPHICAL PERSPECTIVE: ISRAEL-SUR-SEINE

INTRODUCTION

In *La Grande Illusion* by Jean Renoir, Erich von Stroheim plays a German aristocrat and prison commandant in World War I. We see him commiserate with a captured French noble about the passing of their aristocratic way of life. Pointing to the French prisoners and pronouncing their ordinary bourgeois names (including one Jewish one), the German officer declares them the only victors of the war. The war to end all wars destroyed a great delusion—La Belle Epoque.

Proust was aware of the disruption of the old social order and the ascendance of the bourgeoisie, and that this had begun to take place as early as the time of the Dreyfus Affair. As we have seen in the preceding chapters, Proust attempted to show the movement of time and social change through Marcel's world view and the changing nature of the different social institutions and their inhabitants. Since Proust wished to present Belle Epoque society and its evolution succinctly, he chose characters who would represent the many "worlds" and castes of life. A Proustian character thus fulfills many distinct functions: (1) He is first of all the reflection of the impressions left on the narrator's mind; (2) he is a caste representative, whether he is immobile or changes his social surroundings; (3) he conveys tragedy, comedy, or melodrama; (4) he manifests social and psychological laws; (5) and he serves as the living allegory of passing time.

With Mme Verdurin's matinee Proust demonstrates the effects of time and social change upon the individuals gathered for it. It is the social changes in the guests and not their aged physical appearance that interests and amuses us. As time has passed all have lost their personalities and seem to wander about with only their names as badges of identity. At the matinee we find the status-conscious people, the "mobile" members who have generally started their lives in rather different surroundings. In Mme Verdurin's salon, one can see that every class is represented (see Appendix I, p. 237).

In each class, however, there are "immobile" members who are not found at the matinee. They are the classic types which Proust creates to serve as a landmark to show the distance covered by the mobile members as well as to display the typical characteristics of the caste. The "immobile" people tend to be the normal healthy types; the mobile are generally neurotic. The mobile person is not content with his lot; he wants something he does not have and thinks it can be found in the class above him. In all cases, though, the rising Proustian character is totally ignorant of the life of the upper class. He has his own splendid dream of what it is, but it in no way conforms to reality. The climber is looking for identity and acceptance in a world other than his own, and even if he does not arrive at the top, he will correct his dream so that he can still live happily in his new milieu.

The snob's climb depends on many elements: his background; his charm; his desirable skills as a writer or performer; his social, political, or religious opinions; his mystery. Society craves novelty and will destroy itself to have it. "The persons who, according to the old social code, should not have been there were, to my great astonishment, on terms of close friendship with others of excellent family who had been willing to come and be bored at the Princesse de Guermantes' only for the sake of meeting their new friends. For the distinguishing characteristic of this social set was its prodigious aptitude at wiping out social classifications" (II, p. 1058; PIII, p. 957). This is corroborated by the sociologists Lipset and Bendix when they say, "the summary of mobility studies around the world is that no known complex society may be correctly described as 'closed' or static." [1] Time, above all, permits the social climbers to enter high society. The following chart showing the castes, some of the typical members of the castes, and their mobility, should help us appreciate the panorama of the Proustian community.

Caste	Immobile	Upward Mobile—For What Reason—How Accomplished	Downward Mobile—For What Reason
Aristocrats	Queen of Naples Princesse de Parme les Courvoisier M. de Norpois	Mme de Saint-Euverte—need of prestige among her peers—salon, selectivity and fawning-patience Mme Molé—social prestige—her charm and cultivation of proper people Marquis Hannibal de Bréauté-Consalvi—social prestige—selectivity	Charlus—excessive exclusiveness and homosexuality Oriane de Guermantes—need for new pleasures, seeks too many actresses, time Mlle de Saint-Loup—love of an artist
Bourgeoisie	Marcel's grandmother and parents Aunt Léonie	Mme Verdurin—fulfillment of her need for "social security" and love of power—her salon, the external events (Affair, War, death of M. Verdurin), marriage The Legrandin family—fulfillment of a snob's dream—marriage Marcel—fulfillment of a poetic, illusion—good contacts through family and personal charm	Saniette—poor *salonnard* Brichot—poor *salonnard* Mme Leroi—lost favor, became old hat, time
Jews	Bloch family	Albert Bloch—need of acceptance—offers services of playwright Rachel—for artistic fulfillment—acting ability	Swann—bad marriage
Demi-mondaines		Odette de Crécy—to be where it is "chic"—salon, maintains correct political attitudes, uses her body Albertine—to be "chic"—use of contacts, sin of Gomorrah	A demi-mondaine can only be immobile or upward mobile

Caste	Immobile	Upward Mobile—For What Reason—How Accomplished	Downward Mobile—For What Reason
Artists	Vinteuil	Bergotte—liked to be fêted—successful writer Morel—need of success and appreciation—becomes a salon performer	Elstir—self revelation; he wasted his time in society
Lower Class	Françoise	Jupien's niece—escape from her origins—because of Jupien's relations with Charlus who gives her a title	—

The most interesting people in the novel are those caught up in the changes of society. In this chapter we will study one group and its individuals: the Jews. As a small but well-developed group, the Jews are perhaps the best gauge to the working of society, for having been traditionally outside society (in both the sociological and "worldly" senses), their pereginations in society, and especially in high society, depend heavily on the mood of the moment. The Jew accordingly reveals what the majority is thinking by their reactions to him. In *A la Recherche* the Jews emphasize the social and political history of the age (the Dreyfus Affair and its social consequences), the passing of time, certain dramatic incidents (Swann's love affair, the red shoes scene) and comic moments (Bloch's blunders, Nissim Bernard's homosexuality), the psychological laws of inadequacy and inferiority (Bloch's usual behavior), and the social laws of assimilation (all the Jews in the novel to a greater or lesser extent).

We have already seen in the historical perspective that Proust was intimately involved with the Jewish question if only because his mother was Jewish. He was a Dreyfusard, but more out of principle than Jewish allegiance. Proust was in fact rather ambivalent toward the Jews, although he was fascinated by the historic continuity of their "race." In the following excerpt, notice also that, through the use of the words "our" theaters and offices, the Jews are seen as foreigners. "Marvelous racial power which from the dawn of time thrusts to the surface, even in modern Paris, on the stage of our theatres, behind the pigeonholes of our public offices, at a funeral, in the street, a solid phalanx, setting its mark upon our modern ways of hairdressing, absorbing, making us forget, disciplining the frock coat which on them [the Jews] remains not at all unlike the garment in which Assyrian scribes are depicted . . ." (I, p. 851; PII, p. 190).

Proust is repulsed by the Jews' social-climbing aspirations. (It may well be that Proust himself saw them as personal rivals.) Proust, for example, expresses a hint of disdain touched with personal snobbery in the following letter from Cabourg: "Tell me if you intend to come to Tourville or even to Cabourg, I will try to put you up at the hotel . . . what a gathering! You'd be hard put to find someone with a name. Some vain Jewish 'goods merchants' are the local aristocracy." [2] And yet this same Proust goes out of his way to thank Lucien Daudet, brother of the notorious anti-Semite Léon Daudet, for saying that he is free of anti-semitism: "I thank you for what you have had the kindness to tell me concerning the Jews." [3] Proust also gives credence to slanderous reports about Jewish avariciousness. For example, when Gilberte gives her mother very little money Proust wonders "what Israelite strain controlled Gilberte in this" (II, p. 861; PIII, p. 684). Perhaps Proust's very ambivalence makes him an ideal observer of the Jews. In any case, the appearance of the Jews in a French novel is quite significant.

The political and social history of the Jews in France should be reviewed briefly before we examine the role of the Jews in *A La Recherche*. France has hardly ever known the Jews. In the Middle Ages, however, French Jewry, in Provence or along the Seine, lived in a golden age of learning and creativity. Although ignored by the West (with the exception of the misleading poems of Heine or a few obscure scholarly works devoted to early French Jewish history), it was truly a golden age, expressed in Hebrew. (The French Jew used Hebrew as the French Catholic used Latin, while in everyday activities both used the *langue d'oïl* or *langue d'oc* as a mother tongue.) The Crusades terminated this age and destroyed Jewish-Gentile relationships; by the end of the thirteenth century Philip the Fair ordered their expulsion—though for purely venal reasons. (In 1310 Geoffroy of Paris in his delightful *Chronicles* complains of this event because Tuscan bankers were charging higher interest rates than the Jews!) No Jews were found in the French realm until the sixteenth century, when some Portuguese Jews escaping the auto-da-fé arrived, posing as "New-Christians," in Bordeaux and Bayonne. Montaigne's mother was a member of this group, which became assimilated. The Papal enclave of Avignon contained the only continuous Jewish community in France except for the Alsace-Lorraine Jews, who became chattel of the crown when these provinces were conquered by Louis XIV.

It is with the French Revolution that the status of the Jew changed in France, and shortly after, throughout Europe. In 1791 the National Assembly enfranchised the Jews as citizens of the state. While the monarchy found it suitable to maintain Jews as a separate group—and some Jews saw this as a means of self-preservation—the Republic earnestly wished to integrate all groups into a unified country. Most Jews favored this change; it was a chance to shed their inferior position in society and to partake in the world around them.

Though this enfranchisement was a great act of tolerance, it had its shortcomings for the Jews. The Jew had to shed any nationalist tendencies, abandon his own cultural heritage, and accept eventual assimilation. The national religion of the Jews became a religious denomination at most. Though this all seems quite rational viewed from the Republic's standpoint, in the eyes of a nationalist or religious Jew it means the end of Judaism.* Yet by 1800 most French Jews were proud of finally being Frenchmen.

These new Frenchmen quickly fled their ghettos. Many went to Paris and vigorously entered the only trade they knew—business, especially banking. We tend to think that all these Jews were Rothschilds, but that Jewish family was merely a rich exception. Still, the old role of the Jew as *Hofjude* was not lost, for the Bourbon, Orleanist, and Bonapartist restorations relied on

---

* Crane Brinton, in *The Jacobins* (New York: Russell and Russell, 1931), offers contemporary documents dealing with the Jews, Judaism, Jewishness and the various solutions offered to the Jewish question.

the Jews to keep the state solvent. Sir Rufus Israels "had for several generations managed the affairs of the Orleans Princes" (I, p. 396; PI, p. 518). The Houses of Rothschild and Pereire were at the height of their prosperity and influence under the Second Empire.[4] The first intermarriages between the aristocracy and rich Jews took place; the Jews were assimilating so rapidly that even their religion was disappearing.

With the establishment of the Third Republic, the situation of the Jews began to change. Jewish banks became less important, for the Parliament itself could raise vast sums of money. But the Jewish banker's powerful image still captured the public eye, especially when the Union Générale, which was formed as a Catholic banking firm against Protestants and Jews, fell in 1882.[5]

At the same time the pogroms in Russia and Rumania set off waves of Jewish emigration leading to Vienna, Paris, London, and New York.[6] The presence of the Eastern European Jews, almost the *Urjude,* emphasized again the differences that still existed between the old believer, the assimilated Jew, and the Gentile, although the old Jewish-French families were in fact as scornful as their Gentile counterparts of these newly arrived Jews. (It is known that the Dreyfus family itself disdained the immigrant Jews.) Two historians, Chapman and Byrnes, state that in 1880 there were no more than eighty thousand Jews in France; by 1900 Chapman counts two hundred thousand, the majority of whom spoke Yiddish.[7] The anti-Semite, Céline, in his *Bagatelles pour un massacre,* states that in 1848 eighteen thousand Jews lived in Paris, in 1870 thirty thousand, and in 1914 ninety thousand.[8] The Jewish population was doubling every twenty years, though numerically two hundred thousand Jews living among forty million Frenchmen is indeed small. But since the Jews were concentrated in Paris—as in Vienna or New York—their numbers seemed much larger, particularly to the more conservative elements of society.

Race theories were growing popular in the last quarter of the nineteenth century, and the Jews were coming to be seen less as a religious denomination and more distinctly as a race, an alien race. At this same time in Germany, Helmuth von Treitschke was giving antisemitism "the halo of scholarship and respectability,"[9] and in 1886 Edouard Drumont published *La France Juive,* the first *Mein Kampf,* which placed antisemitism on a racial basis: "The Semite is mercenary, greedy, scheming, clever, cunning; the Aryan is enthusiastic, heroic, chivalrous, unselfish, frank, trusting to the point of naivety." [10] (Drumont is even mentioned ironically by Proust [II, p. 407; PIII, p. 42].)

On April 20, 1892, the first antisemitic daily newspaper, *La Libre Parole,* was begun with Drumont as its editor.[11] Drumont raged ineffectively against Jewish financiers like the Rothschilds, Ephrussis, Bambergers, and Cahen d'Anvers, and inveighed against the pollution of French aristocracy through the intermarriage of Jews with the families of Breteuil, Richelieu, Gramont, Rochechouart, Wagram, Faucigny-Lucinge, and others. But at the same time the old Jewish-French bankers, the Rothschilds and Pereires, were entering the basically antisemitic aristocratic society and dreaming with them of financing an Orleans or Bonapartist return. Baron Hirsch gave enormous sums to the Duchesse d'Uzès to back the Boulanger attempt of 1889.[12] During the early 1890s, many Jews were admitted into high society. In 1893, the Panama Scandal broke out, incriminating the state and especially two crooked Jewish financiers, Baron Jacques de Reinach and Dr. Cornelius Herz. Both were *naturalized* French citizens who had been dealing with the Republic in place of the old Jewish financiers (the old Jewish bankers were concerned with the salons and had few direct dealings with the government). Drumont exploited the situation fully in *La Libre Parole.*

In 1894 the first news appeared of the sentencing of a Captain Dreyfus to Devil's Island for espionage. (That a Jew could be a member of the General staff is proof in itself of how far the Jew had traveled on the road of assimilation.[13]) Rumblings appeared about a miscarriage of justice and in 1898, with the demand for a retrial, the battle of the Dreyfus Affair blazed forth. The country was bitterly divided. Dreyfus, as a Jew, represented the Republic and all that was new to the conservative enemies of the state. One became Dreyfusard or anti-Dreyfusard not primarily because of antisemitism but because of one's attitude toward the Republic. Antisemitism was considered to be akin to antirepublicanism. People soon turned from expressing their position in conversations and jokes into riots and attacks. Feelings against Jews ran so high that the Jews of Dijon and Langres were forced to flee.[14] Antisemitic clubs sprang up all over the country. This new antisemitism resulted from the distrust many Frenchmen felt who were distraught with the new social and economic changes represented by the Jews.

The Dreyfus Affair marked a point in Jewish history that is as significant as the second destruction of the Temple or the expulsion of the Jews from Spain. Its reverberations urged on the pogroms of Tsarist Russia, the direct result of which flooded the Western European ports with Jews fleeing to the Golden Land. But above all, it helped bring about Zionism; in 1897 the first international Zionist Congress was held in Basel.[15] The Jews of France, or rather Frenchmen of Jewish origin, were embarrassed, but the antisemites took up Herzl's slogan, *"Wir sind ein Volk, ein Volk,"* to prove the international conspiracy. The Dreyfus Affair would pass. The poisons, however, remained, and European Jewry was eventually exterminated. Assimilation had failed.

Even before the Affair, not too many Jews had fully penetrated into high society. It was one thing to be accepted into bourgeois social functions, but high society represented a different world (which a Jew undertook for the same psychological reason as his Gentile bourgeois counterpart: snobbery). For the most part, the Jews still maintained their own closed world. The family was still the key to Jewish existence, and Proust gives us a graphic description of a typical upper-middle-class Jewish family, the Blochs. However, rich Jews, especially during the Affair, imitated the society above them so consciously that one wonders if there was anything Jewish left in them besides their origin. This strange existence can be seen in this *mondanité* in *Le Gaulois* of January 5, 1898.

> Very lovely dancing party, the evening before last, from nine o'clock to midnight, at Mme Charles Weiswiller, née Fould, in her magnificent mansion on Rue Nitot. An enormous fir tree, overflowing with cotillon objects each more delightful and more charming than the other, and

> hung with electric light bulbs the light of which played on its branches, stood impressively in one of the rooms.
>
> The cotillon was conducted by Mlle Weiswiller in a charming dress of white moire faille, with bouquets of roses as the corsage, and M. de Fouquières. In attendance: Mme Eugène Pereire, Baronne Piérard, Mme Halphen, Auboyneau nee de Flers, Theodore Reinach, Sassoon, Dreyfus, Deutsch, Verde-Delisle, Dubufe, Blumenthal, Oppenheim, du Buit, etc. etc. After the ball, supper was served at separate tables.

This is mainly a society of prominent Jews. The life which they led imitated exactly the eminently aristocratic world just above them. Look at the names: The Bordeaux Jews, Pereire; the Alsatian Jews, Dreyfus, Deutsch; the English Jews, Sassoon; the German Jews, Reinach and Blumenthal. They are all from financier families like Swann's. This is the world of Lady Rufus Israels in *A La Recherche:*

> Perhaps that special class of society which included in those days women like Lady Israels, who mixed with the women of the aristocracy, and Mme Swann . . . that intermediate class, inferior to the Faubourg Saint-Germain, since it "ran after" the denizens of that quarter, but superior to everything that was not of the Faubourg Saint-Germain, possessing this peculiarity that, while already detached from the world of the merely rich [like the Blochs, who are nouveau riche], it was riches still that it represented, but riches that had been channelized, serving a purpose, swayed by an idea that was artistic, malleable gold, chased with a poetic design, taught to smile. (I, pp. 485-486; PI, p. 639)

This was also the time when the Jewish intelligentsia was

truly coming into its own. The parents and grandparents had created an economic base, and the sons accordingly could enter the liberal professions or pursue intellectual endeavors. It is easy to cite Jewish intellectuals of 1900, such as Julien Benda, Henri Bergson, Léon Brunschvicg, and Bernard Lazare, whose paths were already prepared by 1885 by the Darmesteter brothers, Joseph and Salomon Reinach, Adolphe Franck, and Ludovic Halévy, the first members of the Institut de France.[16] But they sought and obtained renown as *Frenchmen* and not as Jews. Most were nonreligious or were atheists, and they accepted their Jewish origins as vestigial. Had antisemitism not become so virulent, their Jewish ancestry would have been as insignificant as the provincial origins of other French intellectuals. If they appear to "socialize" often among themselves, it was not always out of choice.

Jewish salons were developed which were, for the ambitious, stepping stones to such salons as that of the Guermantes. Mme Caillavet nee Lippmann and Mme Straus nee Halévy (widow of Georges Bizet) provided the rendezvous for Jewish and Gentile intellectuals. M. de Fouquières, who knew all the different societies (no doubt because of his paid function in leading cotillons), lists the people one could meet at Mme Straus' salon: Fernand Gregh, Robert Dreyfus, Daniel Halévy, Léon Blum, Henri Bernstein, Reynaldo Hahn, Joseph Reinach, Porto-Riche, Maurice Sachs, Abel Hermant, Henri Barbusse, Louis de Turenne, Madrazzo, doctor Pozzi, Prince d'Arenberg, Paul Hervieu, Réjane, and so forth.[17] The first nine people mentioned were Jews or of Jewish origin. The Gentiles, of course, are all pro-Dreyfus.

The Jewish salon, as I have mentioned above, promoted contact between liberal aristocrats and Gentile and Jewish intellectuals, and, at times, some intellectuals were drawn into the Faubourg Saint-Germain or the H.S.P. (Haute Société Protestante, obviously a Faubourg term. The Jewish salon of Mme Straus and the Gentile salon of Mme de Loynes differed only in political and literary sentiments. They functioned as intellectual salons in exactly the same way, but separately. This seems to be the classic Jewish condition: a sense of alienation, deriving from their own lax customs and especially the barriers imposed upon them by society. The Jews of 1900 could climb if they wished, as we shall shortly see, but the majority stayed in this Jewish world just described.

It was inevitable that some Jews, the very rich and especially the intellectuals, should try to reach the Faubourg Saint-Germain. The Jews wished to conquer the respect even of "Old France," the one group surely opposed to their emancipation and bitter at their successes. Even if the Jew did succeed, he could at best be a parvenu, someone everyone enjoyed, but, like Charles Haas, an old parvenu to the end. Yet a good many chose to try. As Hannah Arendt points out, "To live in the aura of fame was more important than to become famous, thus they became outstanding reviewers, critics, collectors, and organizers of what was famous The 'radiant power' was a very social force by which the socially homeless were able to establish a home." [18] Proust noted that Swann is comforted by "the thought that, if he were seized by a sudden illness and confined to the house, the people whom his valet would instinctively run to find would be the Duc de Chartres, the Prince de Reuss, the Duc de Luxembourg, and the Baron de Charlus" (I, p. 238; PI, p. 310). Swann is the very image of the dilettante, a fancier of historic objects, even down to an historic house on the quai d'Orléans, so that he could send his roots deep into the history of France: "having always had a craze for 'antiques' and pictures, he now lived and piled up his collections in an old house" (I, p. 13; PI, p. 16).

The addresses in the novel in fact offer insights into many of the characters. Mme Verdurin, for example, moved from Rue Montalivet (II, p. 520; PIII, p. 202) to her "hôtel des Ambassadeurs de Venise" and Quai Conti (II, p. 520; PIII, p. 202), symbolizing a move from Republican sentiments (Rue Montalivet is one block from the Palais de l'Elysée) toward growing conservative tendencies—which meant aligning herself with the class she hoped to conquer. Her proper neighbor at Quai Malaquais is an old noble lady friend of Mme de Villeparisis (I, p. 856; PII, p. 198). Odette forces Swann to move to her idea of a chic address, near the Etoile off the Avenue du Bois (I, p. 315; PI, p. 413), which emphasizes her nouveau riche and parvenu tendencies, for the Faubourg Saint-Germain members tend to shun that area. The Prince de Guermantes is domiciled at Rue de Varenne (II, p. 352; PII, p. 1094) near the heart of the classic old Faubourg Saint-Germain, revealing his conservative and ultra-aristocratic tastes. A Courvoisier is their neighbor at Rue de Grenelle (I, p. 1035; PII, p. 443), underscoring a state of mind tied to a geographical location. The more liberal and socially active aristocrats live on the Right Bank. Mme de Saint-Euverte lives in the Park Monceau area (I, p. 1140; PII, p. 596); the Duc de Guermantes lives on the Right Bank ten minutes at most from the Park Monceau (I, p. 140; PII, p. 596); and one could guess that Oriane lived on Rue d'Astorg (where the queen of society, Comtesse Greffühle, lived), or at 102 Boulevard Haussmann, next to the Place St. Augustin where Proust lived and wrote the work. Other Jews lived on the rue d'Aboukir (I, p. 559; PI, p. 738).

The Jew's entry into high society was furthered because the members of high society had a constant thirst for novelty to entertain themselves, for people who were interesting and even a little notorious. This is evident when we consider Oriane's interest in actresses, Charlus' in valets, and Saint-Loup's in Rachel, "La Belle Juive." Swann was the archetype of the successful Jewish *salonnard,* "the particular friend of the Comte de Paris and the Prince of Wales, and one of the men most sought after in the aristocratic world of the Faubourg Saint-Germain" (I, p. 12; PI, p. 16). Swann originally fulfilled that strange role of being at once exotic and familiar, as Bloch was to do later when he entered a salon for the first time: "An Israelite making his entry as though he were emerging from the heart of the desert, his body crouching like a hyena's, his neck thrust obliquely forward, spreading himself in profound 'salaams,' completely satisfies a certain taste for the oriental" (I, p. 851; PII, p. 190). "What non-Jewish society demanded was that the newcomer be as 'educated' as itself, and that, although he not behave like an 'ordinary Jew,' he be and produce something out of the ordinary, since, after all, he is a Jew." [19] Swann also had a charming wit and connoisseurship. (Although he was a Catholic, his family's conversion having taken place two generations earlier [I, p. 237; PI, p. 335], to high society he remained a Jew.) As the Marquise de Gallardon bitterly exclaimed, "fancy a Jew here, and she the sister and sister-in-law of two Archbishops" (I, p. 257; PI, p. 334).

Thus only exceptional Jews were admitted to society: virtuosos in language (like Proust himself), people who were exciting, strange, but tame. The assimilated Jew was half proud and half embarrassed by his heritage. It allowed him to enter into society but never to disappear to remove the stigma. At the beginning of the century a Heinrich Heine who wanted to enter the best society needed only to convert to Catholicism to be admitted.

By the end of the century baptism was no longer "the entrance ticket" to European society. The racism of Gobineau and Drumont had triumphed. Judaism had become Jewishness, which was not convertible. It was a racial stain, an inherent vice. The assimilated Jew became acceptable only because he was different, unnatural, and a tempting vice (anything Jewish was traditionally evil) for a bored society. If Judaism was a social crime exonerated by conversion, Jewishness as a vice could only be cured—if one wished to—by extermination.[20] The religious antijudaism of the Middle Ages became modern-day racial antisemitism.

Actually the Jew appears in the French novel quite rarely. When the Jew is depicted in medieval works it was usually as a usurer, nonbeliever, or Christ-killer. With the Renaissance, Robert Garnier presented Jews with sensibility in the tragedy *Les Juives,* where he stripped them of their medieval robes and gave them an antique garb, as did Racine in *Esther.* Voltaire reintroduced the "Shylock" Jew in his *Philosophic Dictionary.* Chateaubriand had few good words for the Jews in his *Mémoires d'Outre-Tombe,* mainly because he was a spendthrift who was jealous of the imagined Jewish wealth. Balzac presented the Jew as an unsavoury banker, as did Zola in *Son Excellence Eugène Rougon* and *Nana* respectively. Gide in his *Journals* portrayed the Jew as a money shark; Jean Giraudoux in *Pleins Pouvoirs* felt the Jews were destroying French traditions, and Céline in *Bagatelle pour un massacre* prepares the cattle cars for Auschwitz. The Jew in French literature, in short, fares neither better nor worse than in any other European literature. Shylock remained the archetypal image of the Jews in Western civilization—the financier and devoted father appears in some form in every Jewish character. Swann is the modern example.

Jewish writers, however, began to appear for the first time in the 1880s. Unlike contemporary Jewish-American writers who seek, in part, to recreate the themes and styles of Yiddish literature in English by choosing familiar settings in the Jewish-American world, the *fin de siècle* French Jew had no Jewish literary base and would have avoided it had there been one. Urged on by the trend of assimilation, dazzled by French literary history, educated in Western thought, ignorant of his ancestor's heritage, the Jewish writer plunged into the literary movements of the day. The poets included Gustave Kahn, Marcel Schwob, Catulle Mendès, Bernard Lazare, and Ephraim Mikhaël who were decadents and symbolists; writing in the wretched theater of the age were Georges de Porto-Riche, Tristan Bernard, Romain Coolus, Edmond Sée, and Henri Bernstein. Their work was totally French; the Jewish element was nonexistent. It was this type of Jew, like Albert Bloch in Proust's novel, who wanted to enter high society and offered his artistic talents as qualification for acceptance.

The antisemitic novel appeared in French literature for the first time in 1886, partly as a result of the polemics of Drumont. Earle Stanley Randall, in his book *The Jewish Character in the French Novel, 1870-1914,* attempts to trace the development of this movement, and he leaves us with the impression that the hate directed against the Jews was due to the new social position the Jews had attained and their "parasitic" wealth, which robbed Aryan France of her inheritance.[21] The Jews also were accused of ill-breeding, lack of national sentiment, and continual opportunism. Examples of the antisemitic writers of the age are Léon Daudet and the popular Gyp, an aristocratic lady who in such works as *Baron Sinai* (1897) or *Israel* (1898) sketched Jewish upstarts taking advantage of the impoverished but idealistic nobles. Léon Daudet is the master of violent antisemitism and a clear forerunner of Goebbels. Here is a typical passage written by Daudet: "They bantered, touched, and meddled about with one another, as kikes do in the ghettos, while in rags and tatters. Or, slouched in some leather armchair, in order to take a rest from their accounts, they spluttered out obscene stories of brutal sexuality, in the fashion of Henri Bernstein's 'society' dialogues or the madrigals of Porto-Riche, then shamelessly cut wind." [22] One wonders how Proust could still dedicate the *Guermantes Way* to such a man—unless it was with irony or in excessive payment for the highly coveted Goncourt Prize.

Antisemitic novels were especially popular during the time of the Dreyfus Affair and for some time after. Most Jewish French writers were a spineless lot and made little attempt to stem the vicious flow. Only Bernard Lazare in *L'Antisémitisme* (1894) attempted to expose the movement for what it was; Henri Bernstein made one effort in his worthless *Israel* (1908) but evaded the real problem. André Spire was the only halfway successful Judeo-French poet to cry out for social justice for Jews not only in France but throughout the world. A few Gentile French writers, though they were rare, offered some objectivity and even an appreciative portrait. The character of Worms-Clavelier in Anatole France's *L'Orme de mail* and Woldsmuth (supposedly Bernard Lazare) in *Jean Barois* by Roger Martin du Gard are examples.*

Proust's interest in Jews is generally limited to the social scene. He studied what people think of Jews and how they react socially to them as well as the Jew's reactions to the outside world. Proust treats Jews as part of the caste system in France, but he also—for almost the first time in a novel if not in sociology—examines the different Jewish classes within the Jewish stratum. However, he examines only those involved with the social transformation of France and not the Jews of the Marais. To accom-

* Notice the use of obviously Jewish names, particularly Alsatian-German names; these are generally used to underline the foreign origin of Jews and to impugn their honor by making them like Germans—national enemies. Proust was not insensitive to these two currents on the Jewish question, which was hotly debated and is still unresolved in this century. Indeed, if we look at European literature of the early twentieth century we are struck by the massive concern over the question "What is a Jew?" There seems to be no answer, for the modern Jew *is* modern man removed from his traditional roots, a creation of modern society. Witness Leopold Bloom in *Ulysses,* Leon Naphta in the *Magic Mountain,* Swann and Bloch in Proust, K. in Kafka and Zeno in Svevo, each a different angle of vision on the paradox of Jewish continuity as well as an individual alienated from himself and the Western community.

plish this task he creates the Swann family circle and the Bloch family circle and concentrates on the persons of Bloch and Swann.

Proust points out a distinct image of turn-of-the-century French Jews in the novel: They desire to climb socially; they have artistic inclinations (Swann collects art and plans to write a book on Vermeer, Albert Bloch is a playwright, Bloch's father is vaguely interested in art, Rachel is a dramatic actress); the family is important; and they lack any Jewish religious, cultural, or social interests.

The Dreyfus Affair upsets this group as much as it does their neighbors. It jars their social positions and disturbs their routine. Proust uses this external event to probe into the problem of interpersonal and intergroup relations in the Gentile soul as well as the Jewish one. He was fascinated with the Jews' desire to assimilate into high society, for the Jew had to contend not only with normal social exclusivity but also with his own condition of being Jewish. What did he gain by such activity? Bloch in particular will draw our attention to this point as well as expose a typical Proustian character.

ANTISEMITISM AND SOCIAL STATUS

Antisemitism serves as the focal point of many of society's hates and fears. Proust uses antisemitism to illuminate an individual's response to the empirical conditions of the world and thereby probes the internal forces which determine that individual's character. And, as an analyst of his age, Proust delved into antisemitism quite thoroughly and presented several different views of the subject.

Every member of the Proustian community is or has been antisemitic to varying degrees, the most traditional type of antisemitism betraying the dislike and possible fear of anything foreign. It generally accompanies a sense of ethnocentism (I, p. 1010; PII, p. 408). Albertine, in her childish manner, blurts out: "When I told her on this first day that his name was Bloch, she exclaimed: 'I would have betted anything he was a kike.' Trust them to put their foot in it!" (I, p. 661; PI, p. 881). Albertine had been taught by Mme Bontemps to hate Jews (I, p. 973; PII, p. 356). She considers them to be foreigners and Christ-killers and considers it valid to attack them (especially if they do things which conflict with one's own way of life). In the above quotation Proust simply illustrates how the Jewish name sets off a mechanical response, the smear word "kike" establishing not only that Bloch is foreign but that he is a member of an inferior group.

Nor is a mature person like Marcel's grandfather totally free of doubt concerning the Jews:

> It is true that my grandfather made out that, whenever I formed a strong attachment to any one of my friends and brought him home with me, that friend was invariably a Jew; to which he would not have objected on principle—indeed his own friend Swann was of Jewish extraction—had he not found that the Jews whom I chose as friends were not usually of the best type. And so I was hardly ever able to bring a new friend home without my grandfather's humming, "O, God of our fathers" from *La Juive,* or else "Israel, break thy chain."
>
> Before seeing them, merely on hearing their names, about which, as often as not, there was nothing particularly Hebraic, he would divine not only the Jewish origin of such of my friends as might indeed be of the chosen people, but even some dark secret which was hidden in their family. (I, p. 69; PI, p. 91)

Grandfather's olfactory sense is amazing—like that of a truffle hound after the hidden delicacy. This drive to "look for the Jew" expresses an unhealthy manifestation of the average Frenchman's curiosity to see "if he is one of us or not." Like Albertine, Marcel's grandfather catches at the name with a knowing understanding and does not even need to see him. *Petit bourgeois grand-père* must assure himself of his own slight superiority, be it over Jew or Gentile of his caste. This love for the dark secret in someone else's family leads Marcel's grandfather to discover the obscure origins of the Verdurins as well (I, p. 152; PI, p. 199). The arias from *La Juive* which he hums knowingly become comic indeed and we may even be drawn to the grandfather for this foible, but it makes clear the subtle scorn this typical happy French provincial family holds for its Jewish neighbors. Marcel's attempt to protect his grandfather by saying "his own friend Swann was of Jewish extraction" should draw an incredulous smile today.

The bourgeoisie usually is the most openminded concerning the Jews. The traditional aristocratic temperament, the most narrow-minded in France, can bear only disdain for the Jew, since he is not only foreign to the aristocrat's way of life but once served as aristocratic chattel. If, however, a Jew somehow is accepted into the very highest aristocratic circles, his acceptance may be rationalized in the following way: "If he [Prince de Guermantes] was at home to Swann, whose friend he had been since their boyhood . . . this was because, knowing that Swann's grandmother, a Protestant married to a Jew, had been the Duc de Berri's mistress, he endeavored, from time to time, to believe in the legend which made out Swann's father to be a natural son of that Prince. By this hypothesis, which incidentally was false, Swann, the son of a Catholic father, himself the son of a Bourbon by a Catholic mother, was a Christian to his fingertips" (II, p. 51-52; PII, p. 668). This rationale is patently ridiculous and only underlines the blind prejudice of social and racial elitism. In Bloch's case the Duc de Guermantes emphasizes his dislike of Jews by purposely mispronouncing Bloch's name: "M. de Guermantes, perhaps to give to an Israelite name a more foreign sound, pronounced the 'ch' in Bloch not like a 'k' but as in the German 'hoch' " (I, p. 1077; PII, p. 505). It is actually like Albertine's special pronunciation of Israelite. "Her way of pronouncing the word—'Issraelites' instead of 'Izraelites'—would in itself have sufficed to show . . . no feeling of friendliness toward the chosen race" (I, p. 677; PI, p. 903). The pettiness of these people is clearly underscored by the manner in which they express their antisemitism.

Yet if the antisemitism of the aristocrats is traditional, it became in modern times a battle of social superiority, for the theatening invasion of emancipated Jews could destroy the last position of power held by an aristocracy now shorn of political and economic control. "The Princesse de Silistrie went about uttering loud cries, expatiated upon the social importance of Saint-Loup, and proclaimed that if he should marry Odette's daughter by a Jew then there was no longer a Faubourg Saint-Germain" (II, p. 846; PIII, p. 66). Though the Princess appears foolish, she does lucidly bewail the plight of her "crumbling" world: marriage of a Jew to an aristocrat destroys the exclusiveness of the aristocracy and its *raison d'être*. (Remember that Gilberte is a fourth generation Catholic—there is no escape from *déclassant* Jewish origins.)

In terms of social history, the aristocracy was continually in need of money and only certain fabulously wealthy Jews could "regild their escutcheons." The Jews in their turn wanted the status and acceptance which only a title could give. These two factors produced the marriage of convenience, of which the case of Saint-Loup and Gilberte is an example. Each was aware of what the other wanted and in the final accord the aristocracy was enabled to perpetuate itself with but a slight alteration in its makeup. Saint-Loup's cynicism erupts when he attacks the Jewish women for their desires and does not realize that he is describing his very own situation. "I am sure . . . in all the large hotels the American Jewesses were to be seen in their nightgowns, clasping to their scrawny bosoms the pearl necklaces that are going to make it possible for them to marry penniless dukes" (II, p. 915; PIII, p. 759).

Saint-Loup's anti-Jewish feelings are based on his feeling of helplessness and resentment over the fact that these Jews are assaulting the ramparts of the Faubourg Saint-Germain—and winning. He realizes this not only because marriages with Jews were taking place, but because they were being admitted to the clubs: even Le Cercle de la Rue Royale once presided over by his father is now considered to be *déclassé* because it has Jewish members (I, p. 585; PI, p. 775). We have already seen that Mme de Gallardon's antisemitism is based on her jealousy at seeing Jews bypass her and be received in Oriane's salon, which she herself cannot enter. She protects herself by antisemitism, and as Sartre has so brilliantly pointed out, it makes her feel she belongs to an elite

—although an elite of mediocrity.[23] Mme de Marsantes, in fact, exposes the positions of Mme de Gallardon and Swann vis-à-vis Oriane. "While we had old friends, country cousins, people of our own flesh and blood on whom we shut our doors, we threw them open to Jews" (I, p. 897; PII, p. 253).

The really comic figure in our discussion of antisemitism and social status is the Baron de Charlus. He mixes religious hatred, tied to a fascination with these foreigners, and his own exalted lineage. He is outraged when a Lady Rufus Israels (notice that a Jew with a title can still not escape his origins) buys an estate which once belonged to his family. "After being a home of the Guermantes to belong to Israels!!!" (I, p. 578; PI, p. 764). He wants the Jew to stay where he belongs as much for "esthetic" reasons as social ones. "But after all a ghetto is all the finer, the more homogeneous and complete it is" (II, p. 360; PII, p. 1106). And he goes into ecstasy about the *Judengasse* of Paris: "That is where M. Bloch ought to reside" (II, p. 360; PII, p. 1106). Charlus is the extreme. He wishes no real social intercourse between Jews and Christians.

In Paris, the ghetto lies in the heart of the Marais, and the fact that the formerly most aristocratic corner of Paris, so rich in history, is in the hands of the Jews makes Charlus furious. He is especially upset about the historic Rue des Blancs-Manteaux where M. Bloch, *père,* has his offices. "What sacrilege! Imagine that these White Mantles polluted by M. Bloch were those of the mendicant brethren, styled serfs of the Blessed Virgin, whom Saint Louis established there" (II, p. 360; PII, p. 1106). The traditional prejudice finally pours out in the following words: "You may be sure, moreover, so far are business instinct and avarice mingled in the race with sadism, that the proximity of the Hebraic street of which I was telling you, the convenience of having close at hand the fleshpots of Israel will have made your friend [Bloch] choose the Rue des Blancs-Manteaux" (II, p. 360; PII, p. 1106).

Charlus does not even consider Jews in terms of society. He has maintained, above all, the religious hate of a medieval aristocrat and can hardly consider Jews as human—at best they are enemies of his God harboring all the seven deadly sins and more. The key word to understanding Charlus' antisemitism is sacrilege.

The Jew destroys all that is holy—his God, his country, his caste, his way of life. Here is a whole series of sacrileges:

> As soon as a Jew has enough money to buy a place in the country he always chooses one that is called Priory, Abbey, Minster, Chantry. I had some business once with a Jewish official, guess where he lived: at Pont-l'Evêque [Bridge of the Bishop]. When he came to grief, he had himself transferred to Brittany, to Pont-l'Abbé. When they perform in Holy Week those indecent spectacles that are called 'the Passion,' half the audience are Jews, exulting in the thought that they are going to hang Christ a second time on the Cross, at least in effigy. At one of the Lamoureux concerts, I had a wealthy Jewish banker sitting next to me. They played the *Boyhood of Christ* by Berlioz, and he was quite shocked. But he soon recovered his habitually blissful expression when he heard the Good Friday music. (II, p. 359; PII, p. 1105)

We can laugh at this madness easily—but how it is fraught with sinister meaning!

In terms of social history, Proust used an antisemite to describe some aspects of Jewish assimilation. A Jew immediately imitates his neighbor by buying an old château, thus rooting himself to France. Notice, too, that the Jews fill half of the concert halls. This is one more example of Jewish assimilation in the West and underlines the cultural explosion among the Jews in the Paris of 1900. The Rothschilds, the Israels, the Swanns, and even the Blochs are to be counted in the above group. The Jewish banker may well have been a Pereire or Blumenthal who was probably more unprepared for than "shocked" by the music he heard. The very "sacrilege" of the Jews in attending a religious concert further underscores the intellectual curiosity of these liberal Jews who were "soaking up" a new culture and making it a part of their own as quickly as possible. Nor should one simply laugh at the word "shocked," juxtaposed with "Good Friday's" blissful expression. Charlus believes this just as firmly as Albertine and other bourgeois "brought up in God-fearing homes . . . ready to believe that the Jews were in the habit of massacring Christian children" (I, p. 677; PI, p. 903). The source of Charlus' madness is found in his esthetic antisemitism: a mixture of social superiority, religious intolerance, and historic fascination.

Proust does not develop the antisemitic social superiority felt by much of the bourgeoisie (in the business community, for example) as much as he does the snobbery of the aristocracy. But Marcel's grandfather is a fine connoisseur of Jews, and so is Marcel's entire family. Before Swann arrives, Grandfather makes fun of Swann's father and refers to Swann as "young Swann" (I, p. 13; PI, p. 1), not unlike the aristocratic lady who asks for "mother Verdurin." Even Marcel's father was an anti-Dreyfusard and therefore less than tolerant. In short, Marcel's bourgeois family displays the typical prejudices of the age. As a bourgeois snob, Aunt Léonie thinks Swann should feel honored to enter her home. She is mortified, of course, to learn that he has outstripped her socially, and so to ease her own bruised ego she interprets Swann's social rise as "condemned to utter degradation" (I, p. 16; PI, p. 21). Even Marcel's beloved mother mocks the dialect of *"La mère Moser"* (Swann's mother) with her *"Ponchour mezieurs"* (II, p. 943; PIII, p. 659). By mimicking an accent one makes fun of the person's origin, his strangeness, and at the same time gains a sense of personal superiority. The accents of the newly arrived Jews enabled the French (who have been xenophobic since the 1870 defeat) to identify them easily as despised foreigners, if not enemies. Proust may well have gotten his *"Ponchour mezieurs"* from Balzac, if not from Léon Daudet—a master of "Judeo-French."

Antisemitism becomes a more serious matter when it be comes less a caste hate than a racial blood distinction. That Gilberte and Swann are still considered Jews after generations of conversion portends evil. The Duc de Guermantes takes great pride in being free of any Jewish blood: "I will undertake to prove that there has never been a drop of Jewish blood in my family" (II, p. 998; PII, p. 239). In this little remark, Proust has captured the essence of modern racial antisemitism. Comte Boni de Castellane, one of the most celebrated dandies of the Belle

Epoque, states directly: "Although I don't have a drop of their blood in my veins, I understand Jewish schemes wonderfully and possess a certain aptitude for their trade." [24]

If one extends the logic of Castellane's remark, the Jew seems to be the member of a rather unpleasant alien race. Accordingly, a Jew can never be completely trusted as a citizen, as the following exchange with Charlus points out. "I replied that Bloch was French. 'Indeed,' said M. de Charlus, 'I took him to be a Jew' " (I, p. 922; PII, p. 288). Assimilation, to the antisemite, is impossible. It is therefore clear that Swann must always remain a Jew in aristocratic eyes. One can imagine what such antisemites thought of Dreyfus.

The attainment of wealth by Jews is another source of antisemitism, and successful Jewish bankers in Paris were hated. Drumont in *La Libre Parole* on March 1, 1899, cried out in the headline: "The Jews are rich; they own the gold." Even today, this is probably the most widely believed misapprehension in France. One has only to ask one's conciege or a cafe owner or any of the petty bourgeoisie about the Jews and inevitably Jewish wealth is mentioned. Reason is useless; Jewish wealth (and Jewish women's sensuality) are part of a European myth. Charlus is convinced of it (II, p. 360; PII, p. 1106) and so is Morel. Indeed Morel is the novel's lower class representative, and his antisemitism echoes that of his class. After Morel had borrowed five thousand francs from Bloch's uncle, Nissim Bernard, Bloch, who collected the debt as Morel paid it back piecemeal, apparently underestimated how much Morel owed him, and Morel, not wishing to pay back any of the sum, created a scene in which he refused to reimburse his creditor. Proust wryly comments that Morel's antisemitism was "the natural effect of a loan of five thousand francs from an Israelite" (II, p. 415; PIII, p. 54). It was also encouraged by Nissim Bernard's preference for the violinist Thibaud over Morel.

Many aristocrats hate the Jews because certain rich Jews used their wealth for social climbing purposes. They do not forgive Edward, the former Prince of Wales and a friend of Swann's, for living off the wealth of Jewish financiers whom he dubs baronets (I, p. 1093; PII, p. 528). That Swann could be friendly with the Prince of Wales is in fact historically plausible, for Edward was very partial to Jewish friends and in the novel even takes the Baron Hirsch to Oriane's salon (II, p. 51; PII, p. 668).

The Jew, however, is not entirely unattractive to the anti-semite. Charlus is sexually attracted to Jews. They satisfy his erotic needs by their exoticism and pariah status, as he sees it. Charlus' "esthetic interest and love of local color" (I, p. 851; PII, p. 190-191) leads him to ask Marcel what happened to "your young Hebrew friend, whom we met at Douville [sic] . . . one might invite him to the house one evening" (II, p. 530; PIII, p. 216). But notice why he wants Bloch! "He might perhaps take a hall, and give me some biblical entertainment. . . . You might even arrange parties to give us a good laugh. For instance a battle between your friend and his father, in which he would smite him as David smote Goliath. That would make quite an amusing farce. . . . We like exotic spectacles, and to thrash that non-European creature would be giving a well-earned punishment. . . . As he poured out this terrible, almost insane language, M. de Charlus squeezed my arm until it ached" (I, p. 922; PII, p. 288-89).

Charlus is the representative of a group of reactionaries whose wild thinking would dominate Europe forty years later. The essential words "to thrash that non-European creature would be a well earned punishment" proclaims the madness of European racism. But this is France in 1900! Is it any wonder that some Jews, sensing their rejection as Europeans, accepted the challenge and became Zionists?

Charlus takes such physical pleasure in this scene that he squeezes Marcel's hand severely. The homosexual motif is clear. If homosexuality is a vice and the homosexual a social pariah, so, too, are the Jews in Charlus' mind. By combining his homosexual vice with the exotic Jew, the Baron heightens his sexual pleasure. Furthermore, Jews, as sacrificial victims in his fantasy, beat each other as just punishment for the vice of being Jewish and "non-European creatures." He takes a sadist's delight, subconsciously participating in an act of sodomy. Since Charlus' homosexuality causes him to establish rapport with the social pariah Jews which is unpleasant to him, he takes out his frustrations upon one who is his equal as a social misfit. Morel, who is no fool, realizes the sexual fascination which Bloch offers the Baron and is content when Bloch departs because Bloch threatens his new and socially advantageous position. (Antisemitism can also serve as an expression of class struggle between Jews and the lower class for upward mobility.)

In short, almost every character in *A la Recherche* is antisemitic for one or more reasons, but in each case the knowledge of why the character is antisemitic offers a significant insight into the pathology of the individual. That antisemitism is used deftly to draw out individual character flaws is the triumph of Proust's psychology and his technique of character delineation.

THE DREYFUS AFFAIR

The Dreyfus Affair is the most important political event in the novel which directly affects the social world; it appears from *In a Budding Grove* through *Cities of the Plain*. The main discussions of the Affair take place at Doncières, the salon of Mme de Villeparisis, and at the salon of the Prince de Guermantes. Political discussions of the affair are not so important in the novel, however, as is the revelation of character that comes out of the discussions. The absence of all but the most superficial political concern reveals in the characters a lack of political responsibility. The preservation or improvement of social status appears to be the main concern of the French citizen in the Proustian community vis à vis the Affair. The intensification of latent antisemitism for primarily social reasons in *A la Recherche* becomes the key to the shifts in the social kaleidoscope. "It was true that the social kaleidoscope was in the act of turning and that the Dreyfus case was shortly to hurl the Jews down to the lowest rung of the social ladder" (I, p. 851; PII, p. 190). The Affair is the focal point for many of society's hates which find their easiest expression in antisemitism. Léon Blum saw the rapid rise of antisemitism in the salon and its social consequences, exclusion, as "the indiscrete intrusion of *nouveau riche* Jews [Rufus Israel] or the penetration, judged too rapid, of studious Jews [Bloch]." [25] The observation is typical of the age.

The only pro-Dreyfus characters in the novel are: Swann, Bloch, Mme Sazerat "alone of her kind at Combray" (I, p. 823; PII, p. 153), Saint-Loup, and eventually the Prince and Duc de Guermantes. Proust has given us in this small group a Dreyfusard from each social caste, and the development of their sympathy for Dreyfus is interesting. Swann and Bloch easily decided to support Dreyfus—they were Jews. The narrator mocks Bloch's logical deduction and at the same time lends credence to the Jewish stereotype: "Bloch believed himself to have been led by a logical sequence to choose Dreyfusism, yet he knew that his nose, skin, and hair had been imposed on him by his race" (I, p. 928; PII, p. 297). This remark also underlines Proust's belief that our positions are already determined and that our reason only builds a framework for our emotional persuasion. "Imposed by his race" is a key word, for Proust is here clearly a determinist, more subtle than Zola but from the same school. Swann cannot escape his origins either. M. de Cambremer, no great thinker, becomes an anti-Dreyfusard (II, p. 259; PII, p. 965) because of his family background and social caste, again supporting Proust's theory of determinism.

Mme Sazerat is the only bourgeois Dreyfusard in the novel except for the narrator. (Mme Verdurin switches sides in order to be on the socially advantageous one.) Mme Sazerat represents the Republican sentiment, the spirit of '89; she has rallied to the government because *La Gueuse* is threatened. Yet Mme Sazerat embodies an extraordinary paradox: she is antisemitic and pro-Dreyfus!

> My friend's father [Bloch, *père*] had found Mme. Sazerat charming and was particularly gratified by the antisemitism of the lady, which he regarded as a proof of the sincerity of her faith and the soundness of her Dreyfusard opinions, and also as enhancing the value of the call which she had authorized him to pay her. He had not even been offended when she said to him stolidly: "M. Drumont has the impudence to put the Revisionists in the same bag as the Protestants and the Jews." "Bernard," he said with pride,

> on reaching home, to M. Nissim Bernard, "you know, she has that prejudice!" (I, p. 923; PII, p. 289-90)

One might almost accuse Proust of merely juxtaposing opposites for literary variety, but the truth is that there were many in the Mme Sazerat category, the most famous being Colonel Picquart.[26]

Saint-Loup becomes a Dreyfusard because he is under the influence of his Jewish mistress, Rachel. Saint-Loup's family, however, reacts according to Proust's contention that one follows his race and social caste: "when one goes by the name of 'Marquis de Saint-Loup' one isn't a Dreyfusard; what more can I say?" (I, p. 884; PII, p. 235). The Prince and Duke become Dreyfusards late in the campaign and for different reasons. The Prince admits he has his prejudices. "But I come of a family of soldiers, I did not like to think that officers could be mistaken. I discussed the case again with Beauserfeuil, he admitted that there had been culpable intrigues, that the *bordereau* was possibly not in Dreyfus's writing, but that an overwhelming proof of his guilt did exist. This was the Henry document. And, a few days later, we learned that it was forgery. After that, without letting the Princess see me, I began to read the *Siècle* and the *Aurore* every day; soon I had no doubt left, it kept me awake all night" (II, p. 79-80; PII, p. 709). The Prince, by making the great effort to be objective, broke with his racial and class prejudices and saw the truth: Dreyfus was innocent. Swann is "profoundly moved" (II, p. 82; PII, p. 712) by this admission, for he had attacked the Prince as a typical antisemitic anti-Dreyfusard aristocrat.

Proust points out that objectivity is the one element missing in the Affair. In this sense the Prince's change of attitude is enormous and noble, for while Swann may be emotionally correct about Dreyfus' innocence, he has not arrived at this conclusion as did the Prince, through rational deduction in the light of objective fact.

In contrast to the Prince's noble deduction is the newfound Dreyfusism of the imbecile brother Basin, the Duc de Guermantes. Incapable of thought, antisemitic, and naturally anti-Dreyfusard, he is converted by an Italian princess and her sisters-in-law. At first hesitant, he is impressed with the ladies' intellect and their pro-Dreyfus dialectic. But he is mainly convinced "from cowardice and the spirit of imitation" (II, p. 101; PII, p. 740). And so, finally, "the Duke had returned to Paris a frantic Dreyfusard" (II, p. 102; PII, p. 740), having adopted the new trend to support Dreyfus.

But Proust noted bizarrely that the upper crust of the aristocracy was sympathetic to Dreyfus: The Duc and Prince de Guermantes, the Grand-Duke of Hesse, the Empress Eugénie, and the Prince Royal of Sweden, for example (II, p. 77; PII, p. 705). The social queen, the Comtesse Greffülhe, even expressed her feelings of Dreyfus' innocence. As Léon Blum states, "The situation of the royalists and Bonapartists was curious, in the sense that they were in a body violently anti-Dreyfusards, while their natural leaders, the Princess, pretenders, members of the royal and imperial family didn't doubt the innocence of Dreyfus." [27] Proust thus corroborates an extremely interesting division within the aristocracy, the effects of which would forever destroy its unity, its political power, and its social exclusiveness.

On every level of society, of course, there were some people who expressed their doubts about Dreyfus: Aimé at the hotel (I, p. 608; PI, p. 806), Marcel's parents (I, p. 823; PII, p. 152), Mme Swann (II, p. 104; PII, p. 744), M. de Norpois (I, p. 882; PII, p. 233), the Marquis de Cambremer (II, p. 259; PII, p. 965) and all the great nobles of the Guermantes-Bouillon-Bavarois family, Les Courvoisier, and the rest. Those who were antisemitic before the Affair became anti-Dreyfusard during the Affair (with the exception of Mme Sazerat) and even more violently antisemitic.

While most are hotheaded about the Affair, M. de Norpois "guards his opinions" and seems the master diplomat and tactician throughout his long discussion with Bloch at Mme de Villeparisis' salon. Though M. de Norpois actually is an "ardent anti-Dreyfusard" (I, p. 882; PII, p. 233), he takes no stand and thereby avoids any argument with Bloch, who is, in Sartre's term, *très engagé*. Charlus makes more audacious remarks. We have already heard that Bloch was considered Jewish and not French, which freed the narrator to exclaim, "His assertion of this incompatibility made me suppose that M. de Charlus was more anti-Dreyfusard than anyone I had met" (I, p. 922; PII, p. 288). The Baron's nationalist and racial thinking could only dismiss the Jew as an outsider, a foreigner, a guest of France. It is only logical that with the Dreyfus Affair he would say, "Your Dreyfus might rather be convicted of a breach of the laws of hospitality" (I, p. 922; PII, p. 288). These bizzare and amusing words are almost the same as those uttered by a popular anti-Dreyfusard of the day, Maurice Barrès: "But they are right, because a Jew is never a traitor, he is not of our nation, how can he betray it?" [28]

Charlus, in fact, is certain that to be a Dreyfusard means that something is wrong with the individual, for to be a Dreyfusard is not to be a normal healthy red-blooded one hundred per cent Frenchman: "Every time you find a Dreyfusard, scratch a little. You won't find yourself far from the ghetto, the stranger, inversion, or Wagnermania" (From Notes and Variants, Fr. ed., PIII, p. 1185). The ghetto means Jew; the stranger means German; inversion, abnormality; Wagnermania, the enemy. As an example of this view actually expressed, *La Libre Parole* (February 6, 1899) listed prominent Dreyfusards and their German, i.e., untrustworthy, relations: Dreyfus' brother is German. Joseph Reinach's father and uncle were Germans. Zola is the son of an Italian. Scheurer-Kestner is a German manufacturer. Barrès wrote, "At the Jews' homes . . . we are in the salons of their wives, their honorableness; their facade. And during that time the husband is given to intrigues where he destroys our traditional ideals and our country, our ideas and our realities." [29] Proust's friend the Comte de Montesquiou attacks the author while revealing a violent antisemitism worthy of Léon Daudet: "At the time of the Dreyfus affair . . . given the extreme position that he [Proust, who was Dreyfusard] believed should be adopted in this conflict of races, the best, for him, was not to appear." [30] Charlus holds the most bitter anti-Dreyfusard feelings; he provides the most composite view of the anti-Dreyfusard.

The Duc de Guermantes is also an antisemitic anti-Dreyfusard because that is what he is expected to be. He becomes violent later on when he is directly affected by the Affair. In any case, he offers the classic "conspiratorial" argument that the Jews are united to destroy us. "They are to some extent forced to give their support to anyone of their own race, even if they do not know him personally. It is a public danger" (II, p. 59; PII, p. 680). His conclusion is rather simple and very typical: "[We] ought to have driven out all the Jews" (II, p. 407; PIII, p. 42). If one expels the Jews the health of the nation will return. It is frightening to think that at the very same time Gyp, in *La Libre Parole* (March 21, 1899), is offering a more modern solution: "It would be so easy to suppress "supprimer" them [the Jews] in an excess of anger that the entire world would absolve." The Duc, like a child, pins his hate upon the few Jews he knows, the Rothschilds (II, p. 406; PIII, p. 41) and Swann (I, p. 1128; PII, p. 578). "We have evidently been too easy going, and the mistake Swann [a Dreyfusard] is making will create all the more stir since he was respected, not to say received, and was almost the only Jew that anyone knew" (II, p. 59; PII, p. 680). The proof of Jewish conspiracy is the stand in favor of Dreyfus taken by the Rothschilds and especially by Swann. Basin's great pride has been hurt when he is abandoned by those whom he expected would honor his opinion on all matters since he is by rank their superior and therefore should command obedience. He is not racially antisemitic, but socially antisemitic: that is, his opinions change as popular opinion changes. He is perhaps more dangerous than Charlus, who at least remains faithful to his false principles; Basin can be an unforeseen menace. When it was chic to have Jews, Swann entered; now that it is not correct to have Jews—particularly those who disagree with his own opinions—the Jews clearly become a social liability. In short, the anti-Dreyfusism of a Charlus builds on a quack nationalist racial theory while the Duc's is based on the maintenance of caste position.

Worried about maintaining his social prestige the Duc is afraid that the Marquis de Saint-Loup, who is pro-Dreyfus, may not be elected a member of the elite Jockey Club. The aristocracy of lower rank who are violently anti-Dreyfusard expect their traditional leaders, the highest aristocracy, to support their view. They can take revenge on a pro-Dreyfusard high aristocrat in the clubs by voting to deny him entrance, thus threatening the prestige of his family. "You will agree that if one of our family were to be pilled at the Jockey, especially Robert, whose father was Chairman for ten years, it would be a pretty serious matter" (I, p. 884; PII, p. 235). Ordinarily Saint-Loup would be elected without hesitation because of his almost royal ancestry, but his pro-Dreyfus sentiments endanger his chances for acceptance. Thus the Dreyfus Affair is a nuisance because it upsets the normal run of social affairs. Great bitterness overcomes the Duc when he is refused the presidency of the Jockey because many petty aristocrats remember the pro-Dreyfus stand of the Guermantes (II, p. 405; PIII, p. 40). The Dreyfus Affair marks the first step in the loss of prestige of the ducal House of Guermantes.

Oriane and the other smart salon women went out of their way to ignore the Dreyfus Affair. Oriane realized its potential threat to her salon and tried desperately to laugh off Dreyfus and the entire Affair as a great bore: " 'In any case, if this man Dreyfus is innocent,' the Duchess broke in, 'he hasn't done much to prove it. What idiotic, raving letters he writes from that island. I don't know whether M. Esterhazy is any better, but he does show some skill in his choice of words, a different tone altogether. That can't be very pleasant for the supporters of M. Dreyfus. What a pity for them there's no way of exchanging innocents' " (I, p. 887; PII, p. 239). Oriane appears despicable, but her action must be taken as typical of the age. She wishes to protect her salon. Other salons were destroying their "standards" by allowing in nationalists of petty aristocratic or bourgeois origins whom Oriane wishes to avoid at all cost. But salon life cannot remain stagnant, and members of lower society had to be accepted.

With the proof of Dreyfus' innocence, the anti-Dreyfusards felt threatened socially, and to protect their prestige they baited the Jews more. "The anti-Dreyfusard opposition had doubled its violence, and from being purely political, had become social" (II, p. 59; PII, p. 679). The politically defeated nobles and bourgeois wished to prevent the Jews from staging a comeback.

The nationalist bourgeois women especially appreciated the Affair because they had been permitted to enter society, as if to replace Jews, during the stormy days of the Affair. Mme de Marsantes, who had become violently antisemitic (I, p. 897; PII, p. 253), permits the nationalist women to enter her salon—the major step that led to the destruction of the exclusively aristocratic Faubourg Saint-Germain. Oriane declaims bitterly: "But on the other hand I do think it perfectly intolerable that just because they're supposed to hold 'sound' views and don't deal with Jewish tradesmen, or have 'Down with the Jews' printed on their sunshades, we should have a swarm of Durands and Dubois and so forth, women we should never have known but for this business, forced down our throats by Marie-Aynard or Victorienne. I went to see Marie-Aynard a couple of days ago. It used to be so nice there. Nowadays one finds all the people one has spent one's life trying to avoid, on the pretext that they're against Dreyfus, and others of whom you have no idea who they can be" (I, p. 886; PII, p. 238). Oriane clearly describes the new social makeup of society. She realizes that these people are exploiting the Dreyfus Affair to climb, and she is obviously annoyed since she understands that they are a possible threat to her social position and salon.

Charlus, who is as perspicacious on social conditions as Oriane, notes the same changes but reveals his greater understanding of the problem. "All this Dreyfus business . . . has only one drawback. It destroys society by the influx of Mr. and Mrs. Camels and Camelries and Camelyards, astonishing creatures whom I find even in the houses of my own cousins, because they belong to the Patrie Française, or the Anti-Jewish League, or some such league, as if political opinion entitled one to any social qualification" (I, p. 923; PII, p. 290). The last line contains the insight. But Charlus is helpless: The barrier has been breached. The bourgeoisie will eventually take over. "The reason that they were nationalists gave the Faubourg Saint-Germain the habit of entertaining ladies from another class of society; the reason vanished with nationalism, the habit remained" (II, p. 544; PIIII, p. 235-36). The aristocracy gambled on the support of the bourgeoisie and offered as a reward social advancement; little did the Faubourg realize it had destroyed its most sacred possession—aristocratic exclusiveness. But the fact that the bourgeoisie could and did advance underscores that movement in society was not only possible but could lead to considerable social transformation.

Among the first to profit, temporarily at least, from the Dreyfus Affair were the military leaders. M. de Froberville found himself in a position of favor which he greatly exploited (II, p. 57; PII, p. 676). But the most successful climber was Mme Swann. Odette was not really anti-Dreyfusard. "She has been the first to assure me that she was convinced of Dreyfus's innocence" (I, p. 905; PII, p. 264). But in order to climb socially, she realized that it was necessary to appear to be anti-Dreyfusard. She convinced her husband not to talk of the Affair, joined the Ligue de la Patrie Française and other nationalist groups and became known as "sound" (II, p. 104; PII, p. 744). Such a fine record permitted her to enter Mme de Villeparisis' salon. Here are some of her ploys:

> Mme. Swann, seeing the dimensions that the Dreyfus case had begun to assume, and fearing that her husband's racial origin might be used against herself . . . had besought him never again to allude to the prisoner's innocence. When he was not present she went farther and used to profess the most ardent Nationalism; in doing which she was only following the example of Mme. Verdurin, in whom a middle-class antisemitism, latent hitherto, had awakened and grown to a positive fury. Mme. Swann had won by this attitude the privilege of membership in several of the woman's leagues that were beginning to be formed in antisemitic society, and had succeeded in making friends with various members of the aristocracy. (I, p. 896-897; PII, p. 252)

Although better-known Jews were excluded for a while because of the Dreyfus Affair, "Bloch, whom no one knew, might pass unperceived" (I, p. 851; PII, p. 190). That is, Proust notes that there was a contradictory pattern in social movement during the Affair: At the same time Jews were being excluded due to antisemitism there was a "more abundant movement towards the penetration of society by Israelites" (II, p. 786; PIII, p. 574-75). Even a Jew could enter French society during the Dreyfus Affair as long as he was interesting and discreet.

Proust also uses the Affair to convey the continual yet hardly perceptible changes brought about by the passage of time. He shows that a few years after the Affair, society began to accept Dreyfusards; Marcel records that a Mme Alphonse Dreyfus was present at the salon of Charles de la Trémoïlle (II, p. 406; PII, p. 41), certainly one of the four most aristocratic families in France. By the end of World War I, "Dreyfusism had now been given its place in a whole category of respectable and accustomed things. As for inquiring into its real merits, nobody dreamed of doing that now before approving it, any more than they formerly had before condemning it. It was no longer 'shocking' " (II, p. 895-896; PIII, p. 727). Thus an event is confronted by society, jolts it, and through the passage of time old hates and contradictions caused by the event are resolved and dissolved as new positions and concerns are taken up to meet more contemporary problems. Thus Proust remarks:

> But, like a kaleidoscope which is every now and then given a turn, society arranges successively in different orders elements which one would have supposed to be immovable, and composes a fresh pattern. Before I had made my first Communion, ladies on the "right side" in politics had had the stupefaction of meeting, while paying calls, a smart Jewess. These new arrangements of the kaleidoscope are produced by what a philosopher would call a "change of criterion." The Dreyfus case brought about another, at a period rather later than that in which I began to go to Mme. Swann's and the kaleidoscope scattered once again its little scraps of color. Everything Jewish, even the smart lady herself, fell out of the pattern, and various obscure nationalities appeared in its place. The most brilliant drawing-room in Paris was that of a Prince who was an Austrian and ultra-Catholic. If instead of the Dreyfus case there had come a war with Germany, the base of the kaleidoscope would have been turned in the other direction, and its pattern reversed. The Jews having shown, to the general astonishment, that they were patriots also, would have kept

> their position, and no one would have cared to go any more, or even to admit that he had ever gone to the Austrian Prince's. All this does not, however, prevent the people who move in it from imagining, whenever society is stationary for the moment, that no further change will occur. (I, p. 394-395; PI, p. 517)

Many Jews were accepted into society during Proust's lifetime, though always treated as favored guests. The Dreyfus Affair stands out in the age, then, as a major turning point in altering the social character of high society and especially in crystallizing antisemitic reaction which would have significant repercussions decades later.

Proust therefore had multiple ends in depicting the Dreyfus Affair: He again serves as a social historian, recording the passions and hates generated by the political event; he reveals how an external event can cause a change in the "quality" of high society by encouraging the socialites to admit people who merely support the thinking of the old habitués. Proust describes the various aspects of antisemitism and its importance as a focal point for much of the social, political, and economic tensions of the age, He depicts the total apathy of French high society to social justice and its abandonment of civic duties. Concerning the novel itself, he offers one more insight into each of his characters by describing the reaction of each to the event. In addition, the varying reactions to the Affair throughout the novel underline the basic theme of the march of time. Finally, the narrator's disgust at the cowardice and fickleness of high society that was revealed in part by the way people either ignored or quickly forgot the Affair, destroys Marcel's dream of fulfillment in the outside world and eventually leads to his abandonment of this social whirl for a life dedicated to Art.

UN DINER EN FAMILLE

(PARIS, CE 13 FÉVRIER 1898)

PAR CARAN D'ACHE

— Surtout! ne parlons pas de l'affaire Dreyfus!

... Ils en ont parlé...

The Dreyfus Affair. Caption I: "Above all, let's not talk of the Dreyfus Affair!" Caption II: "They talked about it . . ."

At Dieppe in 1880. Left to right: Count Robert de Montesquiou, Marquis du Lau (friend of Comtesse Greffülhe), the Prince de Sagan, Prince Edmond de Polignac, Charles Haas (Proust's Swann), and an unknown person. Photograph courtesy of the Librairie Académique Perrin.

SWANN, THE ASSIMILATED JEW, AND THE FORCE OF HEREDITY

The Dreyfus Affair affected no one in the novel more than it did Swann. He was not excluded from high society because of his Jewish origins but he was deeply hurt by the antisemitism that was expressed around him. Swann's great discovery was that he could not escape his origins, and he decided to take a stand for the first time in his life. But before we turn to the changes Swann underwent, let us look at him as the man who was the personification of social success for young Marcel, the type of the ideal gentleman before his fall from favor.

Was it irony that made Proust present Swann from the beginning as the most elegant gentleman of his age? (I, p. 12; PI, p. 15). Swann, a third-generation Catholic of Jewish origin, portrays the assimilated Jew, and encompasses "all the stages through which his race had passed, from the crudest and coarsest form of snobbishness up to the highest pitch of good manners" (I, p. 332; PI, p. 432). Swann is the gentleman one reads about in *Le Gaulois,* like Charles Haas attending a social function—a funeral, for example:

> The funeral of the Countess de Ludre, nee Beauveau took place yesterday, at ten o'clock in the church of Saint-Honoré d'Eylau. The Dukes de Montmorency, Bisaccia, d'Estissac, de Noailles, de Blacas, de Clermont-Tonnerre, de Mouchy, Prince Murat, Prince de Poix, Marquis de Breteuil, Baron Adolphe de Rothschild, Countess Paul de Pourtalès, Count de Noailles, Count Charles de Breteuil, Marquis de Lau, Count Aimery de la Rochefoucald, M. Lavedan, M. Charles Haas. (*Le Gaulois,* June 12, 1898—in the middle of the Dreyfus Affair.)

That Swann is a gentleman is confirmed by his membership in

the exclusive Jockey Club, which cultivated the arts of the leisured gentleman, the dandy. He also proffers the Guermantes wit, a delicate frivolity, a certain conventionality of mode with a dash of originality—"with such mastery, with such absolute sureness did he play the social game" (I, p. 1129; PII, p. 579). Swann imitates the idealized English gentleman who, on a wintry afternoon, sips tea with cream in the intimate surroundings of his mistress' salon (I, p. 170; PI, p. 221). Swann is indeed the pride of the Faubourg Saint-Germain.

With deliberate irony, Proust uses the elegance of Swann, an assimilated Jew, to show up the aristocrats and their pretensions, for Swann fulfills the ideals of high society far better than any of the Guermantes. The aristocracy flounders in its attempt to live up to its greatest ideal: *otium cum dignitate*. Even when Swann becomes a Dreyfusard the Duc, though perturbed and puzzled, still compliments him for having earlier followed the social code which Swann seems now to have broken. "I should never have believed it of him, an epicure, a man of practical judgment, a collector, who goes in for old books, a member of the Jockey, a man who enjoys the respect of all who know him, who knows all the good addresses, and used to send us the best port wine you could wish to drink, a dilettante, the father of a family" (II, p. 58; PII, p. 677). But Swann, a devoted Dreyfusard, still will not permit Bloch to petition the Prince de Guermantes, who confided his own pro-Dreyfus stand to Swann: it would be unbecoming of a gentleman. "But Swann, blending with his ardent conviction as an Israelite the diplomatic moderation of a man of the world . . . refused to allow Bloch to send the Prince a circular to sign. . . . 'If he were to sign your list, he would simply be compromising himself with his own people, would be made to suffer on our account, might even repent of his confidences and not confide in us again' " (II, p. 82; PII, p. 712). Swann's sensitivity to another's social position can play havoc with his sense of social justice. Even though he personally has become a Dreyfusard, Swann remains the assimilated Jewish nineteenth-century gentleman, while Bloch is the new Third Republic *arriviste* and polemicist whose game rules are in keeping with the contemporary fray.

Society is taken by surprise when Swann supports Dreyfus;

even the reader is a bit jolted. However, when the Dreyfus Affair blew up around him, Swann was beginning to grow old. Though Proust never gives any reasoned explanations of Swann's conversion to Dreyfusism, he interprets Swann's choice in the deterministic mode of the time: "After a certain age, and even if different evolutions are occurring in us, the more we become ourselves, the more our characteristic features are accentuated" (II, p. 188; PII, p. 862). The force of heredity was making itself felt.

> Perhaps too in him, in these last days, the race was making appear more pronounced the physical type that characterizes it, at the same time as the sentiment of a moral solidarity with the rest of the Jews, a solidarity which Swann seemed to have forgotten throughout his life, and which, one after another, his mortal illness, the Dreyfus case, and the antisemitic propaganda had revived. There are certain Israelites, superior people for all that and refined men of the world, in whom there remain in reserve and in the wings, ready to enter at a given moment in their lives, as in a play, a bounder and a prophet. Swann had arrived. (II, p. 67; PII, p. 690)

Everywhere Proust sees the Dreyfus Affair pulling people back to their hereditary origins (see I, p. 1128; PII, p. 578). Proust wonders about M. Reinach, one of the great pro-Dreyfusards who did so much for the retrial: "perhaps this rationalist manipulator of crowds was himself the puppet of his ancestry" (II, p. 928; PII, p. 927). Saint-Loup too is limited and "undergoing an evolution in which heredity played a large part" (II, p. 916; PIII, p. 760). If Jewish traits become apparent because of the Affair, Christian origins also make their appearance:

> I knew that, as deep, as ineluctable as is their Jewish patriotism or Christian atavism in those who imagine themselves to be the most emancipated of their race, there

> dwelt beneath the rosy efflorescence of Albertine, Rosemonde, Andrée, unknown to themselves, held in reserve until the circumstances should arise, a coarse nose, a protruding jaw, a burst . . . ready to "come on," just as it might be a burst of Dreyfusism, or clericalism, sudden, unforeseen, fatal, some patriotic, some feudal form of heroism . . . from a nature anterior to that of the man himself, by means of which he thinks, lives, evolves, gains strength himself or dies, without ever being able to distinguish that nature from the successive phases which in turn he takes for it. Even mentally, we depend a great deal more than we think upon natural laws. . . . For we can see only the derived ideas, without detecting the primary cause (Jewish blood, French birth, or whatever it may be) that inevitably produced them, and which at a given moment we expose. (I, p. 669; PI, pp. 891-92)

Swann appears to be as Jewish to Proust as he does to a Mme de Gallardon. One can never escape his origins, he implies, for they will always appear at moments of great stress. "But Swann belonged to that stout Jewish race, in whose vital energy, its resistance to death, its individual members seem to share. Stricken severally by their own diseases, as it is stricken by persecution, they continue indefinitely to struggle against terrible suffering which may be prolonged beyond every apparently possible limit" (II, p. 77; PII, p. 704). Proust has marked out Swann's path back to his "race"; in dialectical fashion Proust unveils in the Gentile aristocracy the lurking atavisms triggered by Swann's Dreyfusism.

> I [the Duc de Guermantes] have always been foolish enough to believe that a Jew can be a Frenchman, that is to say, an honorable Jew, a man of the world. Now Swann was that in every sense of the word. Ah well! He forces me to admit that I have been mistaken, since he has taken the side of this Dreyfus (who guilty or not, never moved in his world, he cannot ever have met him) against a society

> that had adopted him, had treated him as one of ourselves. (II, p. 58; PII, p. 678)

The Duc not only considers Swann guilty of treachery by association because of his origins, and therefore a traitor like Dreyfus, but also attacks him for abandoning his social caste. In the Duc's eyes, such abandonment meant that Swann became *déclassé*. "This new loss of caste would have been better described as a recasting, and was entirely to his credit, since it made him return to the ways in which his forebears had trodden and from which he had turned aside to mix with the aristocracy" (I, p. 1131; PII, p. 582).

The narrator is proud of Swann for taking an honest stand, for returning and defending his people. Yet Proust is properly annoyed at him when he makes broad remarks about the goyim as the Gentiles make about the Jews. "What can you expect, all these people belong to a different race, one can't have a thousand years of feudalism in one's blood with impunity" (I, p. 1130; PII, pp. 581-82). Obviously neither the Duc nor Swann are concerned about Dreyfus but about *race*.

> "At heart all these people are anti-Semites," replied Swann, who, all the same, knew very well from experience that certain of them were not, but, like everyone who supports any cause with ardor, preferred, to explain the fact that other people did not share his opinion, to suppose in them a preconceived reason, a prejudice against which there was nothing to be done, rather than reasons which might permit of discussion. (I, p. 1130; PII, p. 581)

Such squalid thinking leads Swann to base "all his admirations and all his contempts to the test of a new criterion, Dreyfusism" (I, p. 1131; PII, p. 582). The Affair so constricts Swann's intellectual horizon that he can say: "I should like to live long enough to see Dreyfus rehabilitated and Picquart a colonel" (II, p. 83;

PII, p. 714). Swann eventually will die (II, p. 293; PII, p. 1013) without having logically understood the reasons for Dreyfus' innocence.

Proust leaves us with some unanswered questions concerning Swann. Why should the usually enlightened Swann become so intolerant and even fanatic about Dreyfus and the Jewish question, while the Prince de Guermantes becomes suddenly so objective and escapes his usually racist thinking? That Swann's Jewish heredity led him to a fanatic defense of Dreyfus becomes an indefensible explanation since the Prince, too, should behave according to his heredity. Or does the Aryan heredity in crisis contain greater tolerance or logical abilities?

Perhaps Proust himself, in his concept of personality, was not certain of the extent to which heredity affected behavior or the extent rationality did. His demonstration of the forces of heredity appears absurd when he pushes Swann to adopt the faith of his ancestors, even though the family had been converted to Catholicism three generations earlier. We may ask whether, having pushed Swann to one extreme, Proust needed to counterbalance the characters by suddenly bringing lucidity, without any preparation, to the Prince's mind, thus showing by exaggeration the whirl of the social kaleidoscope caused by the Affair. Or we may see this as an esthetically ineffective switch, although it may prove Proust's contention that we can never really know another person—or another fictional character, in a novel or in life.

Proust was only aware that antisemitism, not the question of Dreyfus' innocence or the need for social justice, was the issue that concerned high society, and he used the Dreyfus event primarily as a means to reveal unexpected new traits of character. Proust showed that the typical *mondain,* like Swann, had no objectivity; he makes judgments about issues based on his caste origins and feelings. He also showed that, because Swann was "racially" still a Jew, he remained an outsider to the caste of which he considered himself a member. And because of this, the Dreyfus Affair exposed Swann's life as a living fraud, just as his love had been, for he wasted his time in a world which was not his own and in which he could no longer believe. He dies forgotten shortly after the Affair, a man who had created nothing, a failure.

BLOCH, THE ASSIMILATING JEW

Bloch is the Jew par excellence of the novel. Whereas Swann represents the socially assimilated Jew, Bloch is the young unknown who dreams of breaking into French high society. Proust portrays Bloch as an unpleasant brassy Jew who, though bright, aggressive, and ambitious is equally tactless, indiscreet, and tasteless, as well as a pompous intellectual. Actually Bloch resembles a rich, third-generation Jewish-American snob who wishes quick access to the best of American society. A strange and complex character, Bloch serves as Proust's whipping boy of Jewish snobbery.

Most critics, Carmen Castro, for instance, feel that Proust used Bloch for comic relief: "[Bloch] remains in the novel in the role of a stupendously comic clown." [31] Roland Donzé, in his book *Le Comique Dans L'Oeuvre de Marcel Proust* sees Bloch as "a comic failure" perhaps because of his Jewish background, but unfortunately he never pursues this point.[32] Actually most of Bloch's gaffes are not funny; they are generally pathetic and vulgar. Whereas Molière brings sympathy to his description of the vulgarity of M. Jourdain, Proust brings none. Proust, for all his usual delicacy, is rather heavy-handed in destroying Bloch's social pretensions.

Bloch is a young, third-generation Jew haunted, in the word of Van Praag, by *Geltungsbedürfnis*.[33] Bloch's father is a typical second-generation businessman whose office is in the heart of the Jewish ghetto in Paris at Rue des Blancs-Manteaux (II, p. 228; PII, p. 1106). He has watched with pride his little Albert write a thesis on Philip II (II, p. 1071; PIII, p. 975), and receive his *agrégation* (I, p. 586; PI, p. 776) and a *cum laude* (I, p. 559; PI, p. 738). But whereas his father is content to remain among his own, Albert Bloch has higher pretensions. He dreams of becoming a playwright, perhaps à la Henri Bernstein or Georges de Porto-Riche. To be a writer brings fame (he does not need the fortune), social admittance, and acceptance—the one thing a rich Jew does not have.

> Socially the Jewish intellectuals were the first, who, as a group, needed and wanted admittance to non-Jewish society. Social discrimination, a small matter to their fathers who had not cared for social intercourse with Gentiles, became a paramount problem for them.
>
> Searching for a road into society, this group was forced to accept social behavior patterns set by individual Jews [Swann] who had been admitted into society during the nineteenth century as exceptions to the rule of discrimination. They quickly discovered the force that would open all doors, the 'radiant Power of Fame' (Stefan Zweig) which a hundred years' idolatry of genius had made irresistible.[34]

Bloch falls squarely into this pattern. And to Proust's amusement he picks Sir Rufus Israels as the image of the highest and most successful Jew whom he could imitate (I, p. 872; PII, p. 218).

But another interpretation of Bloch is possible: perhaps he is not just a vile Jewish pedant and snob who serves as comic relief, but rather the image of a pathetic soul caught in the terrible position of being a "man without a country." Though Bloch's father is a successful businessman, he is still an unassimilated Jew who is proud of being French. And though he "died during the war from the shock . . . of seeing France invaded" (II, p. 1036; PIII, p. 928), he nevertheless has little or no social intercourse with his Christian neighbors but lives in his family circle according to the fading code of Abraham, Isaac, and Jacob. Young Bloch had not been taught to live according to this tradition. He knows no Hebrew; he may understand some Yiddish but does not speak it; he is not religious; he has no Jewish culture: he has only Jewishness, which is, as for Heine, *ein Unglück*. He is a Jewish Frenchman who has yet to absorb all the French traditions and values. Bloch is a trapeze artist who has let go of one bar and who, floating free, is trying to grasp the next one. He is swinging from the Jewish world to the French world in the novel. From Combray until the matinee we observe his mistakes and vulgarities, which are brought on more by ignorance and the desire to be accepted than by willful acts of malice—except when they are compensatory reactions to hide his pitiful sense of inferiority. It is to the honor of F. C. Green that he alone among the critics has seen in Bloch more than an assemblage of unpleasant stereotyped Jewish characteristics.[35] Bloch, in summary, is the young Jewish intellectual desperately looking for acceptance in a world basically hostile to him. His objective is to enter what is considered truly "Old France," the Faubourg Saint-Germain, and this occupies his efforts for three thousand pages. In one brilliant passage, Proust sums up the impossible conditions from which Bloch was attempting to escape:

> Bloch was ill-bred, neurotic, a snob, and, since he belonged to a family of little repute, had to support, as on the floor of the ocean, the incalculable pressure that was imposed on him not only by the Christians upon the surface but by all the intervening layers of Jewish castes superior to his own, each of them crushing with its contempt the one that was immediately beneath it. To carve his way through to the open air by raising himself from Jewish family to Jewish family would have taken Bloch many thousands of years. It was better worth his while to seek an outlet in another direction. (I, p. 563; PI, p. 744)

Before Bloch can even make a move, he is recognized; his name defeats him. "Bloch" was most likely chosen, because it is a typical Ashkenazic Jewish name which evokes anything east of Reims. Bloch, besides, is a most popular name in French jokes about Jews. Thus, in one collection of *Histoires Juives* (which often appear as chapbooks) published by NRF Jews named Bloch appear in forty stories out of a total of two hundred.[36] Two examples are these:

> Bloch is eating in a restaurant run by Mme Dreyfus. It is summer and it is warm. Bloch takes off his coat, puts it on the back of his chair, and continues to eat. Mme Dreyfus

approaches him: "Say, M. Bloch, if you were at Marguery's [a very fine restaurant around 1910] and if you took off your coat, what do you think M. Marguery would say?"

"What would M. Marguery say to me? Well, M. Marguery would tell me: My friend Bloch, if you wish to take off your coat, go eat at Mme Dreyfus's." [Raymond Geiger, *Histoires Juives* (Paris: NRF, 1923), p. 49.]

Bloch and one of his friends, a Catholic, meet each other at a burial. The Christian makes the sign of the cross. "Why do all you Catholics make the sign of the cross?" "It's in remembrance of the crucifixion of Our Lord Jesus Christ." "Tell me. What would you do if He had been impaled?" (*Ibid.,* p. 80)

The only other name used as much was "Lévy." Since Proust names Bloch's cousins Lévy, I believe we have an "in-joke." In fact, all Proust's Jewish names but Swann are borrowed from Jewish jokes.

Besides his unfortunate name, Bloch has a Jewish face, not unpleasing but so rich in Semitic qualities that Swann's description of him is compared to Bellini's portrait of Mohammed II: "He has the same arched eyebrows and hooked nose and prominent cheekbones. When his beard comes he'll be Mahomet himself" (I, p. 74; PI, p. 97). We learn shortly after that he had grown a small beard like Nissim Bernard (I, p. 585; PI, p. 774). And a little later: "He had his chin pointed now by a goat-beard, wore double glasses and a long frock coat, and carried a glove like a roll of papyrus in his hand" (I, p. 851; PII, p. 190). In short, Bloch is the image of the unassimilated Jew in the salon. "But Bloch, not having been rendered supple by the gymnastics of the Faubourg, nor ennobled by a crossing with England or Spain [an allusion to Sephardic Jewry's claim to royal Davidic ancestry], remained for a lover of the exotic as strange and savoury a spectacle, in spite of his European costume, as one of Decamp's [a 19th-century painter of Algerian Jews] Jews" (I, p. 851; PII, p. 190).

But in this last quotation we are rushing things a bit. Actually Bloch, like Swann and Marcel, starts out from Combray. Proust has not explained what a Jew is doing in such a tiny town, although Bloch's family, like Swann's, wanted roots perhaps in a small town. In any case, neither Swann nor Bloch are really part of the community.

Bloch stages his first social maneuver in Combray at the house of Marcel's Aunt Léonie. Entering clumsily, he assails all present with verbal exaggerations and pompous intellectual virtuosity. When asked if it were raining or not, Bloch responds "I never allow myself to be influenced in the smallest degree either by atmospheric disturbances or by the arbitrary divisions of what is known as Time. I would willingly reintroduce to society the opium pipe of China or the Malayan kriss, but I am wholly and entirely without instruction in those infinitely more pernicious (besides being quite bleakly bourgeois) implements, the umbrella and the watch" (I, p. 70; PI, p. 92). "Next, Bloch had displeased my grandmother because, after luncheon, when she complained of not feeling very well, he had stifled a sob and wiped the tears from his eyes" (I, p. 70; PI, p. 92). Obviously such theatrics ring false and lead to the first of his many social disasters. He is never invited to return. But Bloch will not desist, and at Balbec he will try another step upward by inviting Saint-Loup to dinner—addressing him in Greek apostrophes (I, pp. 565-566; PI, p. 747). His verbal facility, however, will be valuable later when he learns to discipline himself and his knowledge. His remarks, of course, were meant to impress.

In the dinner scene we can glimpse Bloch in the intimacy of his home and understand better why he so desires to climb socially. We also discover new traits in him. The dinner party brings together Bloch, Saint-Loup, Marcel, and the Bloch family. The social milieu is a Jewish world speaking French. The boisterous conversation, the blatant materialism, cry out *nouveau riche*. Bloch's father and Nissim Bernard are the first native-born French children of Jews who trekked westward from the townships of Alsace, Germany, and the Pale. They act like Sholem Aleichem's *shtetl* Jews attempting to assimilate French customs. The old Jewish values have already been discarded, for the most part, by the second generation. These Jews, though, can still speak some Judeo-German in the privacy of their home, which Proust shows by the words *schlemihl* (I, p. 584; PII, p. 773) and *meshorès* (I, p. 585; PI, p. 774), which "delighted M. Bloch in the family circle, but struck him as vulgar and out of place before strangers" (I, p. 584; PI, p. 773). They are still proud of their "twofold distinction of being 'masters' " (now that they can afford *meshorès*—servants) and at the same time Jews. But their pride in being Jewish is a household secret. When speaking Yiddish, Bloch's father is embarrassed less for reasons of etiquette than because he reveals his "Oriental side" (I, p. 585; PI, p. 775), which makes him feel inferior. This same complex affects Bloch greatly, and he will suffer further the more he climbs into French society and increasingly becomes the victim of cross-cultural conflict: *Yiddishkeit* versus French values and customs.

The Bloch family is a distinct unit, a microcosm of the Jewish colony of Balbec which itself was "always together, with no blend of any other elements" and "more picturesque than pleasant" (I, p. 559; PI, p. 738-739). An inner warmth unites the family, which is considered sacred and must be protected. The father enjoys enormous respect (I, p. 583; PI, p. 771), and he in turn offers "a warmth of heart, a breadth of mind" (I, p. 1010; PII, p. 408), against which an aristocratic parent, like Mme de Marsantes, appears as a "poor moral figure."

Bloch's desire to climb socially is but the furtherance of his own father's hidden desires. Bloch's father enjoys telling intimate jokes about the Baron de Rothschild, Sir Rufus Israels, and Bergotte as if he knew them personally, even though "M. Bloch knew them only 'without actually knowing them,' from having seen them at a distance in the theatre or in the street" (I, p. 581; PI, p. 769). He boasts like a social climber about his private select club "Le Cercle des Ganaches," a club as easy to enter as any local American fraternal organization (I, p. 879; PII, p. 228). Young Bloch would boast about his sports club "La Boulie" in the same manner.)

Albert Bloch's vulgarity also comes from his father and uncle. Bloch's father tells boring, tasteless jokes (I, p. 581; PI, p. 769). He outrageously tries to pass off on Marcel and Saint-Loup a painting as a Rubens saying that "he had had the signature cut off to make it fit the frame" (I, p. 586; PI, p. 776). He ostentatiously rides about in a "post chaise, with postilions in livery" (II, p. 356; PII, p. 1101). His avariciousness appears when he buys orchestra seats instead of boxes for Albert and his friends, claiming that the boxes were sold out (a lie) and that one saw the stage better from the orchestra (I, p. 586; PI, p. 776). Albert's uncle is no better. Nissim Bernard flaunts his wealth by having his valet bring him his newspaper at the hotel (I, p. 585; PI, p. 775). He is also a perpetual liar. When Bloch discovers that Nissim actually knew Saint-Loup's father, he declares "To think that for once in his life he wasn't lying! It's incredible" (I, p. 914; PII, p. 277).

Nissim also ties the Jewish inferiority complex to the shame of homosexuality. Not only Nissim (II, p. 174; PII, p. 843) but also Bloch's sister (II, p. 173; PII, p. 842) and his cousin Esther Lévy are sexually abnormal (II, p. 437; PIII, p. 85). Proust compares Jews and homosexuals to reveal the problem of social inferiority and of passing for what one is not. Both are pariah to society. Both desperately want acceptance and go out of their way to hide their background (Charlus by a display of virility, Bloch by a change in name). Like the Jews, the homosexuals avoid one another "seeking out those who are most directly their opposite, who do not desire their company" (II, p. 14; PII, p. 616). Both Jews and homosexuals, however, will rally around one of their own if a great misfortune falls. From this point of view Proust sees the homosexuals as a persecuted race like the Jews. Once again it is scintillating to see Proust take two seemingly unrelated subjects and show their similarity. This explains a Jew's appeal and repulsion to a homosexual and vice versa; they are common sufferers but still dislike each other. Charlus' behavior towards Bloch is particularly revealing in this respect. Proust's Jewish family is, in the end, as corrupt as any other in French society.

The dinner party ends abruptly. Whatever Bloch hoped to gain by the "wining and dining" approach was foredoomed by his tactlessness and too-obvious social desires, which destroy his relationship with Saint-Loup. Shortly after the dinner, Bloch vulgarly attempts to force Saint-Loup to introduce him to his uncle, Charlus (I, p. 587; PI, p. 777). "He [Bloch] carried indiscretion to a pitch that was almost maddening" (I, p. 652; PI, p. 867), which is social disaster. The social barrier remains. Antisemitism plays no part in his social failures; his undoing comes from his own weakness of character, the social conditions, and his ignorance of French social customs.

Unfortunately Bloch never realized how useful Saint-Loup could have been for him, nor did he totally appreciate the world Saint-Loup represented. Chance permitted him to stumble upon the best society, but like all other socially mobile characters Bloch had other images and names which represented the fairy Faubourg, and so his social rise to the top was set back at least thirty years. Bloch does get a foothold into the Faubourg, though at the discredited edge, the salon of Mme de Villeparisis; here his tactlessness, combined with his expression of a "nationalist" hostility, again prevents his acceptance into high society. But he discovers, at last, the key which unlocks the salons: he is a writer of witty sketches (I, p. 851; PII, p. 189) and therefore a valuable asset for a hostess.

Many of Bloch's erratic habits can be traced to his Jewishness. We must never forget that many of Proust's characters have problems arising from heredity, and Bloch is no exception. "There was, then, embedded in my friend Bloch a father Bloch who lagged forty years behind his son" (I, p. 581; PI, p. 769). Whereas his father is content to remain a Jew, or better, a Jewish-Frenchman, Bloch desperately wants to be French and wants others to accept him as such. He wants no other appellation, and he remains profoundly aware and ashamed of his Jewish origins. "Bloch was able to make fun of Jews and blushed if the word Jew was uttered in his hearing" (II, p. 600; PIII, p. 317). Bloch is in that pitiful position of no longer having any commitment to his past yet not being allowed to forget it because of his home environment and the outside world. When, for example, he foolishly attemps to discuss the Dreyfus Affair with the Duc de Chatellerault, he is rebuffed by a blatantly antisemitic sally:

"You must not ask me, sir, to discuss the Dreyfus case

> with you; it is a subject which, on principle, I never mention except to Japhetics." Everyone smiled, except Bloch, not that he was not himself in the habit of making scathing references to his Jewish origin, to that side of his ancestry which came from somewhere near Sinai. But instead of one of these epigrams (doubtless because he had not one ready) the operation of the internal machine brought to Bloch's lips something quite different. And we caught only: "But how on earth did you know? Who told you?" as though he had been the son of a convict. Whereas, given his name, which had not exactly a Christian sound, and his face, his surprise argued a certain simplicity of mind. (I, p. 893; PII, p. 247)

Bloch is extremely naive. His ignorance of French values and society is one of the basic traits of his personality. He is the little Jewish boy who, leaving the protection of his warm Jewish household where he is adored as nothing less than a genius, enters the world of the majority, terribly aware of his unappreciated background, which he wishes to hide even though society has only admitted him in the first place because of his strange origins and his value to them as a novelty. He falters, naturally, because he applies the values and concerns of his own world, and an overweening intellectual curiosity, to this new world. The rebuff underlines the fact that any Jew is susceptible to unmasking, derision ("everybody smiled"), and expulsion. The Jew therefore is tolerated as a court jester or the *Hofjude*. Had Bloch only performed the way they wished him to, he would not have been so cruelly insulted. But since he was insulted, all the shame and embarrassment of being a Jew is exposed.

Bloch's feelings of inferiority make him unsure of his relationships with people. He is either too friendly or too arrogant. This leads to many small squabbles, the ending of friendships, and an excessive need to be forgiven. " 'You cannot imagine my grief when I think of you,' Bloch went on. 'When you come to think of it, it is a rather Jewish side of my nature,' he added ironically, contracting his pupils as though he had to prepare for the microscope an infinitesimal quantity of 'Jewish blood' " (I, p. 565; PI, p. 746).

Bloch is haunted by his Jewish origins. Usually he quickly disassociates himself, as the quotation in the paragraph above indicates, from his "Jewishness." But the pride-shame dichotomy in his feelings about his Jewish origins sometimes pulls him in the other direction: " 'I rather like,' he continued, 'to find room among my feelings for the share (not that it is more than a very tiny share) which may be ascribed to my Jewish origin.' He made this statement because it seemed to him at once clever and courageous to speak the truth about his race, a truth which at the same time he managed to water down to a remarkable extent" (I, p. 565; PI, p. 747). If, as Proust says, "every class of society has a pathology of its own" (III, p. 388; PIII, p. 16), then the Jewish one is insecurity stemming from feelings of inferiority which are based on real Jewish persecution. Bloch is a tortured victim of this circumstance. It eventually leads him to take revenge on himself by acting like the Japheth who attacks his brother Shem.

Bloch would not commit suicide—he was too vain for that—but he did express antisemitic self-hate pitifully in the following scene:

> One day when we were sitting on the sands, Saint-Loup and I, we heard issuing from a canvas tent against which we were leaning a torrent of imprecations against the swarm of Israelites that infested Balbec. "You can't go a yard without meeting them," said the voice. "I am not in principle irremediably hostile to the Jewish nation, but here there is a plethora of them. You hear nothing but, 'I thay, Apraham, I've chust theen Chacop.' You would think you were in the Rue d'Aboukir." The man who thus inveighed against Israel emerged at last from the tent; we raised our eyes to behold this anti-Semite. It was my old friend Bloch. (I, p. 559; PI, p. 738)

The quotation underlines the tragic implications of the Jewish condition in France of the Belle Epoque.

Bloch, being an intellectual, soon joins the pro-Dreyfus movement. He insists he is a Dreyfusard by logical deduction, but we have already seen that Proust feels that ascendancy contributes not a little to such a decision. Bloch runs about with petitions (II, pp. 82-83; PII, p. 713) and is annoyed if fellow Jews refuse to sign them; he attends the Zola trials in 1898 "thanks to a Nationalist lawyer of his acquaintance" (I, p. 883; PII, p. 234); he sits at the cafes and discusses the Affair with his Jewish cronies. In short, he takes a stand and does not hide or keep silent as did most Frenchmen of Jewish origin. That Bloch should take such a strong stand is not surprising. The Dreyfus Affair gains him the acceptance of many of his intellectual peers, but in greater part it permits him to reveal the Jewish Bloch fully: the right of Dreyfus to have the Liberté, Egalité, and Fraternité which, as a Jew, Bloch himself especially wants, drives Albert to associate himself with Dreyfus, the victim. Since Bloch feels himself the victim of anti-semitism, without égalité and fraternité, now is his chance to defend himself by defending Dreyfus against *their* common enemies. From this point of view the aristocrat was not wrong in tying Jew and Republic together, for the Jew found his human dignity under the principles of the French Republic.

Because he is ignorant of the ways of the salon, Bloch insists on questioning people about the Dreyfus Affair. Proust takes him to task because it is indiscreet to talk of politics or religion in a salon. Bloch, unacquainted with this interdiction, appears the foolish *salonnard.* But surely, with his intellectual curiosity, his most esteemed asset, he really wants to learn—with a fairly open mind—other people's opinions, especially those of the celebrated ambassador, even though his questions may be stated with a juvenile "tone of sarcasm, so as not to appear to be rating himself below the Ambassador" (I, p. 872; PII, p. 219). Once again Bloch's defenses are up because he is unsure of himself. But instead of hating him for his poor salon manners, we should pity the embarrassment which the lack of worldliness in his background causes him. One is tempted to think that Proust has not lost all his *mondain* attitudes as he consciously attacks Bloch's sad attempts to gain access to society. "He, however, being little used to society, felt bound before leaving the room to take leave of them all, to show his manners, but without any friendliness . . . Mme de Villeparisis stopped him" (I, p. 871; PII, p. 217).

Unfortunately, Bloch becomes impossible to handle, and, fearing he may hurt M. de Norpois' position as well as wishing to please the antisemitic archivist, Mme de Villeparisis performs her memorable grande dame scene. If ignorance leads to social errors, then Bloch's clumsiness only increases our scorn for him as a courtier. Bloch, for example, knocks over a vase and spills the water all over (I, p. 869; PII, p. 215). The archivist, who is admiring the Marquise as she is painting, says: "Really, you have the fingers of a fairy." Thinking it meant for him, Bloch retorts, "It's not of the slightest importance; I'm not wet" (I, p. 869; PII, p. 215). His action is clumsy, his reply insolent, but how much more significant that he should mistake the archivist's remark and defend himself so quickly. This is not only the reaction of a poor *salonnard,* but the reaction of a person whose automatic defense mechanisms protect an easily exposed inferiority and sense of inadequacy. "He was one of those susceptible, highly strung persons who cannot bear to think of themselves as having made a blunder which, though they do not admit even to themselves that they have made it, is enough to spoil their whole day. In black rage, he was just making up his mind never to go into society again" (I, p. 870; PII, p. 217). His inadvertent blunders also lead him to snub a woman whom he thought socially unimportant—his snobbery being one of his most unattractive traits. Unfortunately, the lady was, he later discovered, the Baronne de Rothschild: "If I'd only known!" (I, p. 1078; PII, p. 506). Actually, Bloch's social snobbery is obnoxious to us only because it is so poorly carried off, for in truth we feel no repulsion to Marcel's social pretensions, and we accept Odette's and Mme Verdurin's as a natural part of their characters.

Bloch displays poor breeding in many other ways, for example, when he opens the windows of the salon without awaiting Mme de Villeparisis' permission, which actually is denied (I, p. 872; PII, p. 219). He implies his own superior intellectual gifts—

no doubt in compensation for his social deficiencies—by mocking M. de Norpois' essay on why Russia would conquer Japan, an essay published before the Russo-Japanese War (I, p. 873; PII, p. 220). He has the cheek to ask what type of stocks Saint-Loup possesses and how much real estate he owns (I, p. 871; PII, p. 218). (Clearly this interest comes from his background, since his father is in business.) Out of jealousy of Saint-Loup's social status, he foolishly and meanly attacks Saint-Loup publicly so that "everybody was shocked" (I, p. 878; PII, p. 228). Bloch's social aspirations increase his vulgarity and erode his character.

When Bloch is finally banished from the salon, it is not because of antisemitism, as in the case of Lady Israels. Though the Dreyfus Affair is beginning to reach some intensity, "a young man like Bloch, whom no one knew, might pass unperceived" (I, p. 851; PII, p. 190). But Bloch could not discipline his tongue, his clumsiness, or his general appearance. Had he, like Marcel and Odette, remained silent or flattered the Nationalist cause, he would have had less difficulty as a *salonnard*.

If Bloch is a poor *mondain,* let us observe him as a friend of Marcel's. We have deduced Bloch's personality from the images which impressed Marcel most, and by looking at Marcel's very reactions and his personal relations with Bloch we may gain more insight into both men.

Bloch appears very early in the novel as an older friend who introduces Marcel to the works of Bergotte and the Parnassian poets (I, p. 68-69; PI, p. 90). Throughout the novel Bloch encourages Marcel to write (I, p. 133; PI, pp. 173-74). Whereas Swann introduces Marcel to the world of art, Bloch introduces Marcel not only to contemporary literature but also to the world of the senses. "Bloch overthrew my conception of the world and opened for me fresh possibilities of happiness . . . it was he who took me for the first time into a disorderly house" (I, p. 438; PI, p. 575). Thanks to Bloch, Marcel finds that beauty—on all levels—can be experienced if we recognize the charm of a being or object. For example, "What I sought for in her [Mme de Guermantes] was the charm of her historic name" (I, p. 1076; PII, p. 503). And even three thousand pages later Marcel honors Bloch for the new sensual world which he revealed: "he had made the world so fair to me by showing me . . . the universality of desire" (II, p. 810; PIII, p. 610). It is certainly important to note the overwhelming influence two Jews have on Marcel's character. For the first time in a major European novel, Jews play significant and honorable roles vis à vis the hero. They appear as more than stereotypes. Bloch is a lady's man; he talks of the "delights of Eros" (I, p. 587; PI, p. 778), and we learn that he plans to frequent a lovely woman whom he met in the Metro, who is none other than Mme Swann! This explains that strange scene in the Jardin d'Acclimation where Mme Swann calls Bloch "M. Moreul" in her embarrassment at this unexpected and unpleasant meeting (I, p. 587; PI, p. 543). Once again Proust tries to knit all his personages to one another. Bloch, oddly enough, is sexually quite normal; perhaps he is displaying that "power of the race" which Marcel admires. (Only Jews or people of Jewish origin reproduce in the novel.) In any case Bloch is useful, though Marcel will not forgive him for taking him to a second-rate brothel. Bloch, a connoisseur, perhaps did not think that Marcel was ready for more than *"Rachel quand du seigneur."*

Marcel and Bloch finally become rivals at Balbec, where their social aspirations clash. Each accuses the other of snobbery and social pretension. Bloch shouts: "You must be going through a fine crisis of snobbery. Tell me, are you a snob? I think so, what?" (I, p. 560-561; PI, p. 740). And Marcel retorts: "When Bloch spoke to me of the crisis of snobbery . . . I might well have replied: 'If I were, I should not be going about with you.' I said merely that he was not being very polite" (I, p. 563; PI, p. 744). Marcel in fact is quite enchanted with his new-found noble friend Saint-Loup-en-Bray, and Bloch is obviously jealous because Marcel has socially outstripped him. But Bloch's query touches the sensitive area of Marcel's new aspirations. Bloch, of course, rushes to make Saint-Loup's acquaintance and even that of M. de Charlus. Ever mindful of a chance to rise, Bloch sees everyone else as a competitor, if not an enemy, and he outrageously considers Marcel a rival attempting "to put a spoke in his wheel and to prevent him from making friends with them" (II, p. 358; PII, p. 1104). But if this only serves to reveal Bloch's slight paranoia, perhaps the sense of Jewish persecution and fear of antisemitism are at the roots of his hostility. Suspicion obviously does not aid the friendship.

From Balbec on, the friendship between Bloch and Marcel becomes increasingly difficult. Bloch needs, as we have seen earlier, constant attention and the knowledge of being wanted. "A week's silence was at once interpreted by him as meaning a deliberate coldness" (I, p. 913; PII, p. 275). His violent reactions swing from "the effect of a keen affection" to a lack of interest in others. "And so I have never believed that his most violent outbursts as a friend . . . went very deep" (I, p. 913; PII, p. 275). Marcel and Bloch squabble several times and break off the friendship, only to take it up again. The first break is over Charlus' friendship with Bloch (I, p. 991; PII, p. 381), which does not last long (II, p. 179; PII, p. 850). The second comes over a misunderstanding at a railroad station. Marcel does not want to leave Albertine alone, so he avoids leaving the train to speak to Bloch. Albert, seeing Charlus with Marcel, thinks that he is being snubbed. "From that day he ceased to show me the same friendly spirit and, what pained me more, had no longer the same regard for my character" (II, p. 357; PII, p. 1102). Shortly after, they become friendly again (II, p. 383; PIII, p. 9), but at this point the friendship survives mainly by inertia. Marcel does nothing to help or to destroy it. However, the relationship is further jeopardized when Marcel brings Albertine home and becomes so jealous of her that he deliberately keeps Bloch ignorant of what is going on for fear that Bloch may fall in love with her and become his rival (II, p. 417; PIII, p. 56). Marcel in love, it appears, is as suspicious as Bloch in his passionate social climbing. When Albertine flees, Bloch, who by now knows about the tryst, tries to bring Albertine back to his friend by making an unsolicited and "indiscreet intervention." Since Bloch is clumsy—though his actions are motivated by friendship—he interferes greatly with Marcel's plans. "I boiled with rage . . . I heaped every imaginable reproach upon Bloch" (II, p. 693; PIII, p. 443). Marcel admits: "he could be, and was at times quite charming" (I, p 565; PI, p. 746). This action of Bloch's reveals Marcel's intolerance more than Bloch's lack of tact.

The friendship between Bloch and Marcel continually falters

and we are given to understand that Bloch, because of his ostentation and vulgarity, is mostly to blame. Marcel says a friendship "more precious than Bloch's is not, for that matter, saying very much. He had all the faults that most annoyed me" (II, p. 357; PII, p. 1102). But we must remember that the above words are written by the non-omniscient narrator expressing his own feelings. How do we know that Bloch might not say the same thing about Marcel? Never in the novel does the narrator admit to an error of taste or tact or an act of indiscretion. If we believe Marcel, the narrator, he is the only good person in the world and the rest are just petty schemers. His friendships with Bloch and Saint-Loup permit us to see aspects of his character in relief. If Bloch is a poor friend, Marcel appears little better. Both use friendships to climb. Both are high-strung persons who demand delicate handling. Both enjoy ripping apart the intellectual and social pretensions of each other and everyone else. Bloch and Marcel have quite similar attitudes toward the world: the outside world is not made to their image of it, and they are both lonely unfulfilled boys looking for love and recognition. Their friendship is doomed because they cannot provide for one another what they both need.

Marcel's only other friendship points out the unhealthy attitude of his interpersonal relationships. Saint-Loup is presented as the finest of friends. He admires and praises Marcel's brilliant intellect and introduces him flatteringly to his soldier friends. Saint-Loup treats Marcel with great deference—which later turns out to be pure etiquette if not discreet homosexual advances—and performs little niceties such as offering to introduce Marcel to the Duchesse de Guermantes. Saint-Loup looks upon Marcel as an older brother does upon a younger one. Bloch can do none of these things which Marcel's ego demands because his own needs are as great and similar.

Saint-Loup—noble, handsome, seemingly so virile, elegant—is all that Marcel desperately wants to be. Theirs is not a friendship of equals but the warm benevolence of a hero who appreciates the worshipper; Saint-Loup is Marcel's god. Bloch, who has only the blood of Moses and not of Charlemagne, cannot compete in such an uneven contest, for Bloch is handsome but not ablaze with the golden hair of the Guermantes—virile, but without the

Marquis' harem at Rivebelle. Bloch's inadequacies appear neurotic and vulgar next to the self-assured Saint-Loup, a living work of art (I, p. 558; PI, p. 737). Bloch is a rather lukewarm friend from the ordinary world; Saint-Loup is a vital part of Marcel's illusion. Yet when Marcel finally discovers his delusion about Saint-Loup, friendship becomes impossible.

One can legitimately ask what Marcel expects of a friendship and what he has done to make it viable. Ideally, a Proustian friendship is a union of two people who have complete intellectual and emotional rapport. But in Marcel's relationships, friendship is a one-way street. Marcel wants all the attention and love without having to reciprocate. "I congratulated myself on being liked, admired, by so good, so clever, so rare a creature as Saint-Loup" (I, p. 680; PI, p. 907). Yet what has Marcel done to further the friendship, what initiative does he bring, what warmth does he return? Marcel arrives with illusions, social-climbing pretensions, and an overweening sensitivity which can be easily offended. Bloch, though he acts rather clumsily, does make overtures of friendship, does come over to visit, does encourage Marcel to write. Bloch's gaffes and tactlessness stem from his psychological problems, but at least he is trying to overcome them and find a meaningful relationship in life. Marcel describes a scene in which Bloch ostentatiously carouses with his university friends, and he bitterly reproaches him for this vulgarity while he, Marcel, eats with the elegant Saint-Loup and his wife (II, p. 858; PIII, p. 680). From the narrator's point of view, this scene is supposed to underline once again Bloch's disgraceful behavior. From a more objective perspective, this scene points out (1) Marcel's pettiness in insisting upon Bloch's poor etiquette and praising dull Saint-Loup's manners as exquisite—as if manners make the man; and (2) an unbelievably jealous attack on Bloch who, for all his vulgarity, is having a grand time "with the boys." Bloch's conversation may be meaningless, yet Bloch can enjoy the cheer of good companionship—something quite unknown to Marcel; he is enviously ridiculed by the unhappy, sterile Marcel, who mopes about quite like a Mélisande, melancholic, wanting someone to make him happy. Neither Bloch nor Saint-Loup can possibly do this. Marcel, in short, is not only a poor friend but, more important, is seemingly incapable—if not unwilling—of friendship. It follows that Marcel will eventually admit that friendship is unimportant, as useless to him as conversations which permit no real contact or rapport (I, p. 679; PI, p. 907).

If we have insisted in the last two paragraphs upon Marcel's inadequacies in his relations with Bloch and Saint-Loup, it has been done, in part, to show that Bloch is essentially the creation of the narrator's mind and need not necessarily be viewed in the way the narrator presents him; in part to show that the failure of Bloch's friendship is as much Marcel's fault as his own, and thereby to underline the importance of Bloch in the structure of the novel in terms of understanding Marcel's character development; and finally, to display how Proust's favorite technique of playing individuals against each other in generally unpleasant interpersonal relationships reveals the true psychological, if not pathological, states of the characters' minds. "Over his face I saw in imagination that sickly and garrulous expression, that feeble nodding of the head which so quickly comes to a stop and in which I would have recognized the erudite weariness of amiable old men if I had not, after all, recognized my friend standing before me and if my recollections had not animated him with that erstwhile incessant youthful gaiety which he seemed now to have gotten rid of" (II, p. 1037; PIII, p. 928).

Proust also presents Bloch, like Odette, Mme Verdurin, Legrandin, in the novel not only to show the transformation of high society but to expose the effects of the passage of time, which slowly but inevitably conquers all. Physically Bloch has changed considerably since we last saw him at the salon of Mme de Villeparisis. Like Odette (I, p. 647; PI, p. 861), he has changed his style of dress and makeup. "And thanks to his hair style, to the shaving of his moustache, to his elegance, to his will power, his Jewish nose disappeared. But above all, as soon as Bloch appeared, the import of his physiognomy was changed by a redoubtable monocle . . . his traits no longer expressed anything" (PIII, p. 953). Physical assimilation has taken place. Bloch has been dejudaised to the point that he looks like Swann. That physical Jewishness which made him exotic but still too foreign has disintegrated into a faceless mask hidden behind a fashionable monocle.

Bloch has cut the ties to his "old social life" and entered postwar society; "launching out upon a new phase of his career, full of honor and glory, he had made his entry as a great man" (II, p. 1060; PIII, p. 959).

Bloch attained his new position because of his success as an author, for during the war he published many popular works. "He had not ceased publishing those books of his, the absurd sophistry of which I was today striving to demolish so as not to be shackled by it, books devoid of originality but which gave young people and many society women an impression of unusual intellectual eminence, a sort of genius" (II, p. 1060; PIII, p. 958). Bloch does not think he has wasted his time even if he has written worthless books, for he has entered the world he desired, which, if meaningless to us, is everything to him. Marcel's remarks can also be interpreted as those of an author who still has not published much and who is slightly perturbed at another's "unjust" success. [In fact, Marcel claims that Bloch copies Marcel's ideas for *Figaro* articles (II, p. 1113; PIII, p. 1034).] Marcel's feelings arise from a literary rivalry started before the war, when Marcel was published in the *Figaro* before Bloch. Apparently Marcel never forgave Bloch for not congratulating him. Marcel's sour feelings were further aggravated when Bloch was finally published and ran to Marcel seeking a congratulation which he, in turn, never received (II, p. 707; PIII, p. 590). If Bloch appears intellectually dishonest, Marcel is at best rather petty. They both act like spoiled children, which they are. They have no friendship; they have only a lifelong rivalry.

Actually, Bloch does not seem to have changed so much. He still looks for introductions in spite of his popularity. Albert asks his friend Marcel to introduce him to the Prince de Guermantes (II, p. 1054; PIII, p. 953). Furthermore, he is apparently as clumsy as ever. After congratulating Rachel on her recitation, "he turned back and made so much noise regaining his seat that Rachel had to wait more than five minutes before reciting the second poem" (II, p. 1089; PIII, p. 1001). Frankly one is a little tired at this point of hearing about Bloch's lack of elegance and social grace. We cannot even smile. Making this rather petty criticism of the man nonetheless seems to be Marcel's biggest concern. He shows us Bloch's continued innocence as he runs up to Marcel and says: "How funny it is to see Rachel here" (II, p. 1089; PIII, p. 1001), whereas obviously Bloch's presence is just as unusual. It is repeated when Bloch "answered ingenuously" (II, p. 1085; PIII, p. 995) that he preferred going to the Princesse's rather than to La Berma. We also learn that he is ignorant of the guests' origins and their family relationships. He thinks, for example, that the Prince married a great title: Sidonie, Duchesse de Duras nee des Baux, when actually it is only Mme Verdurin (II, p. 1055; PIII, p. 955). He still has not fully learned the ways of the world, and we are really only listening to an echo of the past.

The presence of Bloch in the highest salon of the declining Faubourg Saint-Germain (II, p. 1073; PIII, p. 977) proves that a Jew, even a Jew who was originally so exotic, can climb in society if he wishes. At the end of the novel, Bloch is in the position Swann was in at the beginning of the Third Republic. Thus Proust gives us the span of Jewish assimilation from about 1870 to 1925. Bloch is able to look back on his humble origins, as could Swann (II, p. 1064; PIII, p. 964-65), and see the immense distance he has covered. Even Marcel admits this with pleasure and notes that in the great leap forward "discretion, in both word and deed, had come to him along with social standing and age, with a sort of social age, if one may use the term. It is true that Bloch had formerly been indiscreet, as well as incapable of kindliness or friendly cousel" (II, p. 1068; PIII, p. 969-70).

Bloch and Swann represent the final stages of Jewish assimilation in France. They are still Jews to society, but their children, following in the footsteps of their fathers will be less so, for they are even more intent on escaping their origins. "And Bloch's grandchildren would be kind and considerate almost by birth" (II, p. 1068; PIII, p. 969). They will even be most discreet. One day when one of Bloch's daughters, who married a Catholic, is asked if she was nee Bloch, she answers affirmatively with "a German pronunciation, as the Duc de Guermantes would have done, that is to say, she pronounced *ch,* not like *ck,* but like the Germanic guttural *ch*" (II, p. 960; PIII, p. 823). And Gilberte, "the apple of her father's eye," when asked the name of her father "instead of pronouncing the name 'Souann' she said 'Svann,' a change, as she soon realized, for the worse" (II, pp. 793-794; PIII, p. 585). When Proust says that the children will be more discreet, he means it with *ethnic* overtones as well as in terms of ethics or etiquette. To be more discreet is to be more assimilated, more French—less Jewish. As Bloch and Swann sought to forget their origins, Proust shows that their own children do the same thing—by disowning their parents. The poisons of Jewish origin continue to haunt the next generation, which, even though intermarried, cannot escape its fate. "Israel, break your chain!"

Albert Bloch has already prepared the way for his children to disown his name. He himself changed his name from his pen name to the permanent one of Jacques du Rozier. To which Proust adds: "One would have needed the good nose of my grandfather in order to recognize the 'sweet valley' of the Hebron and the 'chains of Israel' that my friend seemed to have finally broken. An English style had, in effect, completely transformed his look and planed out all that which could be effaced" (PIII, p. 952).

The question of Jewish assimilation has been faced by Jews each time they were dominated, whether by Egyptians, Babylonians, Persians, Greeks, Romans or the West. Each time Israel is divided by those who, like Akiba or Bar Kochba, wish to remain independent and to preserve the ethnic group against the opportunists like Herod or the quisling Flavius Josephus, who collaborate and are assimilated. Bloch wished to assimilate and seems to have succeeded. He follows a typical pattern of socially mobile people. He becomes Jacques du Rozier to escape his Jewish and bourgeois origins.

But does Bloch really escape his origins? Granted he has the *"chic anglais"* and this new mask of "Jacques du Rozier," but a closer look reveals a final irony. Proust, in his farewell to Bloch, has planted a time bomb in Bloch's name. In *Past Recaptured,* Charlus could not remember the name of the *Judengasse* of Paris (II, p. 360; PII, p. 1106), but he says, "That is where M. Bloch ought to reside" (II, p. 360). The name of that *Judengasse,* which is in the heart of the ghetto in the Marais, is Rue des Rosiers. To any informed Parisian who hears "du Rozier"—pronounced almost exactly as "des Rosiers"—Proust's joke is clear: the image of the Jewish ghetto is evoked. So Bloch with all his *"chic anglais"* does not escape from his origins after all. Why, one could ask, did Bloch take such a name, given that he had chosen it and not Proust? Perhaps in his haste to escape his origins Bloch felt a tinge of guilt, and like all social climbers who seek the perfect compromise which can accommodate guilt and desire, decided to choose a double-edged word like "du Rozier." By changing his name, Bloch hoped to escape all references to his Jewish past except for the faintest allusion in his name—like the touch of warmth and friendship and recognition in a Legrandin glance (I, p. 96; PI, p. 125). Such is the ugly picture of European Jewish assimilation in which Jews shed their names, their origins, and their human dignity in order to be accepted.

Bloch's assimilation was accomplished at a time when many Jews really did enter European society, and the major concern of French novelists of the time not unnaturally "turns out to be the Jews' ability or inability to fuse and disappear into another race." [37] Proust obviously believed in assimilation and probably thought that the route his mother took was the best (Proust strongly disliked *sionisme*) (II, p. 17; PII, p. 620). Yet so long as his grandfather had "the good nose . . . for recognizing the 'sweet valley' of the Hebron," the Jew was never assimilated, never safe. Deep in the French mind he remained an alien.

The route Bloch took in the Belle Epoque and just after the war was really the only road a Jewish intellectual could take in Europe unless he became a Zionist. Dual identity in a nation-state like France was and still is frowned upon. France, like the rest of Western Europe in the first part of this century, tolerated the Jew so long as he was willing to assimilate. And yet Jews as assimilated as Gilberte Swann, a fourth-generation Catholic, were plagued by their origins. Obviously Europe was afraid of full assimilation. Jacques du Rozier and his ilk, though, took pride and had a confidence in becoming pure French, pure European.

In summary, Bloch fulfills many functions in Proust's novel. He helps reveal strengths and weaknesses in Marcel, the narrator; he is a typical representative of the Jewish and intellectual social climber, indeed, a perfect specimen of social mobility; he provides us with some comic relief but appears primarily as a pathetic clown à la Rouault; he illustrates the psychological effects derived from feelings of inferiority and inadequacy brought on by cross-cultural conflicts; and finally, through his various transformations in the novel, he serves as a living allegory of passing time. Whereas Bloch is a microcosm of the Jews as a caste, the Jews as a typical social caste with social pretensions also represent all other upward-mobile social castes. Therefore, in having studied the individual Jewish members of a caste we also have discovered an image of the caste or social group itself.

CONCLUSION

We can now legitimately ask if there has been a transformation of high society up to 1925. The superficial glitter certainly has remained the same. Traditions have hardly changed; the famous old names are still very active; on the surface nothing is altered. But this may be deceptive. The play remains the same, yet every night there is a new audience; Proustian high society resembles it in that.

In the Belle Epoque the new members of the Faubourg came from a greater variety of social castes than ever before. The bourgeois continually buy more titles, even capture the greatest ones. Gilberte becomes the Duchesse de Guermantes and Mme Verdurin the Princesse de Guermantes; Mme Swann becomes the Baronne de Forcheville and Renée Legrandin becomes the Marquise de Cambremer. In their wake follow the solicitous artists, the Jewish talent—Bloch, and the valet's son Morel. All these people have changed the traditional origins of the Faubourg Saint-Germain, which supposedly chose its members from the very cream of the old aristocracy. Whereas the old Faubourg Saint-Germain always took for granted both title and bearer, the present Faubourg, though still accepting the fine title, has to accept a strange new bearer whose origins are not commensurate with the traditions of the title.

Of course, the members of the lower classes who have succeeded in reaching the Faubourg have undergone a tremendous change. Mme Verdurin has gained a dignity through age and title;

Bloch has developed an English style; Odette is elegantly but properly dressed; Morel has tamed his vulgarity; and so forth. The transformation we see is not so much of the Faubourg Saint-Germain as it is a transformation of the persons to the ideals and exigencies of the Faubourg. The Faubourg has assimilated these social climbers and not vice versa. We note, besides, that the Proustian hierarchy of castes has not altered at all; only individual members are mobile. If there has been any change to high society, it is that the upwardly mobile can gain acceptance in it more readily, once he fulfills the fundamental demands of the Faubourg Saint-Germain. The Proustian community, therefore, has remained stable while gradually allowing greater freedom of movement within its boundaries.

This study has proceeded chapter by chapter from the general (the conception of the novel based on society and the world view) to the particular (the characters) in order to show that society, the external world—though presented as a mirrored reflection of the author's vision or "point of view from which we come at last to regard the world" (I, p. 649; PI, p. 864) and in which he himself is reflected—*is the all-encompassing shell* within which the narrator discovers his personal concerns, personal solutions, and personal world view. And in which Proust explains the meaning of time, art, and life, and offers, finally, a brilliant study of man's relationship to man during the Belle Epoque. All this is accomplished through a detailed study of the individual, his caste, and the institutions in which the individual exists.

If we reverse the order of the chapters and begin from the particular and proceed to the general, we can see that Proust had a masterly conception of every organizational detail of the work, from the smallest element of the individual to the completely integrated work of art. The novel reflects Proust's conception of life and its hierarchy. At the core of the Proustian universe is man: man, whose mind can transcend time and space but whose body is the victim of time and space. Man is tied to a family, which in turns belongs to a caste within the social structure or hierarchy. Those on the various levels of the hierarchy function according to the different social institutions which Proust analyzes so brilliantly. The entire novel is structurally unified by the world view of the narrator, who has composed this personal view at a certain time—France in the Belle Epoque.

The ideas, the dreams of man, the author himself, must be freed from the chains of time and space, and so the final and highest goal of man in the Proustian vision is Art. Through Art, Man overcomes his humiliating limitations, and captures his own essence and that of the world around him. Art crowns man and renders him immortal. Such is the master conception of *A la Recherche du Temps Perdu,* the fulfillment of the Proustian community.

NOTES

CHAPTER I

1. Henri Duquaire, "A Notre-Dame de Paris," *Le Figaro,* June 12, 1963, p. 9.
2. Girard de Sède, *Petite Encyclopédie des Grandes Familles* (Paris: Société des Editions Modernes, 1962), pp. 154-57.
3. *Ibid.,* p. 9.
4. Samuel Osgood, *French Royalism under the Third and Fourth Republic* (Hague: Martinus Nijhoff, 1960), p. 17.
5. *Ibid.,* p. 10; Gordon Wright, *France in Modern Times* (London: John Murray, 1960), p. 286.
6. Samuel Osgood, *French Royalism,* p. 29.
7. D. W. Brogan, *Development of Modern France* (London: Hamish Hamilton, 1953), p. 141.
8. André Germain, *Clés de Proust* (Paris: Edition Sun, 1953), p. 124; "Mondanités," *Le Gaulois,* August 25, 1898, p. 2;; Paul Morand, *1900* (Paris: Les Editions de France, 1931), p. 218; Marie Riefstahl-Nordlinger, "Proust as I Knew Him," *London Magazine,* VII (August, 1954), p. 60; E. de Clermont-Tonnerre, *Mémoires* (Paris: Bernard Grasset, 1926), p. 21; Arthur Meyer, *40 Years of Parisian Society* (London: Eveleigh Nash, 1912), p. 75.
9. Girard de Sède, *Petite Encyclopédie,* p. 58.
10. *Almanach de Gotha* (Gotha: Justus Perthes, 1912), pp. 255-492.
11. All dates mentioned with names are from editions of those dates of *Le Gaulois* (Paris), "Mondanités," p. 2.
12. Louis Halphen, *Histoire de la Société Française* (Paris: Fernand Nathan, 1953), p. 285.
13. Jacques-Emile Blanche, *Mes Modèles* (Paris: Librairie Stock, 1928), p. 103.

14. Richard Barker, *Marcel Proust, a Biography* (New York: Criterion Books, 1958), p. 28.
15. J.-E. Blanche, *Mes Modèles,* p. 108.
16. *Ibid.*
17. Elisabeth Gramont, *Marcel Proust* (Paris: Flammarion, 1948), p. 30.
18. Antoine Adam, "Le Roman de Proust et le Problème des Clefs," *Revue des Sciences Humaines,* V, 65 (January-March, 1952), p. 51.
19. Marcel Proust, *Lettres à Robert de Montesquiou* (Paris: Plon, 1930), p. 67.
20. Marcel Proust, *Lettres de Marcel Proust à Bibesco* (Lausanne Guild du Livre, 1949), p. 98.
21. *Ibid.,* p. 92.
22. Robert Vigneron, "Marcel Proust et Robert de Montesquiou," *Modern Philology,* XXXIX, No. 2 (November, 1941), p. 160.
23. Princesse Bibesco, *Au Bal avec Marcel Proust* (Paris: Gallimard, 1928), p. 111.
24. Lucien Daudet, *Autour de Soixante Lettres de Marcel Proust* (Paris: NRF, Gallimard, 1929), p. 22.
25. Comte A. de Luppé, "Chez Marcel Proust: Snobs et Mondains," *Le Correspondant,* March 25, 1928, p. 853.
26. Charles Briand, *Le Secret de Marcel Proust* (Paris: Henri Lefebvre, 1950), p. 221.
27. Sylvain Bonmariage, "Faucettes de Proust," *Le Bayou,* Vol. 70 (Summer, 1957), p. 396.
28. J.-E. Blanche, *Mes Modèles,* p. 100; Georges de Lauris, *Souvenirs d'une belle époque* (Paris: Amiot-Dumont, 1948), p. 131; J.-E. Blanche, *Mes Modèles,* p. 100; Robert de Billy, *Marcel Proust* (Paris: Editions des Portiques, 1930), p. 38.
29. George Painter, *Marcel Proust, a Biography* (London: Chatto and Windus, 1959), I, p. 80; Scott Moncrieff (ed.), *English Tribute* (New York: Thomas Settzer, 1923), Stephen Hudson, p. 9 and Ralph Wright, p. 43; Georges Cattaui, *L'Amitié de Proust* (Paris: NRF, 1935), p. 53; Ernst Robert Curtius, *Marcel Proust* (Paris: La Revue Nouvelle, 1928), p. 107.
30. Jean-François Revel, *Sur Proust* (Paris: René Julliard, 1960), pp. 88-89.
31. André Maurois, *Proust* (New York: Meridian Books, 1958), p. 61; Jacques Nathan, *La Morale de Proust* (Paris: Librairie Nizet, 1953), p. 104; Léon Pierre-Quint, *Marcel Proust, Sa Vie, Son Oeuvre* (Paris: Kra, 1925), p. 177.
32. Georges de Lauris, *Souvenirs,* p. 21; Princesse Bibesco, *Au Bal avec Marcel Proust,* p. 170; Henri Bonnet, *Le Progrès Spirituel dans l'Oeuvre de Marcel Proust* (Paris: Librairie Philosophique, J. Vrin, 1947), I, p. 84; Charlotte Haldane, *Marcel Proust* (London: Arthur Barker, 1951), p. 38; Louis Auchincloss, "Proust's Picture of Society," *Partisan Review* (Fall 1960), p. 692.
33. Ernest Seillière, *Marcel Proust* (Paris: Editions de la Nouvelle Revue Critique, 1931), pp. 48-49; Jean Cocteau, *Hommage à Marcel Proust* (Paris: NRF, 1923), p. 91; Edmée de la Rochefoucauld, "Proust,"

Bulletin de la Société des Amis de Marcel Proust, 1953, p. 52; E. de Clermont-Tonnerre, *Robert de Montesquiou et Marcel Proust* (Paris: Flammarion, 1925), p. 203; Marie-Anne Cochet, *L'Ame Proustienne* (Bruxelles: Imprimerie des Etablissements L. Collignon, 1929), p. 106; Clive Bell, *Proust* (London: Hogarth Press, 1928), pp. 35-36; André Germain, *Clés de Proust,* p. 143; Charles Briand, *Le Secret de Marcel Proust,* p. 328.

34. Louis Auchincloss, in *Partisan Review* (Fall, 1960), p. 696; John K. Spagnoli, *The Social Attitude of Marcel Proust* (New York: Publication of the Institute of French Studies, 1936), p. 32.
35. François Mauriac, *Du Côté de chez Proust* (Paris: La Table Ronde, 1947), p. 34.
36. Marcel Proust, *Lettre à Sydney Schiff et al.* (Paris: Plon, 1932), pp. 43-44; Marcel Proust, *Lettres à Mme C.* [atusse] (Paris: Janin, 1946), p. 175.
37. Marcel Proust, *Lettres à Bibesco,* p. 153.
38. Harold March, *The Two Worlds of Marcel Proust* (Philadelphia: University of Pensylvania Press, 1948), p. 22.
39. Antoine Adam, *Le Roman de Proust,* p. 57.
40. Marcel Proust, *Lettres à la Comtesse de Noailles* (Paris: Plon, 1931), p. 128.
41. Louis de Robert, *Comment Débuta Marcel Proust* (Paris: NRF, 1925), p. 45.
42. André Gide, *Journal,* 1939-49 (Paris, NRF, 1949), I, p. 1067.
43. *Ibid.,* p. 692.
44. Marcel Proust, *Lettres à Walter Berry et al.* (Paris: Plon, 1935), pp. 76 and 78.
45. Marcel Proust, *Lettres à Paul Souday et al.* (Paris: Plon, 1932), p. 86.
46. Emmanuel Berl, *Sylvia* (Paris: Gallimard, 1952), p. 134.
47. After reading most of Proust's letters, it is clear that Proust preferred not to see his friends. Over and over again in his letters this verse line from Sully-Prudhomme is repeated: "The truth of friendship is to feel together, not to be with one another" (Louis de Robert, *Proust,* p. 68). This is a strange way to conduct a real friendship. In fact, his enormous correspondence served as an efficient distancing device which permitted him to filter out exactly what he wished to reveal and no more. Proust had little faith in friendship; he saw it as he did love—at best a one-sided affair, at worst an exploitation (Robert de Billy, *Proust,* p. 71). This tragic state explains in part why both Proust and the narrator Marcel finally turn to art as their last desperate gamble to communicate with humanity.
48. M. Vigneron in *Modern Philology,* XXXIX, No. 2, p. 194 sees Proust as a half-breed, a stranger to the aristocracy and to the Jewish and Gentile bourgeoisie; from this isolated position, Proust could thus observe with cold logic high society and its movement. This is one of the more rational explanations of the effects of Proust's Jewish background. However, most critics are simplistic and obsessed with racism. Here is a blatant example of this sort of criticism: "There can be little doubt that the mixture of races played a decisive part in the

formation of his character and the development of his art. From his father he derived his feelings for the historic France which gives his novel strength and solidarity; from his mother his exceptionally delicate sensibility, and possibly his interest in clans and coteries" [Martin Turnell, *The Novel in France* (New York: Vintage Press, 1958), p. 337]. The poetic imaginings of a critic who joins the medieval French peasant from his "Illiersian" fields to a daughter from the tents of Jacob (long camped on the banks of the Rhine) make good "copy" but offer a little insight into the uniqueness of Proust's work. Nor do the Alexandrian lines of Cattaui, a convert whose apostasy colors his criticism, enrich our vision of Proust when he insisted that the author, like all Jews, has "a natural taste for suffering" [Georges Cattaui, "Marcel Proust and the Jews," *Jewish Review,* No. III (December, 1932-March 1933), (London: Soncino Press), p. 91]. M. Saurat stretches a point when he describes Proust's style as "the style of a rabbi commentating the Scriptures" [Denis Saurat, "Le Judaïsme de Proust," *Les Marges,* Tome 34 (1925), p. 84], though Proust knew no Hebrew or anything about the Talmud. M. Fretet in his criticism denounced the Jewish menace everywhere in Proust's work: "The incessant flow of cultural reminiscence calls to mind certain quasi-charlatanical Jewish eruditions. What one calls 'Proustian monadism' could very well be only a manifestation among so many of an essential Jewish trait, irreducible opposition to all unity." [Jean Fretet, *L'Alienation Poétique* (Paris: Janin, 1946), p. 224.] All of these early critics of Proust wrote in the thirties and were victims of that age. Their distinctions of Jewish and French traits—based on no tangible proofs—rather underline the sad fact that too many Frenchmen, including the intellectuals, continue to talk of Jews as a foreign element (as opposed to the Latin genius) in France to this very day. However, the postwar criticism of Briand, Turnell, Barker, and March shows little more enlightenment. It is sad that a Frenchman of Jewish origin must correct the thinking of Gentile critics: "They wished to find an explanation in his Jewish ascendance to certain turns of his mind. These are theoretical deductions, which clarify nothing" (Léon Pierre-Quint, *Marcel Proust,* p. 23). There is a Jewish question, but the racism of these critics only obstructs our view.

49. Hannah Arendt, *The Origins of Totalitarianism* (Cleveland: Meridian Books, 1958), p. 80.
50. Robert Dreyfus, *Souvenirs sur Marcel Proust* (Paris: Grasset, 1926), p. 176.
51. J.-E. Blanche, *Mes Modèles,* p. 115.
52. Richard Barker, *Marcel Proust,* p. 246.

CHAPTER II

1. Edmond Kinds, *Marcel Proust* (Paris: Richard Massé, 1947), p. 63.
2. Jacques Zéphir, *La Personnalité Humaine dans l'Oeuvre de Marcel Proust* (Paris: Lettres Modernes, 1959), p. 63.

3. Ian Watt, *The Rise of the Novel* (Berkeley: University of California Press, 1962), p. 21.
4. Howard Moss, "The Two Ways," *Sewanee Review,* LXX (Summer, 1962), p. 462.
3. Ian Watt, *The Rise of the Novel* (Berkeley: University of California Press, 1962), p. 21.
6. Leo Bersani, *Marcel Proust* (New York: Oxford University Press, 1965), p. 17.
7. Gaëton Picon, *Lecture de Proust,* p. 195.
8. Germaine Brée, *Du Temps Perdu au Temps Retrouvé* (Paris: Les Belles Lettres, 1950), p. 132.
9. Harry Levin, "The Novel," *Dictionary of World Literature,* ed. Joseph T. Shipley (New York), p. 405.
10. Gaëton Picon, *Lecture de Proust,* pp. 107-09.
11. E. E. Evans-Pritchard, *Essays in Social Anthropology* (London: Faber and Faber, 1962), p. 19.
12. Lucien Daudet, *Autour de Soixante Lettres de Marcel Proust* (Paris: NRF, Gallimard, 1929), p. 71.
13. Benjamin Crémieux, *Du Côté de Marcel Proust* (Paris: Lemarget, 1929), p. 55; Léon Pierre-Quint, *Le Comique et le Mystère Chez Proust* (Paris: Kra, 1928), p. 11.
14. Joseph E. Baker, "Ivory Tower as Laboratory: Pater and Proust," *Accent* (Autumn, 1959), p. 212; Ruy Coelho, *Proust* (Sao Paulo: Flama, 1944), p. 21; Lester Mansfield, *Le Comique De Marcel Proust* (Paris: Librairie Nizet, 1953), p. 118; Germaine Brée, *Du Temps Perdu au Temps Retrouvé,* p. 59; Howard Moss, *The Magic Lantern of Marcel Proust* (New York: Macmillan Company, 1962), p. 75; Jean François Revel, *Sur Proust* (Paris: Julliard, 1960), p. 98; Leo Bersani, *Marcel Proust.*
15. Martin Turnell, *The Novel in France* (New York: Vintage, 1958), p. 336.
16. Harold March, *The Two Worlds of Marcel Proust* (Philadelphia: University of Pennsylvania Press, 1948), p. 244.
17. Van Meter Ames, *Proust and Santayana* (Chicago: Clark, 1937), p. 28.
18. Robert Redfield, *The Little Community* (Chicago: University of Chicago Press, 1955), p. 161.
19. Robert Redfield, *The Little Community,* p. 70.
20. J. F. Revel, *Sur Proust,* p. 43; Georges Poulet, *Studies in Human Time* (New York: Harper Torchbook T61004, 1961), p. 176; André Chaumeix, "Le Roman et la Peinture de la Société," *Revue des Deux Mondes* (Paris: 1928, pp. 691-701), T. 44, p. 694; Hans Robert Jauss, *Zeit und Erinnerung in Marcel Proust* (Heidelberg: Carl Winter, 1955), pp. 202-06.
21. Howard Moss, *The Magic Lantern of Marcel Proust,* p. 65.
22. John Gaywood Linn, "Notes on Proust's Manipulation of Chronology," *Romanic Review,* LII, No. 3 (October, 1969), pp. 210-25; J. P. Houston, "Temporal Patterns in Proust," *French Studies* (England, January, 1969), pp. 33-44; in the *Bulletin de la Société des Amis de Marcel Proust et des Amis de Combray* (France), Pierre Jaquillard, "Chronolo-

gies," (1957), p. 284, and Willy Hachez, "Chronologie de Marcel Proust," (1956), pp. 198-206; (1961), 392-95.

23.

Book	Approximate Dates	Season	Some References
Swann's Way	1872-1887	Spring—Combray Winter—Paris	Miss Sacripiant, 1872 (I, p. 639; PI, p. 849); Charity Ball for Victims of Murcia, 1879 (I, p. 172; PI, p. 225); Swann's letter from Twickenham (exiled King since 1885), (I, p. 14; PI, p. 18).
Within a Budding Grove	1887-1896	Summer—Balbec	Dumas novel *Francillon,* 1887 (I, p. 413; PI, p. 542); Talk of *Cavalleria Rusticana* after 1891 (I, p. 663; PI, p. 883); Sadi Carnot, President of France 1890-94 (I, p. 520; PI, p. 686).
The Guermantes Way	1897-1899	Fall (November), 1897—Doncières Winter, 1898—Paris Spring—Mme de Villeparisis Summer—death of grandmother Fall—Mme de Stermaria Spring, 1899 at Oriane de Guermantes	Saint-Loup and another "two partisans of the revision," 1897 (I, p. 789; PII, p. 105); Bloch discusses Zola's trial, Spring, 1898 (I, p. 883; PII, p. 234); death of Empress of Austria, 1898 (I, p. 1080, PII, p. 509).
Cities of the Plain	1899-1907	Late summer (?)—Princesse de Guermantes	*Pelléas et Mélisande,* 1902 (II, p. 152; PII, p. 812); Alfred Capus, revival of *La Châtelaine,* 1902 (II, p. 346; PII, p. 1087); L'Affaire Eulenbourg, 1907 (II, p. 247;

Book	Approx-imate Dates	Season	Some References
The Captive	1907-1914	Winter—Paris	PII, p. 947).
The Sweet Cheat Gone		Late spring	*Les Ballets Russes,* 1909 (II, p. 545; PIII, p. 237); after the Dreyfus Affair "the closing of the churches and deportation" (II, p. 710; PIII, p. 467); Balkan Wars, 1912-13 (II, p. 879; PIII, p. 705).
The Past Recaptured	1914-1925 (?)	Late spring—Tansonville Summer—Paris, second visit Spring—matinee at the Princesse de Guermantes	1914 (II, p. 945; PIII, p. 801); 1916 (II, p. 892; PIII, p. 723); 1925 (?) after "many years" (II, p. 983; PIII, p. 584).

24. Germaine Brée, *Du Temps Perdu au Temps Retrouvé,* p. 35.

CHAPTER III

1. Robert Redfield, *The Little Community* (Chicago: The University of Chicago Press, 1955), p. 88.
2. *Ibid.,* p. 68.
3. Louis de Robert, *Comment Débuta Marcel Proust* (Paris: NRF, 1925), p. 75.
4. Georges Piroué, *Proust et la Musique de Devenir* (Paris: Denoël, 1960), p. 86.
5. *Ibid.*
6. Leo Bersani, *Marcel Proust* (New York: Oxford University Press, 1965), p. 227.
7. Germaine Brée, *Du Temps Perdu au Temps Retrouvé* (Paris: Les Belles Lettres, 1960), p. 59.
8. Georges Poulet, "L'Espace Proustien" (Paris: NRF, 11e année, no. 121, 122, 123), III, no. 123, p. 499.
9. One can almost sense that the work was conceived in sonata form. The overture and Combray represent the exposition, in which the two ways are the themes presented. The development section begins with *Within a Budding Grove,* in which the two themes are restated with some development and bridged by Elstir's art. The *Guermantes Way* develops the Guermantes theme, and *Cities of the Plain* concludes it while it

begins the Swann theme. *The Captive* hints at a possible resolution of the two themes in the septet of Vinteuil and in the involuntary memories (which perform the same function throughout the work, reminding one of Franck's cyclical structure). *The Sweet Cheat Gone* is the last grand development of the Swann theme. The recapitulation begins in *The Past Recaptured* at Combray, in which the two themes are restated clearly and are finally joined and resolved in the coda of the matinee. In short, *Remembrance of Things Past* itself follows the cyclical sonata form presented in the Vinteuil scene. The musical analogy is one more way of looking at the totality of the constructed work.

CHAPTER IV

1. Maurice Allem, *La Vie Quotidienne Sous le Second Empire* (Paris: Hachette, n.d.), p. 39.
2. Maurice Donnay, *Education de Prince* (Paris: Ollendorff, 1895), p. 58.
3. *Ibid.*, p. 148.
4. Paul Hervieu, *L'Armature* (Paris: Lemerre, 1895), pp. 10-11.
5. Robert LeBidois, "Le language parlé par les personnages de Proust," *Le Français Moderne* (June-July, 1939), No. 3, p. 212.
6. Edmond Goblot, *La Barrière et le Niveau, Etude Sociologique sur la Bourgeoisie Française Moderne* (Paris: Librairie Félix Alcain, 1925), p. 168.
7. Paul Poiret, *En habillant l'époque* (Paris: Bernard Grasset, 1930), p. 63.
8. Hugo, *Vingt ans maître d'hôtel chez Maxim's* (Paris: Amiot-Dumont, 1951), p. 157.
9. Comtesse J. de Pange, *Comment j'ai vu 1900* (Paris: Hachette, 1962), p. 72.

CHAPTER V

1. Seymour Lipset and Reinhardt Bendix, *Social Mobility in Industrial Society* (Berkeley: University of California Press, 1959), p. 74.
2. Robert de Billy, *Marcel Proust* (Paris: Editions des Portiques, 1930), p. 209.
3. Lucien Daudet, *Autour de Soixante Lettres de Marcel Proust* (Paris: NRF, Gallimard, 1929), p. 130.
4. Hannah Arendt, *The Origins of Totalitarianism* (Cleveland: Meridan Books, 1958), p. 4.
5. D. W. Brogan, *The Development of Modern France* (London: Hamish Hamilton, 1953), p. 171.
6. Robert Byrnes, *Antisemitism in Modern France* (New Brunswick: Rutgers University Press, 1950), p. 90.
7. Guy Chapman, *The Dreyfus Affair—A Reassessment* (New York: Reynal and Company, 1955), p. 27.

8. Louis-Ferdinand Céline, *Bagatelles Pour Un Massacre* (Paris: Denoël, 1937), p. 242.
9. Robert Byrnes, *Antisemitism,* p. 81.
10. Edouard Drumont, *La France Juive* (Paris: Marpon et Flammarion, 1886), p. 9.
11. Robert Byrnes, *Antisemitism,* p. 324.
12. D. W. Brogan, *Modern France,* p. 202.
13. H. Stuart Hughes, *Consciousness and Society* (New York: Vintage Books, 1961), p. 57.
14. Robert Byrnes, *Antisemitism,* p. 261.
15. Joachim Prinz, *The Dilemma of the Modern Jew* (Boston: Little, Brown and Company, 1962), p. 79.
16. Rabi, *Anatomie Du Judaïsme Français* (Paris: Editions De Minuit, 1962), p. 69.
17. André de Fouquières, "Mon Paris et ses Parisiens," Tome II, *Quartier Monceau* (Paris: Editions Pierre Horay, 1954), p. 246.
18. Hannah Arendt, *Origins of Totalitarianism,* p. 52.
19. *Ibid.,* p. 56.
20. *Ibid.,* p. 87.
21. Earle Stanley Randall, *The Jewish Character in the French Novel, 1870-1914* (Menasha, Wisconsin: George Banta, 1941).
22. Léon Daudet, *Souvenirs* (Paris: Nouvelle Librairie Nationale, 1920), p. 352.
23. Jean-Paul Sartre, *Réflexions sur la Question Juive,* translated as *Anti-Semite and Jew* (New York: Schocken Books, 1948), p. 27.
24. Comte Boni de Castellane, *L'Art d'être Pauvre: Mémoires* (Paris: Editions G. Crès et Cie., 1926). p. 54.
25. Léon Blum, *Souvenirs sur l'Affaire* (Paris: Gallimard, 1935), p. 63.
26. Guy Chapman, *The Dreyfus Affair,* p. 65.
27. Léon Blum, *Souvenirs,* p. 114.
28. Maurice Barrès, *Mes Cahiers* (Paris: Plon, 1929-31), Cahier II (1897), p. 118.
29. *Ibid.,* Cahier, I, p. 232.
30. Robert de Montesquiou, *Les Pas Effacés: Mémoires* (Paris: Emile-Paul Frères, 1923), III, p. 39.
31. Carmen Castro, *Marcel Proust o el Viver Escribiendo* (Madrid: Revista de Occidente, 1952), p. 112.
32. Roland André Donzé, *Le Comique dans l'Oeuvre de Marcel Proust* (Neuchatel: Editions Victor Attinger, 1955), p. 68.
33. J. E. Van Praag, "Marcel Proust, Témoin de judaisme déjudaisé," *Revue Juive de Genève* (1937), no. 48, p. 344.
34. Hannah Arendt, *Origins of Totalitarianism,* p. 52.
35. F. C. Green, *The Mind of Proust* (Cambridge: University Press, 1949), p. 103.
36. Raymond Geiger, *Histoires Juives* (Paris: NRF, 1923).
37. Earle Stanley Randall, *The Jewish Character in the French Novel,* p. 205.

BIBLIOGRAPHY

I
PROUST'S WORKS

1. *A la recherche du temps perdu,* ed. Pierre Clarac et André Ferré. 3 vols. Paris: Gallimard, "Bibliothèque de la Pléïade," 1955-1956. *Remembrance of Things Past,* trans. C. K. Scott Moncrieff. 2 vols. New York: Random House, 1934.
2. *Chroniques.* Paris: Gallimard, 1927.
3. *Contre Sainte-Beuve, suivi de Nouveaux Mélanges,* ed. Bernard de Fallois. Paris: Gallimard, 1954.
4. *Jean Santeuil.* 3 vols. Paris: Gallimard, 1952.
5. *Les Plaisirs et les jours.* Paris: Gallimard, 1924.
6. *Pastiches et mélanges.* Paris: Gallimard, 1937.

PREFACES AND TRANSLATIONS BY PROUST

1. *La Bible d'Amiens.* (John Ruskin). Preface, translation, notes by Marcel Proust. Paris: Mercure de France, 1926.
2. *Propos de Peintre de David à Degas.* (Jacques-Emile Blanche). Preface by Marcel Proust. Paris: Emile Paul, 1927.
3. *Sésame et les lys.* (John Ruskin). Preface, translation, notes by Marcel Proust. Paris: Mercure de France, 1906.
4. *Tendres Stocks.* (Paul Morand). Preface by Marcel Proust. Paris: Nouvelle Revue Française, 1921.

CORRESPONDENCE OF PROUST

1. *Lettres à Walter Berry,* Comte et Comtesse Maugny, Comte V. d'Oncien de la Batie, M. Pierre de Chevilly, Sir Philip Sassoon, Princesse Bibesco, Mlle Louisa de Mornand, Mme Laure Hayman, Mme Scheikévitch. Paris: Plon, 1935.
2. *Lettres de Marcel Proust à Bibesco.* Lausanne, Guild du Livre, 1949.
3. *Lettres à Mme C (atusse).* Paris: Janin, 1946.
4. *Lettres à Robert de Montesquiou.* Paris: Plon, 1930.
5. *Lettres à la comtesse de Noailles.* Paris: Plon, 1931.
6. *Lettres à Paul Souday et al.* Paris: Plon, 1931.
7. *Lettres à M. et Mme Sydney Schiff,* Paul Souday, J. E. Blanche, Camille Vettard, J. Boulenger, Louis Martin-Chauffier, E. R. Curtius, L. Gautier Vignal. Paris: Plon, 1932.

II
REFERENCE WORKS

Almanach du Gotha. Gotha, Germany: J. Perthes, 1890-1914.
Annuaire des Châteaux. Paris: A. La Fare, 1887-.
Bottin Mondain. Paris, 1960.
de Sède, Gérard. *Petite Encyclopédie des Grandes Familles.* Paris: Société des Editions Modernes, 1962.
Tout-Paris, Annuaire de la société parisienne. Paris: A. La Fare, 1900-1914.

NEWSPAPERS AND JOURNALS
1890-1914

NEWSPAPERS:

L'Aurore
La Croix
L'Echo de Paris
Le Figaro (society paper)
Le Gaulois (society paper, rightist)

Gil Blas
*The Herald Tribune (*Paris Edition) (society paper)
L'Humanité (leftist)
Le Journal Des Débats
La Libre Parole (antisemitic)
Lutèce (rightest)
Le Matin (center)
Le Petit Journal
Le Petit Parisien
Le Temps (center)

MAGAZINES AND JOURNALS:

L'Illustration (the French *Life* magazine)
L'Assiette Au Beurre (satiric with cartoons)
Le Rire (satiric with cartoons)
Le Triboulet (satiric with cartoons)

Intellectual and Cultural Journals:

Cahiers de la Quinzaine
Le Correspondant
Gazette des Beaux-Arts
Mercure de France
Nouvelle Revue Francaise
La Plume
La Revue Blanche
La Revue Bleue
Revue de Paris
Revue des Deux Mondes

III
STUDIES OF PROUST AND HIS TIME

BOOKS

Allem, Maurice. *La Vie quotidienne sous le second Empire.* Paris: Hachette, n. d.
Ames, Van Meter. *Proust and Santayana.* Chicago: Clark, 1937.

Arendt, Hannah. *The Origins of Totalitarianism.* Cleveland: Meridian Books, 1958.

Aron, Robert. Les Grandes Heures De La Troisième République. 6 vols. Paris: Libraire Académique Perrin, 1967-68.

Astruc, Gabriel. *Le Pavillon Des Fantômes, Souvenirs.* Paris: Grasset, 1929.

Aubéry, Pierre. *Milieux juifs de la France contemporaine.* Paris: Plon, 1957.

Bailby, Léon. *Pourquoi je me suis battu—Souvenirs.* Paris: Plon, 1951.

Barker, Richard. *Marcel Proust, A Biography.* New York: Criterion Books, 1958.

Barrès, Maurice. *Mes Cahiers.* Paris: Plon, 1929-31.

Baumann, Alphonse. *La vie sociale de notre temps.* Paris: Perrin et Cie., 1900.

Beau de Loménie, E. *Les Responsabilités des dynasties bourgeoises.* Paris: Denoël, 1943.

Bell, Clive. *Proust.* London: Hogarth Press, 1928.

Bell, William Stewart. *Proust's Nocturnal Muse.* New York: Columbia University Press, 1962.

Benda, Julien. *La France Byzantine.* Paris: Gallimard, 1945.

Berenson, Bernard. *Sunset and Twilight—From the Diaries of 1947-1958.* New York: Harcourt, Brace and World, 1963.

Berl, Emmanuel. *Sylvia.* Paris: Gallimard, 1952.

———. *Présence Des Morts.* Paris: Gallimard, 1956.

Bersani, Leo. *Marcel Proust, The Fictions of Life and of Art.* New York: Oxford, 1965.

Bertaut, Jules. *L'Opinion Et Les Moeurs.* Paris: Les Editions de France, 1931.

Bibesco, Princesse. *Le Voyageur voilé.* Genève: La Palatine, 1947.

Bibesco, Princesse. *Au Bal avec Marcel Proust.* Paris: Gallimard, 1928.

Billy, André. *L'Epoque 1900.* Paris: Editions Jules Tallandier, 1951.

de Billy, Robert. *Marcel Proust.* Paris: Editions des Portiques, 1930.

Blanche, Jacques-Emile. *Mes Modèles.* Paris: Librairie Stock, 1928.

Blum, Léon. *Souvenirs sur l'Affaire.* Paris: Gallimard, 1935.

Bolle, Louis. *Marcel Proust ou le complexe d'Argus*. Paris: Grasset, 1967.

Bonnet, Henri. *Marcel Proust de 1907 à 1914*. Paris: Librairie Nizet, 1959.

Borin-Fournet, J. *La Société moderne et la question sociale*. Paris: Librairie Guillaumin, 1893.

Brée, Germaine. *Du Temps perdu au temps retrouvé*. Paris: Les Belles Lettres, 1950.

Vicomte Brenier de Montmorand. *La Société française contemporaine*. Paris: Perrin et Cie., 1899.

Bret, Jacques. *Marcel Proust*. Genève: Editions du Mont-Blanc, 1946.

Briand, Charles. *Le Secret de Marcel Proust*. Paris: Henri Lefèbvre, 1950. (Based on conjecture, this book makes Proust not only a homosexual, but guilty of incest.)

Brogan, D. W. *Development of Modern France*. London: H. Hamilton, 1953.

Burnand, Robert. *Paris 1900*. Paris: Librairie Hachette, 1951.

Byrnes, Robert F. *Antisemitism in Modern France*. Vol. I. New Brunswick, New Jersey: Rutgers University Press, 1950.

Carassus, Emilien. *Le Snobisme et les lettres françaises*. Paris: Armand Colin, 1966.

Castellane, Comte Boni de. *L'Art d'être pauvre—Mémoires*. Paris: G. Crès et Cie., 1926.

Castro, Carmen. *Marcel o el vivir escribiendo*. Madrid: Revista de Occidente, 1952.

Cattaui, Georges. *L'Amitié de Proust*. Paris: NRF, 1935.

Céline, Louis-Ferdinand. *Bagatelles Pour Un Massacre*. Paris: Denoël, 1937.

Chantal, René de. *Marcel Proust*. Montréal: Presses de l'Université de Montréal, 1967.

Chapman, Guy. *The Dreyfus Affair—A Reassessment*. New York: Reynal and Company, 1955.

Chastenet, Jacques. *La France de M. Fallières*. Paris: Libraire Arthème Fayard, 1949.

Clermont-Tonnerre, E. de. *Mémoires*. Paris: Bernard Grasset, 1926.

Clermont-Tonnerre, E. de. *Robert de Montesquiou et Marcel Proust.* Paris: Flammarion, 1925.

Cochet, Marie-Anne. *L'Ame Proustienne.* Brussels: Imp. des établissements L. Collignon, 1929.

Coelho, Ruy. *Proust.* Sao Paulo: Flama, 1944.

Coleman, Elliot. *Golden Angel.* New York: Coley Taylor, Inc., 1954.

Combes, Emile. *Mon Ministère, Mémoires 1902-1905.* Paris: Librairie Plon, 1956.

Crémieux, Benjamin. *Du Côté de Marcel Proust.* Paris: Editions Lemarget, 1929.

Curtius, Ernst Robert. *Marcel Proust.* (Translated from German by Armond Pierhal.) Paris: La Revue Nouvelle, 1928.

Dardenne, Henriette. *Lumière sur l'Affaire Dreyfus.* Paris: Nouvelles Editions Latines, 1964.

Daudet, Léon. *Souvenirs.* Paris: Nouvelle Librairie Nationale, 1920.

Delarue-Mardrus, Lucie. *Mes Mémoires.* Paris: Gallimard, 1938.

Deleuze, G. *Marcel Proust et les signes.* Paris: Presses universitaires de France, 1964.

De Ley, Herbert. *Marcel Proust et le Duc de Saint-Simon* (ISLL, 57). Urbana: University of Illinois, 1966.

Delhorbe, Cécile. *L'Affaire Dreyfus et les écrivains français.* Neuchatel: Victor Attinger, 1932.

Derrick, Leon. *Introduction to Proust.* London: Kegan, Paul, Trench, Trubner and Co., 1940.

Donnay, Maurice. *Education de Prince.* Paris: Paul Ollendorf, 1895.

Donzé, Roland André. *Le Comique dans l'oeuvre de Marcel Proust.* Neuchatel: Victor Attinger, 1955.

Dreyfus, Robert. *Souvenirs sur Marcel Proust.* Paris: Grasset, 1926.

Drumont, Edouard. *La France Juive.* Paris: Marpon et Flammarion, 1886.

Evans-Pritchard, E. E. *Essays in Social Anthropology.* London: Faber and Faber, 1962.

Feigelson, Raph., *Ecrivains Juifs De Langue Française.* Paris: Jean Grassin, 1960.

Ferronnays, Mme de la. *Mémoires*. Paris: Paul Ollendorff, 1900.
Forain, Jean. *La Comédie Parisienne*. Paris: Charpentier et Fasquelle, 1892.
Fouquières, André de. *Mon Paris et ses parisiens*. 3 vols. Paris: Pierre Horay, 1954.
Fretet, Dr. Jean. *L'Aliénation poétique*. Paris: J. B. Janin, 1946.
Geiger, Raymond. *Histoires Juives*. Paris: NRF, 1928.
Genette, Gérard. *Figures II*. Paris: Editions du Seuil, 1969.
Germain, André. *La Bourgeoisie qui brûle*. Paris: Sun, 1951.
Germain, André. *Les Clés de Proust, suivi de portraits*. Paris: Sun, 1953.
Germain, André. *Les Fous de 1900*. Genève: La Palatine, 1954.
Girard, René. *Proust*. New Jersey: Prentice-Hall, Inc., 1962.
Girardet, Raoul (ed.). *Le Nationalisme Français, 1870-1914. Textes choisis et présentés*. Paris: Armand Colin, 1966.
Goblot, Edmond. *La Barrière et le niveau, étude sociologique sur la bourgeoisie française moderne*. Paris: Librairie Félix Alcan, 1925.
Graham, Victor E. *The Imagery of Proust*. Oxford: Blackwell, 1966.
Gramont, Elisabeth de. *Marcel Proust*. Paris: Flammarion, 1948.
Green, F. C. *The Mind of Proust*. Cambridge: University Press, 1949
Guilleminault, Gilbert (ed.). *La Belle Epoque*. Paris: Denoël, 1958.
Gyp. *Le Baron Sinaï*. Paris: Charpentier, 1897.
Hahn, Reynaldo. *Journal d'un musicien*. Paris: Plon, 1933.
Haldane, Charlotte. *Marcel Proust*. London: Arthur Barker Ltd., 1951.
Halévy, Daniel. *La République des ducs*. Paris: Grasset, 1937.
Halicka, Alice. *Hier, Souvenirs*. Paris: Editions du Cavois, 1946.
Halphen, Louis. *Histoire de la société française*. Paris: Fernand Nathan, 1953.
Hermant, Abel. *Souvenirs de la vie mondaine*. Paris: Plon, 1935.
Hertzberg, Arthur. *The French Enlightenment and the Jews*. New York: Columbia University Press, 1968.
Hervieu, Paul. *L'Armature*. Paris: Alphonse Lemerre, 1895.

Hindus, Milton. *The Proustian Vision.* New York: Columbia University Press, 1954.

Hommage à Marcel Proust. Brussels-Paris: Disque Vert, 1952.

Hughes, H. Stuart. *Consciousness and Society.* New York: Vintage Books, 1961.

Hugo, *Vingt ans maître d'hôtel chez Maxim's.* Paris: Amiot-Drumont, 1951.

Jauss, Hans Robert. *Zeit und Erinnerung in Marcel Proust.* Heidelberg: Carl Winter, 1955.

Johnson, Douglas. *France and the Dreyfus Affair.* London: Blandford Press, 1966.

Julian, Philippe. *Prince of Aesthetes: Count Robert de Montesquiou.* New York: Viking Press, 1968.

———. *Esthètes et Magiciens: l'Art fin de siècle.* Paris: Librairie Académique Perrin, 1969.

Kinds, Edmond. *Marcel Proust.* Paris: Richard-Masse, 1947.

Kracauer, Siegfried. *Nature of Film.* London: Dennis Dobson, 1961.

Krutch, Joseph Wood. *Five Masters.* Bloomington: Indiana University Press, 1930.

Lauris, Georges de. *Souvenirs d'une belle époque.* Paris: Amiot-Dumont, 1948.

Lauwick, Hervé. *Jupons et Hauts-de-Forme.* Paris: Plon, 1964.

Lavedan, Henri. *Les Deux Noblesses.* Paris: Calmann Lévy, 1897.

Lazare, Bernard. *Job's Dungheap.* New York: Schocken Books, 1948.

Leblond, Marius-Ary. *La société française sous la Troisième République d'après les romanciers contemporains.* Paris: Félix Alcan, 1905.

Lehrmann, C. *L'Elément Juif dans la Littérature Française.* 2 vol. Paris: Albin Michel, 1960.

Lesage, Laurent. *Marcel Proust and His Literary Friends.* Urbana: University of Illinois Press, 1958.

Levin, Harry. *Contexts of Criticism.* Cambridge, Massachusetts: Harvard University Press, 1957.

Lipset, Seymour and Bendix, Reinhard. *Social Mobility in Industrial Society.* Berkeley: University of California Press, 1959.

Lorrain, Jean. *Sensations et Souvenirs.* Paris: Charpentier, 1895.

(This book contains extraordinary parallels with passages in *A la recherche.*)

Lowenthal, Leo. *Literature and the Image of Man.* Boston: The Beacon Press, 1957.

Lowery, Bruce. *Marcel Proust et Henry James.* Paris: Plon, 1964. (Excellent bibliography)

Mansfield, Lester. *Le Comique de Marcel Proust.* Paris: Librairie Nizet, 1953.

Marcel Proust (ed. Bibliothèque Nationale). Paris: Bibliothèque Nationale, 1965. (Catalogue of the Proust exhibit)

March, Harold. *The Two Worlds of Marcel Proust.* Philadelphia: University of Pennsylvania Press, 1948.

Marrus, Michael. *The Politics of Assimilation.* Oxford: Clarendon Press, 1971.

Martin du Gard, Maurice. *Les Mémorables.* Paris: Flammarion, 1957.

Martin-Deslias, N. *L'Idéalisme de Proust.* Paris: Nagel, n.d.

Maurel, André. *Souvenirs d'un écrivain.* Paris: Hachette, 1925.

Mauriac, François. *Du Côté de chez Proust.* Paris: La Table Ronde, 1947.

Maurois, André. *Proust.* New York: Meridian Books, 1958.

Mendelson, David. *Le verre et les objets de verre dans l'univers imaginaire de Marcel Proust.* Paris: José Corti, 1968.

Meyer, Arthur. *Forty Years of Parisian Society.* London: Eveleigh Nash, 1912.

Mistinguett. *Toute ma vie.* 2 vols. Paris: Julliard, 1954.

Montesquiou, Comte Robert de. *Les Pas effacés—Mémoires.* Paris: Emile-Paul Frères, 1923.

Morand, Paul. *1900.* Paris: Les Editions de France, 1931.

Moss, Howard. *The Magic Lantern of Marcel Proust.* New York: Macmillan Company, 1962.

Nathan, Jacques. *La Morale de Proust.* Paris: Nizet, 1953.

Osgood, Samuel. *French Royalism under the Third and Fourth Republics.* The Hague: Martinus Nijhoff, 1960.

Pailleron, Edmond. *Le Monde où l'on s'ennuie.* Paris: Calmann-Lévy, 1884.

Painter, George. *Marcel Proust—A Biography.* London: Chatto and Windus, 1959.

Pange, Comtesse J. de. *Comment j'ai vu 1900*. Paris: Hachette, 1962.

Picon, Gaëton. *Lecture de Proust*. Paris: Mercure de France, 1963.

Pierre-Quint, Léon. *Marcel Proust—sa vie, son oeuvre*. Paris: Kra, 1928.

Piroué, Georges. *Proust et la musique du devenir*. Paris: Denoël, 1960.

Poiret, Paul. *En habillant l'Epoque*. Paris: Bernard Grasset, 1930.

Poliakov, Léon. *Histoire de l'Antisémitisme*. 3 vols. Paris: Calmann-Lévy, 1955-1968.

Poulet, Georges. *Studies in Human Time*. New York: Harper Torchbook, 1961.

Pouquet, Jeanne Maurice. *Le Salon de Mme Arman de Caillavet*. Paris: Hachette, 1926.

Prinz, Joachim. *The Dilemma of the Modern Jew*. Boston: Little Brown and Co., 1962.

Proustiana brasileira. (ed. Ruy Coelho) Rio de Janeiro: Revista Branca, 1950.

du Puy de Clinchamps, Philippe. *La Noblesse*. Paris: Presses Universitaires de France, 1962.

Rabi. *Anatomie Du Judaïsme Français*. Paris: Editions De Minuit, 1962.

Randall, Earle Stanley. *The Jewish Character in the French Novel 1870-1914*. Menasha, Wisconsin: George Banta, 1941.

Redfield, Robert. *The Little Community*. Chicago: University of Chicago Press, 1955.

Revel, Jean-François. *Sur Proust*. Paris: René Julliard, 1960.

Rheims, M. *L'Art 1900—ou le style Jules Verne*. Paris: Arts Et Métiers Graphiques, 1965.

———. *L'Objet 1900*. Paris: Arts Et Métiers Graphique, 1964.

Rièse, Laure. *Les Salons littéraires parisiens du Second Empire à nos jours*. Toulouse: Privat, 1962.

Robert, Louis de. *Comment débuta Marcel Proust*. Paris: NRF, 1925.

Roblin, Michel. *Les Juifs de Paris*. Paris: A. et J. Picard et Cie., 1952.

Rod, Edouard. *Les Idées morales du temps présent*. Paris: Perrin et Cie., 1891.

Sachs, Maurice. *Le Sabbat*. Paris: Corrêa, 1946.

Sartre, Jean-Paul. *Réflexions sur la question juive*. (Translated as *Antisemite and Jew*). New York: Schocken Books, 1948. (Originally published in Paris, 1946.)

Schlumberger, Gustave. *Mes Souvenirs (1844-1928)*: Paris: Plon, 1934.

Seillière, Ernest. *Marcel Proust*. Paris: Editions de la Nouvelle Revue Critique, 1931.

Seznec, Jean. *Marcel Proust et les dieux*. Oxford: Clarendon Press, 1962.

Shattuck, Roger. *Proust's Binoculars*. New York: Random House, 1963.

Silvera, Alain. *Daniel Halévy and his Times, a Gentleman-Commoner in the Third Republic*. Ithaca: Cornell University Press, 1966.

Sorokin, Pitirim. *Social Mobility*. New York: Harper and Brothers, 1927.

Spagnoli, John J. *The Social Attitude of Marcel Proust*. New York: Publications of the Institute of French Studies, 1936.

Spire, André. *Souvenirs A Bâtons Rompus*. Paris: Albin Michel, 1962.

Thomas, Marcel. *L'Affaire Sans Dreyfus*. Paris: Armand Colin, 1961.

Tõnnies, Ferdinand. *Gemeindschaft Und Gesellschaft*. Leipzig: H. Buske, 1935.

Truffaut, Louis. *Introduction à Marcel Proust*. Munich: Heuber Verlag, 1967.

Turnell, Martin. *The Novel in France*. New York: Vintage Books, 1958.

Uzès, Duchesse de. *Souvenirs*. Paris: Plon, 1939.

Valle, Titta del. *Marcel Proust et il vestito della principessa di Cardignan*. Florence: G. Barberà, 1951.

Veblen, Thorstein. *The Theory of the Leisure Class*. New York: New American Library (Mentor Books), 1953. (Originally published in 1899).

Waleffe, Maurice de. *Quand Paris était un paradis*. Paris: Denoël, 1947.

Watt, Ian. *The Rise of the Novel*. Berkeley: University of California Press, 1962.

Weber, Eugen. *Action Française, Royalism and Reaction in Twentieth Century France.* Stanford: Stanford University Press, 1962.

West, Rebecca. *The Court and the Castle.* New Haven: Yale University Press, 1957.

Wilson. Edmund. *Axel's Castle.* New York: Charles Scribner's and Son, 1931.

Wright, Gordon. *France in Modern Times.* Chicago: Rand McNally & Co., 1960.

Zborowski, Mark, and Herzog, Elisabeth. *Life is with People. The Culture of the Shtetl.* New York: Schocken Books, 1952.

Zéphir, Jacques. *La Personnalité humaine dans l'oeuvre de Marcel Proust.* Paris: M. J. Minard, Lettres Modernes, 1959.

Articles and Periodicals

Adam, Antoine. "Le Roman de Proust et le problème des clefs," *Revue des Sciences Humaines,* Vol. 65 (January-March, 1952), pp. 49-90.

Auchincloss, Louis. "Proust's Picture of Society," *Partisan Review* (Fall, 1960), pp. 690-701.

Baker, Joseph E. "Ivory Tower as Laboratory. Pater and Proust," *Accent,* Autumn 1959, pp. 204-19.

Bardac, Henri. "Proust and Montesquiou," *Revue de Paris* (September, 1948), pp. 142-47.

Barthes, Roland. "Proust et les noms," *To Honor Roman Jakobson.* The Hague: Morton, 1967.

Bertrand, Louis. "Marcel Proust—Les Snobismes littéraires," *Candide,* May 26, 1927.

Bonmariage, Sylvain. "Facettes de Proust," *Le Bayou,* Vol. 70 (Summer, 1957).

Bonnet, Henri. "Proust en 1896," *Europe,* no. 496-497 (August-September, 1970), pp. 120-128. (Issue devoted entirely to Proust.)

Brombert, Victor. "Le Comique dans le roman de Proust," *Littérature Moderne,* II (November-December, 1951).

Bulletin de la société des amis de Marcel Proust. 1950-1970.

Cattaui, Georges. "Marcel Proust and the Jews," *Jewish Review,* III (December, 1932-March, 1933), pp. 60-75.

Chaumeix, André. "Le Roman et la peinture de la société," *Revue des deux mondes,* T. 44 (1928), pp. 691-701.

Dufour, Louis. "Marcel Proust et la météorologie," *Revue de l'Université de Bruxelles,* T. 3-4 (1950-1951).

Duquaire, Henri. "A Notre-Dame de Paris," *Le Figaro,* June 12, 1963, p. 9.

"La Fête des Acacias," *Illustration,* No. 2785 (July 11, 1896), pp. 33-36.

Freeman, Bryant. "Marcel Proust et Pierre Lavallée," *Extrait du Bulletin de la société des amis de Marcel Proust,* No. 11 (1961), pp. 323-363.

Garrett, Helen. "Marcel Proust's Vision of the French Social Hierarchy," *Modern Language Forum,* XL (December, 1955), pp. 95-103.

Girard, René. "Les Mondes Proustiens," *Médiations,* I (March, 1962), pp. 97-125.

Graham, Victor E. "Water imagery and symbolism in Proust," *Romanic Review* (New York), L (1959), pp. 118-28.

Hachez, Willy. "Chronologie de Marcel Proust," *Bulletin de la société des amis de Marcel Proust* (1956), pp. 198-206, pp. 392-395.

Heppenstall, Rayner. "Morel," *Twentieth Century,* CLXV, pp. 482-92.

Houston, J. P. "Temporal Patterns in Proust," *French Studies* (Oxford, January, 1962), pp. 33-44.

Hyde, John K. "Proust, His Jews and His Jewishness," *French Review,* XXXIX, pp. 837-48.

Jacot, Claude. "La signification du costume dans *A la recherche du temps perdu,*" *Le Bayou,* Vol. 70 (1957), pp. 377-91.

Jaquillard, Pierre. "Chronologie," *Bulletin de la société des amis de Marcel Proust,* 1957.

Kallen, Horace. "Can Judaism survive in the United States," *Menorah Journal,* XI, No. 2 (April, 1925), pp. 101-13.

LeBidois, Robert. "Le langage parlé par les personnages de Proust," *Le Français Moderne,* No. 3 (June-July, 1939).

Lesage, Laurent. "Proust's Professor of Beauty: Count Robert de Montesquiou," *The American Society Legion of Honor Magazine,* XXVII (Spring, 1936), pp. 65-76.

Linn, John Gaywood. "Notes on Proust's Manipulation of Chronology," *Romanic Review,* LII, No. 3 (October, 1961), pp. 210-25.

Lunel, Armand. "Proust, sa mère et les Juifs," *Europe,* no. 502-503 (February-March, 1971), pp. 64-67. (Issue devoted entirely to Proust.)

Luppé, A. de. "Chez Marcel Proust: Snobs et mondains," *Le Correspondant,* March 25, 1928.

Maréchal, R. "La Phrase de Marcel Proust," *Le Français Moderne,* (January, 1963), pp. 13-30.

Moss, Howard. "The Two Ways," *Sewannee Review,* LXX (Summer, 1962), pp. 451-63.

Pasquali, Constanza. "Personaggi proustiana: Mme Swann e i suoi vestiti," *Studi Neophilologica* (Uppsala, Sweden), XXXI (1959), pp. 108-27.

Porel, Jacques. "Marcel Proust chez Réjane," *La Table Ronde,* No. 34 (October, 1950).

Poulet, Georges. "L'Espace Proustien," *NRF,* 11e année, Nos. 121, 122, 123 (1962-1963).

Praag, J. E. Van. "Marcel Proust, Témoin du Judaisme déjudaisé, *Revue Juive de Genève,* Nos. 48, 49, 50 (1937).

Rhodes, S. A. "Marcel Proust and his Jewish Characters," *Sewanee Review,* Vol. 39 (1931), pp. 144-57.

Riefstahl-Nordlinger, Marie. "Memories of Marcel Proust," *The Listener* (April 28, 1960), pp. 749-51.

———. "Proust As I Knew Him," *London Magazine,* I, No. 7 (August, 1954), pp. 51-61.

Rièse, Laure. "Proust—salonnard," *Le Cerf Volant,* No. 19 (October, 1957).

Rochefoucauld, Edmée de la. "Proust," *Bulletin des amis de Marcel Proust,* No. 3 (1953).

Roditi, Edouard. "Proust Recaptured," *Kenyon Review,* Vol. 30 1968), pp. 23-29.

Samuel, Maurice. "The Concealments of Marcel Proust's Jewishness," *Commentary,* Vol. 29, No. 1 (January 1960), pp. 8-22.

Saurat, Denis. "Le Judaïsme de Proust," *Les Marges,* T. 34, 1925.

Sobejano, Gonzalo. "Tiempo y recuerdo en la novela," *Insula* (Spain), No. 121 (January 15, 1956).

Spire, André. "Israel in France," *Menorah Journal,* XI, No. 1 (February, 1925), pp. 66-73.

Truc, Gonzaque. "Marcel Proust et le monde," *Comoedia,* May 17, 1927.

Vigneron, Robert. "Marcel Proust et Robert de Montesquiou autour de professionnelles beautés," *Modern Philology,* XXXIX, No. 2 (November, 1941).

Watson, D. R. "Sixteen Letters from Marcel Proust to Joseph Reinach," *Modern Language Review,* Vol. 63 (1968), pp. 587-99.

Werner, W. L. "The Psychology of Marcel Proust," *Sewanee Review,* Vol. 39 (1931).

Wharton, Edith. "Marcel Proust," *Yale Review* (January 1925), pp. 209-22.

Unpublished Material

Clark, Charles Newell. "Elstir: The Role of the painter in Proust's *A la recherche du temps perdu.*" Unpublished Ph.D. dissertation, Yale University, 1952.

O'Neal, Helen H. "A Study of Gilberte, the Duchess of Guermantes and Albertine in *A la recherche du temps perdu* by Marcel Proust." Unpublished Ph.D. dissertation, Tulane University, 1967.

Stern, Peter S. "The Right in France and the Evolution of French War Aims, 1914-1919." Unpublished Ph.D. dissertation, Princeton University, 1971.

APPENDIX

EVOLUTION OF THE VERDURIN SALON

1880 (original clan) First Verdurin salon	1880 Goncourt view	1902 Matinee	1912 La Raspelière	1922 Music Recital
Cottard (doctor)	Cottard	Cottard	Cottard	dead
Brichot (professor)	Brichot	Brichot	Brichot (exiled)	———
Saniette (archivist)	———	Saniette	Saniette (dies)	———
Biche (Elstir) (artist)	Biche (self-exiled)	———	———	———
Dechambre (pianist	———	dead	———	———
M. de Forcheville (low aristocracy)	———	———	———	———
Odette (demi-mondaine)	———	———	———	Mme de Forcheville (nee Odette)
Swann (upper bourgeois) new "faithful"	Swann exiled	dead	———	
	Princess Sherbatoff	Princesse Sherbatoff	dead	———
	Viradobetski (sculptor)	Viradobetski	Viradobetski	Viradobetski
		M. & Mme Cambremer (provincial nobility)	———	M. de Cambremer
		Morel (violinist)	Morel	Morel
		Baron de Charlus	Charlus (exiled)	———
		Marcel	Marcel	Marcel
			Queen of Naples	———
			the brother of the	———
			King of Bavaria	———
			General Deltour	———
			Mme de Montesquiou	———
			Duchesse de Duras, et	———
				Legrandin
				Prince d'Agrigente
				M. d'Argencourt
				Princesse de Nassau
				Mlle de St. Loup
				Jacques du Rozier (nee Bloch)

INDEX